The Intercultural City

The Intercultural City

Planning for Diversity Advantage

Phil Wood and Charles Landry

London • Sterling, VA

First published by Earthscan in the UK and USA in 2008

ISBN-13:   978-1-84407-437-2 hardback
ISBN-13:   978-1-84407-436-5 paperback

Typeset by JS Typesetting Ltd, Porthcawl, Mid Glamorgan
Printed and bound in the UK by Cromwell Press, Trowbridge
Cover design by Susanne Harris
Cover illustration by Christopher Corr (chriscorr@yahoo.com)

For a full list of publications please contact:

Earthscan
8–12 Camden High Street
London, NW1 0JH, UK
Tel: +44 (0)20 7387 8558
Fax: +44 (0)20 7387 8998
Email: earthinfo@earthscan.co.uk
Web: **www.earthscan.co.uk**

22883 Quicksilver Drive, Sterling, VA 20166-2012, USA

Earthscan publishes in association with the International Institute for Environment and
Development

A catalogue record for this book is available from the British Library

Library of Congress Cataloging-in-Publication Data

Wood, Phil, 1959–
    The intercultural city : planning for diversity advantage / Phil Wood and
Charles Landry.
        p. cm.
    Includes bibliographical references.
    ISBN-13: 978-1-84407-436-5 (pbk.)
    ISBN-10: 1-84407-436-6 (pbk.)
    ISBN-13: 978-1-84407-437-2 (hardback)
    ISBN-10: 1-84407-437-4 (hardback)
    1. Multiculturalism. 2. Urban policy. 3. City and town life. 4. Cross-cultural
orientation. I. Landry, Charles, 1948– II. Title.
    HM1271.W66 2007
    305.8–dc22

                                                        2007034784

Contents

List of Boxes

List of Figures

Acronyms and Abbreviations

BAME   black, Asian or other minority ethnic
BJP   Bharatiya Janata Party
BME   black and minority ethnic
CABE   Commission for Architecture and the Built Environment
CCDN   Celebrating Cultural Diversity Network
CD/LEI   Centre for Documentation/Laboratory for intercultural education
CIP   Community Induction Project
CMC   computer mediated communication
ESOL   English for speakers of other languages
HUV   Holbeck Urban Village
IBNIS   Internet-based Neighbourhood Information Systems
ICLS   Intercultural Communication and Leadership School
LDA   London Development Agency
MMOG   massively multiplayer online game

The True Ecology

And where is home? Home is not the neighbourhood, nor in a community. Home is in the unexpected welcome of the stranger. Home is in the charity reflected in the chance encounter. Home is what you want to make of the city when you are the object of kindness. Home is what you return to in the gatherings of people, in coffee shops, street corners – in those zones where you met the human eros. It might have been a tollbooth, at a counter, in a gallery, a parking lot, in the most ridiculous or fortunate of places. The unseen city is in the happenstance – the boulevards and paths and piazzas and atriums or in the choreography of people that build a city as homage to what they have found in each other. The city is built after the architecture of care has been improvised. And the roots of it are not logistical or prudently designed. The roots of it are in the mystery of grace, the appetite for each other, the gusto of being curious about each other before the conventions of the world. It is the invisible city that is the Valhalla of the civic dream. The structure of a city is for the furthering of kindness and inter-civic munificence. We will not have liveable cities until we find a reason for living in each other.

Pier Giorgio Di Cicco (2007)

Pier Giorgio Di Cicco is Poet Laureate for the City of Toronto.

Introduction: Setting the Scene

This is a serious book, but one that approaches its subject matter from some unusual angles and has been written in a way that, hopefully, brings a freshness to a topic often weighed down by its own earnestness. It is challenging and argumentative, sometimes discursive and a little playful, but also highly researched and evidence-based. Ultimately, however, we hope readers will find it helpful – even inspirational – and a spur to take practical and positive action in their work and daily lives.

It is also a personal book drawing from our own life experiences, and this influences both its tone and its conclusions. So we begin with potted histories of our very different lives and then go on to set out some of the ideas with which we have tried to wrestle.

Who Are We?

We are two white guys interested in crossing cultures.

Phil

I live in Huddersfield in the former industrial heartland of the north of England. When I look out of my bedroom window, across a valley of empty textile mills still awaiting conversion to bijou apartments, I can see the former house of my grandparents and next to it the site of the house where I myself was born. In a recent article in the *Observer* newspaper on the incidence and location of surnames in the British Isles, it was noted that there are rather a lot of people called Wood around the country, but the greatest concentration of the tribe can be found in ... Huddersfield.

Dad was the son of a textile engineer and Mum from a family of coal miners, but they met as shop workers. They told me that we are all equal and that regardless of background, it is character that matters. What they gave me was the chance to do things no one in the family ever had the chance to do before: go to grammar school followed by university, leave home and – daringly – Huddersfield and Yorkshire too. But perhaps more than anything they gave me curiosity and the chance to stimulate it through books and then foreign travel. When everyone I knew was going to Scarborough or Blackpool, they took me to strange and fascinating places such as Egypt, Norway, Soviet-era Moscow and the shores of the Caspian Sea. In a way they gave me wings to fly away but also a pride in my roots.

And, after living and travelling around the world following college, I came back to my roots and set out to rediscover the town I had left. I found communities formerly unknown or beyond reach, which now became a fascinating world of new insights and friends. Through my community development job in the local authority I encountered the Sikhs who had built their magical Gurdwara with domes that vie with the mill chimneys. Then there was the extended family of Kashmiris among whom my wife and I lived and who provided their warm and open households, which were the backdrop to my daughter Ruby's happy childhood. Most of all it was the people of the various islands of the Caribbean – Trinidad, Grenada, Barbados and Jamaica – who chose this draughty northern town to settle in and who drove a large, blasting sound system through the middle of its millstone grit Puritanism. I warmed rapidly to this theme, eventually becoming an honorary member of Huddersfield Trinidad and Tobago Ladies Association masquerade camp, learning to jump up with the best of them at the annual carnival. This drew me in to the North Stars Steel Orchestra where I spent many years, helping them eventually to become British champions. And all this has led to a long-term love affair with the island of Trinidad – a fantastically raucous, gaudy and intercultural meeting place of Africa, Asia, Europe and Latin America – where I was eventually adopted as 'deh White Trini'. It's that strange mix of bluff Yorkshireness, an arse-waggling irreverence from Trinidad, and an esoteric introspection that has recently attracted me to what may be my genetic home of Norway that defines my own personal brand of interculturalism and has brought diversity advantage to me and my family.

Charles

In some ways there couldn't be a greater contrast in the background of Phil with that of myself. Landry is a name taken on by my grandfather who was a chemist who then became an opera singer. His name was Schmidt – 'Smith' – the most common in Germany and not distinctive enough in the artistic arena, so he took on a name from his mother's side far back. It is French. My passport betrays the mix 'Charles Rene Schmidt-Landry', a bit of a mouthful. My 'blood', as far as I can discern, is 80 per cent German, 15 per cent Polish, 5 per cent French and 0 per cent British. My nationality is British, although I have a fading German passport somewhere.

My parents escaped from Nazi Germany. They were not Jewish, but worked for a Jewish publishing house and were politically active and so had to leave. They moved to London as refugees and my father was sent to an internment camp. They always had German accents. My father was a journalist who specialized in philosophical writings and my mother, far more practical, started small businesses, including a small toy factory, but she also wrote. They were never able to be successful in the conventional sense in Britain. Their faces did not fit. This is still a sadness for me now. But as bohemian intellectuals they attracted a following of mixed British oddballs who lingered around our house.

Being a bit of a 'Jerry', really, I was seen as odd at school. I tried to integrate and ingratiate myself by being charming and good at sport, but I never passed the pure British test. We all noticed some prejudice, but not on scale that a black person might experience to-day. Aged 11 I moved to Germany and lived there for nine years as a *Britischer Deutscher*. This had an advantage as British pop culture was king. I was an outsider again, and that was alright because I was a bit exotic, but again too bohemian for our German friends. The family moved on to Italy, but I studied in the UK and then in Bologna, worked in Brussels at the EU before, via an extended route, setting up Comedia in 1978.

With three cultures and languages racing around my blood it feels natural to want to 'see the world through other eyes' and to focus on what we share rather than what divides us. Oh, and there is another quirk since adolescence – I have had a recurring dream that in a former life I was really Chinese.

WHY INTERACT?

Humans, it is said, are social beings. They need to interact for survival and what 'survival' means has changed over time and the millennia. There is the biological urge to mate, there is safety in numbers so addressing security is easier, and there are social needs and the desire for companionship. Let's not forget efficiency, as two hands can get things done more easily and communicating with others leads to greater speed in solving problems and inventing solutions to them. Now, crucially, our culture has invented some threats that could reduce interaction. A risk-averse culture is creating conditions around life in the public domain that creates a 'no culture', which has shaped how space looks, feels, works and how we behave in it. The sign language of cities reminds us what we *can't* do: 'No entry', 'Do not feed the ducks', 'Beware of the dog'. The physical form reminds us of the many 'no-go' areas. Security points control access to buildings. The car-dominated culture of the city demands highways that slice it up, segmenting communities and threatening pedestrian activity, which drives us even further into our metal boxes and away from each other. As a consequence, many choose to cocoon themselves away in gated estates or ghettoes. Technology can help reduce interaction as well as enhance its possibilities. Many people do things now on the Internet that they might have done by interacting with people in shops, libraries, surgeries, and so on. Equally, increasing numbers are migrating to virtual worlds on the Net. 'Second Life', which at the last count had well over 6 million members, is but the latest incarnation of a life imagined and created in cyberspace that avoids face-to-face contact in the material world. These inner worlds are perhaps no better than the ghettoes that exclude.

The Intercultural City argues that we should interact more with each other because we live side by side. Only then will we foster empathy by learning more of each other and reduce the distrust between people. This way we get used to living with difference. In a world of hyper-mobility where the make up of cities is becoming more diverse every day, a new and different type of 'contract' is needed to govern how individuals and groups behave together. The threat of urban breakdown is too strong not to go down this route.

Communicating across cultures and peoples does not necessarily come naturally. There is only a small percentage of people who thrive on the stimulation provided by knowing people and situations different from themselves. On the flipside there is a small group of people who want to keep 'pure' and not be tarnished by contact with other groups. The large majority is somewhere in the middle, preferring to live in a comfort zone of the known and predictable. With encouragement this group can be persuaded, seduced, cajoled into seeing how interaction with the 'Other' is the best way forward.

ACKNOWLEDGING CONFLICT

Communicating across difference is not easy and the greater the cultural distance, the more difficult it gets. There is a lot of room for misinterpretation and misunderstanding, and a lack of knowledge of how people with different values or other cultures work. Cultural literacy is an under-explored discipline. Perfect harmony is not a realistic goal or even a desirable aim, so the capacity to negotiate and mediate difference takes on a more significant role. It could be said that being different and arguing about differences shows you are alive. This process of crossing boundaries and trying to understand the 'Other' can broaden the mind, encourage different perspectives and lead to hybrid inventions. It can generate a special cross-cultural creativity. Arguing in this way might be a cultural version of the biodiversity argument in nature. Without biodiversity, species can atrophy. Similarly, in human terms, a culture cannot develop without diversity. Pick any cultural group throughout history and it is through dealing with the external and the different that they have evolved. Culture, like nature, needs to respond to its evolving environment.

Explicitly recognizing conflict in a politically correct but politically bereft world is not straightforward. There is an institutional inertia to tackle issues of population change and the feelings of disruption, mistrust and even dislike of each other that flow from it. This is not to deny that a substantial group thrives on the stimulations of difference.

We know something needs to be done, as the implications are far-reaching though they often fall into the 'too hard' basket. Politicians mostly prefer to brush over or sweep away the fact that people may not like each other. They use a bland language of 'inclusion' and 'cohesion', although racist parties who are blunt and explicit hover quite close to the surface. Dealing with diversity is seen as a minefield presenting many opportunities to put your foot in it and trip yourself up because you do not understand the cultural nuances. It is a bold politician indeed who sets out to build a career on race relations issues – greater prospects of success, recognition and a quieter life lie elsewhere. This can also be the case for municipal officials such as planners or engineers who would prefer to give the issue a wide berth and leave it to the 'race relations industry' professionals. It seems only when a crisis hits, like the 7/7 bombings in the UK, that suddenly we are all interested and everyone is an expert.

The challenge is to proactively manage conflict by acknowledging the types of problem it creates, such as fear or prejudging people, and then to deal with them in a direct way that does not put either side of the argument down. Conflict and differences can be managed well. The ability to do so is a competency and skill, though sadly it is rarely taught as a day-to-day skill.

RULES OF ENGAGEMENT

What are the boundaries of the public sphere in an age of diversity? What are the rights and responsibilities of individuals from whatever hue and background when they enter the public realm or public life? Does everyone have obligations to a joint public purpose of the country as a whole in which they live?

Every society on the globe struggles with the emerging landscape of diversity as we reconfigure our thinking about who is a citizen and what is the nation state. Almost universally, those that are different suffer discrimination and in turn social and economic disadvantage. Some countries deal with it better than others. The Nordic countries and Canada, while not perfect, are taken as models of good practice, and there are cities such as Stuttgart and Amsterdam that have exemplary codes of practice embedded into policy. Yet while many might criticize the UK, The Netherlands and Germany for their policies, they are at least, in their own imperfect way, all trying to face up to the issues. There are all too many places in the world where the state chooses to ignore diversity or even encourages intercommunal antagonism. Indeed, while this book is primarily about the countries of the West, there is perhaps another to be written on how the newly emerging economic giants will have to face up to the need to balance growth, democracy and diversity.

All societies have rules of engagement – none is a free-for-all. The intercultural city that lives with diversity is different from places that channel people into one worldview. It decries fundamentalisms insofar as they affect public, as distinct from private, life. These are the movements or attitudes that believe in the infallibility and literal interpretation of a particular religion's doctrine and absolute religious authority, and demand that this be legally enforced. They stress strict and literal adherence to a set of basic principles that capture every facet of life. The varieties of these fundamentalisms are extensive and often age-old. The Christian Crusades and the Inquisition constituted older versions; the evangelicals so prevalent in the US are a newer one. Islamic fundamentalism pushes for Sharia law and an Islamic state. This is the legal framework within which public and some private aspects of life are regulated on Muslim principles. It deals with all aspects of day-to-day life including politics, economics, banking, law, sexuality and social issues. Judaism has its version, as does Hinduism – *Hindutva* ('Hinduness') describes movements advocating Hindu nationalism, such as that of the former ruling party in India, the Bharatiya Janata Party (BJP). These are enclosing and all-absorbing worlds that prefer not to let the outsider in.

In fact the term 'fundamentalism' has now even wider use to include movements such as 'free market fundamentalism' (coined by George Soros) to challenge the philosophy that the free market is always beneficial to society.

Inevitably, fundamentalisms come into conflict with the concept of the democratic state, which in its essence allows for competing voices. A second conflict surrounds secularism, which most fundamentalists believe is the cause of most of the world's problems. *Secularism* has two primary meanings. The first asserts the freedom from government imposing a religion or set of beliefs upon people. The state is neutral on matters of belief and gives no privileges or subsidies to religions. In its second sense it argues that activities and decisions, especially political ones, should be based on reasoning and evidence and not religious influences.

The intercultural city or society cannot be religiously affiliated by definition. It argues that each of us gives up a bit of our private beliefs, desires and preferences when we are in the public realm – and where these boundaries are constantly negotiated through public debate. It says 'yes' to every place having a dynamic and challenging interfaith forum and serious teaching about world faiths in the classroom, but would happily see the fading away of faith-based schools.

As any society would, the intercultural society contains core beliefs to govern relations between people, yet it is not as prescriptive at the level of detail as fundamentalism. It allows for people to grow together and to create and recreate the society within which they live. It privileges civic values that in essence seek to foster competent, confident and engaged citizenship. It does not decry the sustenance that religion or other belief systems give. It is simply that its focus is on human ethical values and how people live together. It argues for reasoning and conversation without reference to higher authorities. It claims life can be best lived by applying ethics, the attempt to arrive at practical standards to guide our common views and behaviour, and to help resolve conflicts. It provides a frame within which difference can be lived out and shared with mutual respect.

This is the secular humanist position. It has been drained of confidence, feels exhausted and consequently it is mistakenly accused of being 'wishy-washy' or as having an 'anything goes' ethos with no apparent point of view. Or as fundamentalists would claim, its apparent 'vagueness' is the source of our problems. But this could not be further from the truth. Nevertheless, its confidence needs to be restored and the intercultural project is part of that process.

The confident secular humanist view proposes a set of civic values and rules of engagement, which include: providing settings for a continually renewing dialogue across differences, cultures and conflicts; allowing strongly held beliefs or faiths expression within this core agreement; and acknowledging the 'naturalness' of conflict and establishing means and mediation devices to deal with difference. It seeks to consolidate different ways of living, recognizing arenas in which we must all live together and those where we can live apart. It generates structured opportunities to learn to know the 'Other', to explore and discover similarity and difference. It wishes to drive down decision-making on the subsidiarity principle, which implies much greater decentralization and devolution of power. Central government takes on a more subsidiary role and the city level increases its power dramatically. This enhances participation and connectivity at a local level. It helps generate interest, engagement, concern and responsibility. This is the frame within which the 'intercultural citizen' would think.

Some will argue that this view is prescriptive, culturally bound and Western. To some extent it is. However, as we will come on to show, throughout history in places as diverse as ancient Persia, China and Muslim Spain there have been societies that have attempted to negotiate and achieve advantage from difference. The West too must face up to the paradox that its reverence for its own liberal secularism, born out of the Enlightenment, can breed its own fundamentalism. Replacing religion with reason alone creates problems if we neglect and allow to wither an open and political public domain. Reason then becomes the domain of the lawyer and the bureaucrat who hand down their judgements to a disengaged public as prescriptively as a priest or imam. A healthy society is not just a place of reason but of passion too, and in the dynamic public domain that passion has to be expressed politically and creatively. Sadly, these are things that have been lost in all too many of our public places and institutions.

And, while not the topic of this book, we cannot overlook the fact that ethnicity is but one of the ways we choose to divide our societies; age, gender, wealth, lifestyle and – let's say it – class are others. Indeed, the rich go out of their way to avoid contact with other income groups at work, at play, on holiday and where they live. They have relative freedom to opt out. With traditional class barriers breaking down, new forms of distinction between rich and poor are constantly being constructed based on lifestyle preferences and the market plays a strong role here. It was ever thus, you may say. But what seems to have changed over recent years is the draining away of empathy and respect across the class divide. Today's polite middle classes, who would never dream of allowing the words 'Paki' or 'Nigger' to pass their lips, nevertheless feel comfortable in vilifying and ridiculing the working class as 'chav'. The law may now prevent the worst excesses of the past but when the mighty lose respect for the meek in such a societal way, one worries for where it might lead.

FROM DIVERSITY DEFICIT TO DIVERSITY ADVANTAGE

We try to be honest in acknowledging that living with diversity is not straightforward but we simultaneously focus on looking at the *diversity advantage* for neighbourhoods, cities and nations rather than the *diversity deficit*. The way you look at a problem determines how you address it. If we see everything as a problem to be solved, the mind and imagination sees more trouble than opportunity. By taking the reverse position, inventiveness grows. The fundamental conviction of this book is, first, that there are enormous untapped resources, which our societies can scarcely afford to forgo, available from the creative power of heterogeneity and dissonance. Our second conviction is that a positive impulse to *intercultural exchange* is vital to encourage cross-fertilization from which innovation can proliferate. Yet the ways to unlock this are often neither simple nor obvious. It will require new outlooks, skills and aptitudes from politicians, professionals and ordinary people. The most important of these are *cultural literacy* and *cultural competence*.

These are also going to require a change in the narrative we have constructed around diversity. The conversation in most of Europe over the last 50 years has been somewhat defensive. There was a sense that people were being asked to adapt reluctantly and accommodate to something unavoidable: 'OK... as long as it doesn't affect the way I lead my life'. The narrative constructed was that immigration would help keep public services and factories running. The strange, unassimilated 'Other' held at arm's length could be experienced as an exotic treat without touching the core of people's lifestyles.

This is not how diversity is perceived in societies where immigration lies at the heart of national identity such as the US, Canada and Australia. Diversity in those countries is widely seen as a source of potential and advantage. The private sector has led and evolved the idea of a 'business case for diversity'. First, it is argued, diverse teams of people bring new skills and aptitudes that broaden a company's business offer and might produce new process and product innovations that advance competitiveness. Second, a business more diverse in outlook will have access to new markets both at home and abroad and, through 'supplier diversity', access to better priced and more interesting goods. The idea has been transferred to the national scale with the notion that a more heterogeneous nation is better equipped than a homogeneous one to weather the storms of globalization and change. Japan and Germany, it is argued, have fallen behind the economic performance of more 'mongrel' G8 member states (Zachary, 2003). Lastly, Richard Florida (2002b) in *The Rise of the Creative Class* contends that the competitiveness of cities is influenced by their ability to offer an open, tolerant and diverse milieu to attract and hold mobile wealth creators – though he never quite spells out how it can be done.

This thinking, or at least this debate, is less advanced in Europe, let alone China, India, Russia or Japan in business circles and in national or local government. Our aim is to shift the focus and mindset to start thinking of their own cultural diversity as an asset rather than a liability, and to explore the advantages – economic, but also social, cultural and political.

When we first sat down together in around 2000, along with valued colleagues such as Jude Bloomfield and Franco Bianchini, and began to sketch out what we meant by the intercultural city and diversity advantage, we did it out of a sense of exasperation drawn from our experience of living and working in multiethnic cities. We were frustrated by the inertia and complacency of the policy imagination in regard to cultural diversity. Whether people feared saying or doing the wrong thing, whether they saw it as the preserve of 'the experts', or because they felt it no longer a pressing issue, they left it alone. For people running cities, if they thought about diversity at all, it was probably with a weary shrug – 'just another complicated problem to make my job more difficult'. We set out to turn the paradigm on its head, to say that diversity is not a threat but an opportunity – not in a happy-clappy way but in a hard-nosed assessment of the social, cultural and economic factors that make cities both functional and good places. Sadly, in that space of time, cultural difference has become an issue but for all the wrong reasons – riots, extremism and terror have become irrevocably linked to it in the imagination of politicians and the public. And it has begat a response – in terms of fear, suspicion and security measures – that may inadvertently entrench the problem.

For all those years when people responsible for running cities blindly thought that ethnic interaction and cooperation was happening, or would happen soon – or that it didn't really matter whether it happened or not – we are now paying a price. Local and national policy-makers are now being reminded in no uncertain terms that these things really do matter.

This book seeks to remind us all that there is a way other than fear. It also seeks to remind the British section of our readership that there is a wider world out there that is facing up to similar threats and opportunities and has some insights and experience to offer. In particular we argue that while the rapid growth of interest in 'community cohesion' in Britain has produced much good new thinking and action it remains rather parochial in its points of reference and narrow in its scope and ambition.

AND THANKS ...

This book is in part based and builds upon research that our organization Comedia undertook for a study that was published and supported by the Joseph Rowntree Foundation called 'Cultural Diversity in Britain: A Toolkit for Cross-cultural Co-operation' (Wood et al, 2006). Within that project we undertook case studies in Australia, New Zealand, Norway and the US and surveyed the European scene. Subsequently we broadened the scope of our investigation, focusing on segregation and mixing and the psychological impact of cultural encounters.

We thank the Foundation and especially Richard Best and Theresa McDonagh for their faith in the initial project. Others who contributed financially to that project were One North East, Bristol City Council, Bristol Cultural Development Partnership, the London Borough of Lewisham, the London Borough of Tower Hamlets and the Arts Council of England. Collaborators from overseas were important, especially Richard Brecknock in Australasia, Benedicte Broegger and Petter Wiberg in Norway and Gregg Zachary in the US. Thanks too to the authors of thematic studies and the expanded team, which helped to drive and inspire this project and provided valuable background knowledge including: Adam Mornement, Lise Bisballe, Maurice Coles, Robert Vincent, Franco Bianchini, Lia Ghilardi, Andy Howell, Tom Fleming, Mandeep Kandola, Peter Kenway, Naseem Khan and Anita Morris. The initial project received guidance from an advisory group including: Professor Waqar

Ahmad, Rumman Ahmed, Professor Ash Amin, Christopher Cripps, Professor Sir Peter Hall, Dr David Janner-Klausner, Ranjit Sondhi, · Hamza Viyani and Joy Warmington. We also thank Professor Leonie Sandercock for her inspiration; Ed Beerbohm for his sharp eye and insightful comments; and our wives, Deryn and Susie, for their support and encouragement.

The core assertion of the first study was that increased interaction between ethnic cultures would produce social and economic innovations that would drive the prosperity and quality of life in our cities. Aimed beyond the 'diversity profession', it argued that for too long discussions about cultural diversity have been the preserve of the few and locked into a formulaic pattern. We noted that if more people do not actively engage with the implications of growing diversity, they were stacking up problems for themselves and their communities in the future.

Our starting point was that practically all countries down to their deepest roots are and always have been heterogeneous and interactive. In the case of the UK for instance we have: the North Africans that patrolled Hadrian's Wall; the interplay of Celtic civilizations with successive waves of mediaeval invaders and settlers; deep-seated communities of Jewish and Huguenot origin; the postcolonial immigrants – African-Caribbeans, Indians, Pakistanis, Bangladeshis and Chinese, but also Europeans from Germans, Italians and Portuguese to Scandinavians, Poles and Russians; and Australasians, Arabs, Nigerians, South Africans, Moroccans, Somalis and South and North Americans.

In terms of policy, we acknowledge the value of multiculturalism as the guiding model over many years in the UK and elsewhere, and do not wish to undermine its achievements, but believe fresh thinking is now needed. This is not the final word but hopefully the opening of a new chapter in the way societies think about and respond to diversity. The creative challenge is to move from the multicultural city of fragmented differences to the co-created intercultural city that makes the very most of its diversity.

1

The Urge to Define, Sort and Categorize

A WORLD OF DISTINCTIONS

Our focus is on human diversity and how in cities we live together with our differences with greater ease. We want to encourage intercultural exchange. Yet our starting point is a much broader frame that acknowledges how very difficult it is to turn this into reality: the deep-seated, cross-cultural, human urge to define, to distinguish, to sort, to categorize, to classify and label.

We create a world of distinctions that help define who we are and what we are not. We build an intellectual architecture so we can categorize things, ideas and people to help decide and specify: Who am I? Who am I not? Who is 'insider' and who is 'outsider'? What is 'in' and what is 'out'? What is significant and meaningful, as distinct from trivial and superficial? What is deemed to be right or wrong, good or bad? Where do 'the high' and 'the low' fit in? In particular we define ourselves relationally, in relation to who we are not, into 'Self' and 'Other'. This is the stuff around which identity itself is constructed.

Establishing distinctions is a fundamental process in identity creation and philosophy – the quest for perceiving clearly, understanding and knowing, as well as judging what is right and wrong. It involves the recognition of two or more things being distinct and different, and building thought structures and value systems around these differences. This process is etched into all cultures and helps distinguish one culture from the next. Accepting differences without ascribing value is, it appears, difficult.

Distinction is not in itself necessarily an evil. Labelling, simplifying, generalizing and abstraction are central to understanding the world and being able to negotiate it at all. How else do we distinguish the raw and the cooked, the clean and dirty, safe and dangerous, and good and bad? Indeed languages are systems of distinction and difference. At its best, distinction reduces the clutter of information, helps lift general concepts out of observations by seeing common features and allows you to jump across themes and subjects and to discern universals and general principles.

But when focus on distinction becomes too sharp it can feed discrimination and prejudice – and these have caused disagreements, conflicts and wars throughout history.

We could imagine the acceptance of difference as a spectrum or continuum. At one extreme there is very active hatred, passing through aversion, which is more a default mechanism, to sufferance, benign indifference, coexistence, tolerance, to active interaction, cooperation and finally co-creation at the more positive end. In *The Intercultural City* we argue that if cities, whether through choice or ignorance, find themselves in the 'aversion' or 'benign indifference' sectors of the spectrum; they will ultimately lose out – in competitiveness or quality of life – to those that actively seek to position themselves in the zone of 'active interaction'.

SORTING AND CATEGORIZING

These categorizing and sorting processes simultaneously define and are shaped by geography, values and understandings of 'blood'. The place focus reminds us how geography, topography, neighbourhoods, streets, cities and countries influence us. We schematize 'blood' and 'belonging' into understandings of families, clans, tribes, races, ethnic groups, cultures, nations and ultimately civilizational realms. The wider the grouping, the more tenuous and unstable they become, except where, as in the case of nation, geography, history and government collude to reify them into actual existence.

Family seems self-evident: mother/father, brother/sister, uncle/ aunt, grandparents, cousins, and so on. There is the sense of immediate relation – heritance, household, close lineage – though any anthropologist can tell you that cultures differ enormously with regard to understandings of kinship. State (inheritance, benefits) and medical ('next of kin') definitions and received cultural norms help stabilize our understandings of family, while marriage, divorce, adoption and friends blur the seemingly crisp distinctions. Family is central to our sense of belonging as it invokes feelings of love, of likeness in terms of shared blood and experiences, and of home – family is integral to living arrangements. And if you don't like the family you're born into, you can always find or start a new one. We need to belong, and so transfixed with belonging are we that many of us seek an extended family of dead relatives. Websites offering genealogies and family trees constitute a growth industry. TV programmes tracing family histories become ever more popular. The fashion for genealogy is a modern form of ancestor worship.

For some if not most people, further, wider affiliations like race and nation are needed. 'Race' describes groups of people and is used as a distinguishing concept though by differing criteria: sometimes by 'common ancestry' or biologically, sometimes geographically or nationally, sometimes by visual distinctions, sometimes by a mixture of all these. The categories black, white, Hispanic, the French, Creole, Asian, Chechen, for example, demonstrate a right royal collection of conflations and confusions. 'Ethnic group' is a similarly fraught concept.

'Nation' may seem a slightly less contentious notion for, as aforementioned, geography and government can make it a real entity. We are 'nationals' of one or more states. Most of us have passports that tell us so. But 'nation' can also conflate geography with a shared history and a common people, if not race. The rise of new nationalisms, and the success of some, demonstrate that nations can be fragile. Yet sometimes this very fragility coexists with vehement nationalism.

Finally, and most ambitious in terms of categorization, are civilizational realms. Understanding them is particularly pertinent in the context of a globalized media where sweeping conceptualizations function critically to represent a world frequently understood to be divided into a small number of camps. These realms are groupings of cultures and subcultures that we perceive to have a binding narrative or common way of explaining the world. They help us understand the big cultural differences, such as assumptions about existence and destiny or even time, as well as the seemingly smaller things that collectively make a culture. We may assume within a realm a loose coherence of values, beliefs, modes of thinking, ideas, prejudices, views of beauty and ugliness, faiths and religion. They are the widest geographical groupings of ideas of who you are, how to live, think and what to believe in that we perceive to be held in common. From a Western perspective we may, for instance, distinguish realms between Chinese, Indian, Islamic, Christian, Japanese and so on. The Western media's construction of the 'Arab street' is another example of such a grouping. A Chinese or Indian's perspective of how to separate the world into different realms will be different, however.

We assumed and believed for a long while that nations linked blood, geography and values. People tried to create a shared narrative of origin, destiny and initial myth. And nationhood has come back with a vengeance in Eastern Europe. So being French, an Arab, or someone from Benin, Croatia or China was key. With so much people movement through time these myths are difficult to sustain.

But TV programmes in Britain such as *Who Do You Think You Are?* and *100% English* have helped to explode the myth of clear-cut groupings of belonging and within that the case for racial 'purity', revealing surprising results. Many participants dropped their jaws as they found themselves with racial origins from Africa, Mongolia, Romany gypsies or the Middle East when they thought they were quintessentially English. This raises the question: When can I become English or an Italian, an Israeli, an Iranian? What are the criteria? Is it merely living there, accepting the customs or faith, or is it more?

The categorizations we use change over time. In one period it is tribe, nationhood or class that is in vogue, in another it is lifestyle categories. They all amount to the same thing – to distinguish one from another and to ascribe value and importance to distinctions. Trees of origin are created out of distinctions to describe how the complex or developed come from the simple. They are the genealogies, typologies and taxonomies that structure our biological world and much else.

This is how people order the world and justify their position in it and differentiate themselves from others, to feel *right*, even *chosen* in some instances. Within such taxonomies we can develop hierarchies and create boundaries. We do it even within institutions and professional associations and, in a capitalist economy, through consumption. Ultimately we build nations on these edifices as well as belief systems such as religion. Faith, what you look like and how you behave have always been great dividers between who is 'in' and who is 'out', who you like and who you hate.

Distinction is a social fact that places different values on different individuals and things. And in spite of our democratic age, making distinctions continues. It drives fashion, from clothes and housing to who we meet and where we go on holiday. Distinction establishes our tastes or aesthetic codes. These may seem trivial but they are still part of the more profound identity creation process. The criteria on which we make such judgements about what is important have always been a matter of controversy. It is the negotiation of the significance of differences that drives and shapes a culture and its resulting rituals.

VALUES AND HIERARCHIES

In biology, the study of taxonomy is one of the most conventionally hierarchical kinds of knowledge, placing all living beings in a nested structure of divisions related to their probable evolutionary descent. Most evolutionary biologists assert a hierarchy extending from the level of the specimen, to the species of which it is a member, to further successive levels of genus, family, order, class, phylum and kingdom.

Given a set of distinctions and difference, the next step in identity creation is to ascribe value to any position, whether you are up or down – that is to rank according to perceived criteria – importance, sacredness, right/wrong, advanced/backward, expedient/foolish, and so on. This defines the parameters and status that circumscribe the relative position or standing of things. With living things – from plants to animals, including humans – it shapes the patterning of reciprocal behaviour. In human terms we recognize throughout history these ranking schemes, such as barbarian, slave, freeman, citizen, noble, ruler – systems of class, caste and status.

We separate physically too and classify areas according to attractiveness and whether they are for 'people like me'. These are hierarchies of taste. At one time the city may have been segregated into quarters based on status, profession or religion. Now it might be housing estates and gated communities. Crossover is not encouraged and market price is the great divider. That world of distinctions is built on and creates bodies of apparent truth, knowledge systems and a canon. That canon is now under threat and radically so.

Hierarchies are powerful ordering devices that result from sorting. At first sight they feel compelling as they seem to be self-evidently true, practical and workable. In a computer, subcomponents or modules, which are themselves created out of smaller components (integrated circuits), which in turn are internally organized using hierarchical methods, fit into a larger structure that makes the computer. But human interaction is not a computer.

A hierarchy orders things or perceptions of people up and down and helps us understand, or rather, constitute our understanding of, the world. But not all hierarchies are necessary and some can hinder lateral, equitable and effective communication between people. So you might find two co-workers, neither of whom is the other's boss, but both of whose chains of command will eventually meet through a complicated, inefficient loop or pathway. And this is why hierarchical structures are increasingly under threat and new more equality-based organizational forms, such as matrix management, are more popular as they give individuals and teams more scope to perform. Hierarchy and respect for diversity are uncomfortable partners.

SIMPLICITY AND COMPLEXITY

A world where 'this is just so', a world of single and simpler 'truths', is easier to deal with than one of multiple truths, varying values, and many interpretations and diversity, or a world where people look different, believe different things and behave not like me. It is easier to slot into the former life – it appears more manageable, simpler and efficient. At one level it is effective, of course. You do not need to think or to challenge yourself. You can get on with life more speedily; there is a structure to life and a pattern. This is etched into the mindset and beliefs and these become self-reinforcing over time. Most things then confirm what we already thought – this is the 'confirmation bias'.

Sorting and categorizing is an attempt to reduce complexity by creating borders and boundaries between people, values and things. But sorting is also a precondition for creating prejudices. In our current period of dramatic change, mobility and information overload these tendencies are reinforced. There is little space for reflection and an urge to reduce every issue to a sound bite problem with a simple solution.

These in turn can themselves become barriers to further understanding as we block things off. Yet the urge to define is sensible. It is an attempt to increase predictability, to allow us to prejudge things by responding to default preferences so we can simplify the world. The key to reducing complexity is to reduce the number of events, variables, thoughts and distinctions you have to handle. This is a form of reductionism. It is embedded in our culture.

These default responses can provide apparent continuity and stability. They are then anchored by set ways of behaviour that become the prejudices.

Being less open has a flipside and a cost. Exploring and easy discovery get lost, stimulation is curtailed, knowledge possibilities are reduced and, ultimately, the potential for enrichment suffers. Ideas and inventions require openness to flourish. This openness in turn needs the ability to live with ambiguity and a lack of certainty and predictability. This is a tall order for some.

BREAKING THE UNIFIED CANON

But everywhere you look there is a breakdown of the simple canon that things are as they seem. Truth systems are collapsing. The natural sciences are one example. For centuries we worked within the sharp distinction of things being objective and sharply separate from the subjective. At the boundaries of physics, chemistry and biological research we now know that it all depends on how you look at things. For example, a conscious decision as to how to look at an electron will determine what it is and its properties. If we ask a particle question we get a particle answer, if I ask a wave question I will get a wave answer (Capra, 1982). The classic distinctions between mind and matter and the observer and observed no longer hold.

Postmodernism has challenged our perceptual and value land-scapes. We see more clearly now the multiple truths as we wrench ourselves out of a singular Eurocentric or Western mindset. Suddenly there are many things to be known and perhaps they are better. Perhaps an Indian, Chinese or Islamic worldview or that of native peoples has something to teach the West. These are well beyond perceptions about how life should be lived, according to what values and what is deemed important. The more collectivist, group or socially oriented thinking suddenly comes into its own when we think of the challenges to address global warming, where individualism shows its limitations. Alternative medicines are gaining credence to the extent that you can receive such therapies free at special National Health Service clinics. You merely need an Internet connection to self-publish to a potentially global audience.

New thinking looks at interdependences, relationships and how assemblies of parts make a whole. It takes complexity as its starting point. It tends to value diversity in thought, ideas and the make-up of people. It sees things organically. You could say it reverses Occam's

Razor principle from 'All things being equal, the simplest solution tends to be the best one' to 'All things being equal, the most complex might open out the most possibilities'. As you switch from a world of more rigid patterns to a world of interrelationships, traditional structures do not work anymore.

DIVERSITY: THE CENTRAL DILEMMA OF THE AGE

Dealing with and valuing diversity, difference and the desire for distinctiveness is the central dilemma of our age. Acknowledging and living at ease with the landscape of diversities is different from focusing on differences. The challenge is to create a coherent narrative for diversity and how it can answer the problems of our age. This is what we attempt to begin in this book.

The drive to prejudge can take on a visceral, sinister and potentially physically dangerous character. While we can pretend having prejudices about how people look or think does not matter or affect us, the reality is that such prejudices jeopardize our well-being and our ability to live comfortably. When we ascribe too much importance to ordering concepts like race or tribe or nationality, we admit the possibility of conflict given the context of the inevitable coexistence in towns and cities of people from different parts of the world. Worse, when faced with crisis, people tend to withdraw further into their self-categorizations to seek solace and stability. When food or fuel is hard to come by, faith, for example, may be the only reliable constant in a person's life to which to turn.

However, the notion of tribe is today being reconfigured beyond bloodlines and geography as groups of the young define their cultural interests as if they were a tribe. Professional associations can even be seen as tribal. So from a diversity perspective it becomes interesting to see what happens when, say, an Islamic planner meets a Western one...

Projecting ahead, say 50 years, will new markers of distinction emerge that cut across lines of colour, class and ethnicity or will one issue like 'ethnicity', 'religion' or 'colour' trump all others? Instead, might attitudes to greenness and sustainability or other ideas suddenly become dominant ways of dividing the world as 'class' once did? Or, even, might completely different worldview contrasts develop such as flash, fast and the mobile versus staid, slow and sedentary?

A final issue. Has acceptance of diversity become a moral universalism and should we make normative judgements about this? Can this concept or doctrine apply to all persons and all things for all times in all situations? Moral universalism is the *meta-ethical* position that applies to all people, regardless of culture, race, sex, religion, nationality, sexuality or any other distinguishing feature. Its justification is only so that the human endeavour can survive given our shared vulnerability to suffering. If this is so, a universal reason applies that overrides all relative moral codes. Many people believe they have more important duties to family members, friends, compatriots and their ethnicity rather than to strangers, foreigners or the planet. The 'intercultural city' notion challenges us to re-engage with the strange and the different and the planet. Indeed, welcoming the stranger is part of the tradition of most cultures.

2

The Context of Diversity

PEOPLE ON THE MOVE

There are now few parts of the world that are entirely homogeneous, while an increasing number of urban communities now routinely comprise dozens of different groups in visible numbers. Major cities are now 'world cities' inasmuch as they are becoming microcosms of the world in all its teeming diversity.

This is no more so apparent than in the UK. London is now more diverse than any city that has ever existed. Altogether, more than 300 languages are spoken by the people of London, and the city has at least 50 non-indigenous communities with populations of 10,000 or more. Virtually every race, nation, culture and religion in the world can claim at least a handful of Londoners. London's Muslim population of 607,083 people is probably the most diverse anywhere in the world, besides Mecca. Only 59.8 per cent of Londoners consider themselves to be 'White British', while 3.2 per cent consider themselves to be of mixed race (Kyambi, 2005).

And while London represents a unique kind of diversity, the rest of the UK is now changing too. In 1997, a total of 63,000 work permit holders and their dependants came to Britain. In 2003, it was 119,000. Altogether, between 1991 and 2001, the UK population increased by 2.2 million, some 1.14 million of whom were born abroad. And all this was before EU enlargement in May 2004, which brought 130,000 more people from the new member states in its first year alone.

There are 37,000 Pakistan-born people in Birmingham and 27,500 in Bradford, 25,000 Indians in Leicester, 4000 Bangladeshis in Oldham and 4000 West Indians in Nottingham. There are now over 1000 French people living in Bristol and Brighton, 650 Greeks in Colchester, 600 Portuguese in Bournemouth and Poole, 800 Poles in Bradford, 1300 Somalis in Sheffield, 770 Zimbabweans in Luton, 370 Iranians in Newcastle and 400 in Stockport, and 240 Malaysians in Southsea. And these figures only represent those who are foreign-born and not the much larger numbers, of second generation and beyond, of people whose nationality and identity are hyphenated.

This phenomenon is familiar – though not uniformly so – across the EU. Over the next two decades the total population of the EU25 is expected to increase by more than 13 million inhabitants from 459 million to 472 million. Growth up to 2025 will be due mainly to net migration (World Bank, 2005). Although we are seeing some migration to rural areas, the impact is largely urban and the population of most large cities in northern and western Europe already comprises between 15 and 30 per cent people of non-European descent.

Net international migration continues to be the main engine of population growth in Canada too, accounting for about two-thirds of the annual increase in 2005–2006. Between 1 July 2005 and 1 July 2006, Canada's population increased by 324,000 to an estimated 32,623,500. During this period, the nation took in 254,400 immigrants, 9800 more than in the previous year. International migration's role in Canada's population growth even exceeds its impact in the US. In 2004–2005, net international migration accounted for two-thirds of Canada's population growth, compared to 38 per cent south of the border.[1] Migration continues to exceed natural population growth in Australia too.[2]

People have always moved – the difference today is the scope and scale of movement. Take worldwide migration. There were 75 million migrants in 1960, 87 million in 1975, 111 million in 1985, 165 million in 1995 and 191 million in 2005. The global count of uprooted people rose to nearly 21 million in 2005 and the annual figure for asylum seekers hovers at around 660,000 (UNHCR, 2005). There are nearly 2 million foreign students studying abroad of which a third are in the US, and the US, UK, Germany, France and Australia account for 66 per cent of all foreign students.[3] In 1950 some 25 million people travelled abroad. By 1960 it had risen to 70 million and 800 million in 2000, with a predicted 1 billion by 2010, an astonishing 40-fold increase over this 50-year period. Further, there are predicted to be 10 billion domestic travellers per annum by 2010.[4]

This said, we should not allow the scale of current migration to obscure the fact that many communities in the world have been bi-polar or multiethnic for decades if not centuries. There are obvious high profile locations such as Palestine, Northern Ireland or Bosnia but very many others through the Balkans, Asia Minor and Central Asia for example where ancient peoples have lived side by side, sometimes in peace and sometimes not. These communities too cry out for an intercultural approach, whether or not their situation has been more recently supplemented by migration.

Let us also explore what is known about the levels of interaction between different people across ethnic lines. A recent study conducted by the Ipsos MORI Social Research Institute for the Commission for Racial Equality (Ipsos MORI, 2006) found that a significant majority of the British public believe that they live in a country that has good relations between different types of people – with only 20 per cent of people disagreeing (see Figure 2.1 below). Furthermore, most people (two-thirds) believe that over the last five years, the level of interaction between groups has remained the same or improved. Members of ethnic minority groups were notably more positive in this regard than the public as a whole.

Beneath these headline figures there is, however, considerable vari-ation in the way that people actually interact. Sixty-two per cent said they mixed socially with people from other ethnic groups at the shops, but only half this number formed meaningful relationships to the extent that they were mixing at home with people from different ethnic backgrounds to themselves (see Figure 2.2 below). While half mixed with people from different ethnic groups at work, school or college, fewer chose to mix socially with people from different ethnic groups after work, and fewer still (32 per cent) mixed with people

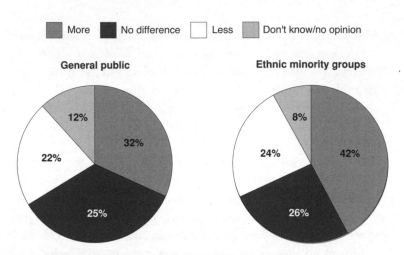

Base: GB residents 15+ years (1,068). Fieldwork: 28 September–3 October 2006
Ethnic minority groups: England residents 16+ years (223). Fieldwork: 15–22 November 2006

Source: Ipsos MORI

Figure 2.1   Growing intercultural mixing?

through hobbies or sports clubs at least monthly. In all cases, white people were the least likely to engage in interaction.

Ipsos MORI (2006) also looked into who was interacting with whom. Perhaps unsurprisingly, greater mixing was closely associated with greater opportunity to mix and so levels of social mixing were much lower among older people, those who were not in work and in areas of lower ethnic diversity such as Scotland (13 per cent) and the South West (15 per cent), in contrast to areas of higher diversity such as London (50 per cent) and the West Midlands (42 per cent) where people were most likely to say they mixed socially with people from other backgrounds at least monthly.

Mixing occurred less among those from lower social grades, those educated to less than degree level, people renting from the council or housing associations, and tabloid newspaper readers. Men were more likely to mix via work, school or college (56 per cent), socially outside work (44 per cent), hobbies and sports clubs (38 per cent), whereas women were more likely to mix socially at home (32 per cent).

	General public	White	Black	Asian
	% mix at least monthly			
Base: All respondents	(1063)	(996)	(114)	(109)
At the shops?	62	60	76	84
At work, school or college?	49	47	75	64
Through hobbies or at sports clubs?	32	30	52	34
Socially outside work?	41	39	71	59
At your home or their home?	30	27	83	58

Source: Ipsos MORI

Figure 2.2 Where, if at all, do we mix?

Seventy-two percent of people who mixed with others at work, school or college at least monthly also chose to mix socially in other circumstances, and this was even higher among ethnic minorities (84 per cent), suggesting that mixing with others is something people do in both formal and informal social situations. Such people who mix in a variety of situations were more likely to be young, to read broadsheet newspapers and live in London. People who mixed in a variety of social situations also tended to be more positive about all measures of diversity and integration.

THE IRREPRESSIBLE URGE FOR CROSS-POLLINATION

We are more intercultural than we think. In many fields it is so ubiquitous we cannot see it. Take the UK. Cultural influence and mixing has etched itself into the fabric of its life for centuries, as it has to the cultures of the peoples who have come here. This is even truer for countries defined by immigration such as Australia or Canada.

Take the quintessential icon of British food: fish and chips. Fried fish came over from Eastern Europe with the Jews and the chips from

Huguenots' France; the Brits put them together as the innovation, fish and chips. Ketchup comes to us from the Cantonese *Kher-Chap*. Chutney feels British but is Indian in origin, as are important ingredients in Worcester sauce and Branston pickle. The origins of tea are Chinese and English breakfast tea came to Britain via India. The haggis reached Scotland from its origins in Greece via France, transmuting along the way. Curry powder sounds Indian but as a mix of spices is a British invention. The pizza we know is an American adaptation of a Neapolitan pastry. Then different cultures add their twist to the pizza – for one it may be pineapple for the other reindeer sausage. The pizza is so resilient because it is so adaptable. Pasta, so quintessentially Italian, has many creation myths from its appearance in Greek mythology to the first certain written record of noodles cooked by boiling in the Jerusalem Talmud, written in Aramaic in the 5th century AD. The Arabs then brought noodles to Italy during their conquest of Sicily in the 9th century. So the romantic myth that Marco Polo brought pasta on his return from China has long been debunked. The vegetables we think of as British come from elsewhere: the potato from America, the brussel sprout from Iran and Afghanistan (Spencer, 2003).

Most of these foods stay largely faithful to their origins – there is a kind of cultural essentialism, they remain recognizable. But they absorb and reject influences as they go through the taste checker. So pizza with chips as a filling did not work, nor pizza with sauerkraut.

Indeed, some cuisines are defined by fusion. Australian food culture received a blast of life from the new immigrants, so liberating itself from the lamb, mash and peas stereotype. The result is a cuisine that truly brings about 'interculturalism' through the fusion of the best of European food traditions and the Asian influences more recently permeating throughout Australian society. It is now a reality that almost all supermarkets in Australian cities include shelves of produce from across the world and TV cooking shows bring fusion recipes into virtually every home.

This conversation across cultures occurs in sports. Take cricket. England, it is said, regained the Ashes in 2005 because of 'reverse swing' bowling. This was a Pakistani invention associated with cricketers such as Wasim Akram and Waqar Younis. When introduced it was seen as a dubious and 'wily oriental trick' probably involving cheating. Later they taught it to English players such as Freddie Flintoff, from there making its way through the system to players like Simon Jones of Glamorgan. It is now England's 'secret' weapon.[5]

Think too of music where cultural mixes create distinct new forms and innovations. The classic example is jazz. It is a combination of African music transmuted through Mississippi delta blues and the gospel churches of the Alabama cotton fields, combined with Caribbean and especially Cuban rhythms themselves responding to their African background, native American influences and then a Western classical music element, which came in via ragtime. Interestingly, all of these musical styles coexisted side by side in New Orleans and might have continued to do so. It took the repressive imposition of the racist 'Jim Crow' laws and particularly the re-designation of the relatively privileged mixed-race Creole people as second-class citizens, which forced them into solidarity with the black population and brought about the fusion of musical traditions from whence came jazz at the turn of the 20th century (Ward and Burns, 2000).

More recently there is house music, a collection of styles of electronic dance music whose earliest forms begin in the early to mid-1980s combining US black disco with German electronic music such as Kraftwerk and Art of Noise. Its two places of origin are Chicago and Detroit clubs. The common element of most house music is a 4/4 beat generated by a drum machine together with a solid (usually also electronically generated) bass line. Upon this foundation are added electronically generated sounds and samples of music such as jazz, blues and synth pop.[6]

Other musical mixes include Chutney, a combination of Hindi and calypso music popular in Trinidad, and Bhangra Beat, a combination of traditional Punjabi music, with Western rock beats that, when mixed further with Jamaican Ragga, transmogrified into Bhangramuffin (Cooper, 2004). More recently Bollywood music now combines distinctively Hindi sounds with Western style rhythms and has even stormed the bastions of London's West End theatres.

With an increased frenzy, fashion has been scouring the world for impulses. Barely a decade ago seasons were twice a year. They are now six. Themes may be territorial – a Russian look here, an African ethnic touch there. They may be subject based – the safari look, the military look, power dressing or tart chic or any combination of them. Anything to get the clothes off the hanger. This mixing can be confusing. Perhaps the threshold has been overreached as the pot-pourri of styles creates an international style of little distinctiveness, here today and gone tomorrow.

Think of gardens. What would our public parks be without gazebos, summer houses, water gardens brought in from Asia and through the Moors, let alone the plants themselves (Turner, 2005)? Consider architecture. At one extreme, perhaps, Brighton Pavillion, the opulent seaside home remodelled in Indian style by John Nash between 1815 and 1823 for George IV, or the Moorish market built in Spitalfields in 1905. Or the more ordinary bungalow. The word derives from the Hindi word *bangla* and means a house 'in the Bengal style', a tiled house surrounded by a veranda. This leaves aside the innumerable decorative touches, with Chinese and Indian elements that mark out houses grand and simple throughout the land. An instance is Edward William Godwin, who promoted Anglo-Japanese taste, who built the Guild Hall, Northampton and Congleton town hall.

Consider too domestic furnishings – the rich have always brought in the fanciful. There is chinoiserie – decorative work produced under the influence of Chinese art. Imitations of Eastern art started to reach Europe in the Middle Ages in the porcelains brought by returning travellers. The East India trading companies of the 17th and 18th centuries imported Chinese lacquers and porcelains. Dutch ceramics quickly showed the influence of Chinese blue and white porcelains. By the middle of the 18th century the enthusiasm for Chinese objects affected practically every decorative art applied to interiors, furniture, tapestries and bibelots, and supplied artisans with fanciful motifs of scenery, human figures, pagodas, intricate lattices, and exotic birds and flowers. Later there was Japonisme in ceramics, furniture and jewellery. Many of these designs are still produced by Wedgwood, Royal Doulton, the textile designers and wallpaper manufacturers. These plates and designs reached the poor as well as the rich. Liberty was opened 1875 as an oriental warehouse bringing in rattan and bamboo. These crossovers were reflected in art movements. Japanese art affected Art Nouveau; Picasso and cubism were influenced by African art and Art Deco by Aztec, Mayan and Egyptian signatures. Bernard Leach brought oriental influences into British pottery and these innovations in turn influenced Japan.

Jumping forward in time the crossovers continue. Sir Terence Conran brought continental taste to Britain (Pearman, 2001). Italian and Spanish pottery designs, duvets from Austria and Switzerland, Scandinavian lighting and cookware, chicken bricks from France. Then as the hippie trail exploded, India and the Far East came back to fashion in the guise of rattan furniture, floral textiles, bedspreads and most notably the waft of incense.

The adept eye can unravel a plethora of cultures and cultural influences in any British, European, Australian or North American household: the food we eat, the clothes we wear, the furniture that surrounds us, the gadgets we use, the entertainment we consume.

Let us not forget language. English itself is a mix of two great language groups within the Indo-European language family, the Germanic and the Romance. Countless words reveal the origins: *stuhl* and stool, *chaise* and chair. The same is true of concepts. Most recently the 'slow food' and 'slow cities' concept came to the rest of the world via Italy, itself having made play on the English 'fast food' by inverting it. Equally, 'peaceful resistance' came to us via India.

In the Muslim world there were the bold inventions in mathematics such as the development of algebra, the invention of the concept of zero, organizing the number system into decimals as well as the principle of the pendulum that was used to measure time – all vital raw materials for the scientific revolution. Muslims not only passed on Greek classical works but also introduced new scientific theories, without which the European Renaissance could not have occurred.

The flow of exchange and weft and wove of interchange strengthens cultures and feels comfortable as long as cultures do not feel they are giving up too much of their identity and the traffic is not one way. It is these contrasts that the great city negotiates.

EXPLORING THE LANDSCAPE OF DIVERSITY

We set out to reread much of the classic literature on migration, race and ethnicity, which might appear to have an influence on the way urban policy addresses cultural diversity. It soon dawned there is an awful lot of it. From Europe the work of John Rex, Stuart Hall, Paul Gilroy, Ulf Hannerz, Tariq Modood, Pnina Werbner, Les Back and John Solomos; and in the US, George Borjas and Alejandro Portes, to name but a few. And all have inspired subsequent generations of adherents and critics. Important as this literature is, it can tend to dominate the field of vision and cast a long shadow, leaving little space for other perspectives.

So, while according due respect, we have tried to approach our reading for this book from another angle. Simplistically, instead of starting from diversity and looking outwards to think about the city, we have started from several separate but related standpoints to home in on diversity. We do not claim to have a new paradigm on diversity. Yet by starting from unfamiliar or unexpected places both for ourselves and our readership we hope to stimulate a series of jolts. These might help fresh interpretations of an old idea or even new insights into a crowded and sometimes rather insular field.

We started by thinking about the city and looking at what energizes and drives it, what divides and unites it, what agitates and soothes it. We have thought about spaces within a city – physical and social but also spaces of the mind that subconsciously influence how positively or negatively we feel towards a place and its people. In particular we have sought the sources of energy – particularly in the form of social, economic, technological and cultural innovations – that can determine whether a place is vibrant or stagnant, open or closed. We have looked a little at how new ideas and trends are born and what can aid or inhibit their spread and adoption and have asked to what extent cultural diversity can be seen as a stimulant or an inhibitor of this urban innovative energy. From the level of the city we have also tried to zoom down to the level of the mundane individual interaction of citizens to try and understand what fuels the almost routine attractions and aversions that choreograph our daily lives.

So our reading has taken us at times quite a way off the beaten track that may only be familiar to specialists and professionals in the race relations field.

Aside from the classics noted, there are five principal strands of literature which have informed this project:

- the literature on cities and the factors – economic, social and cultural – that influence the direction they take;
- studies of impact of diversity within groups, organizations and companies;
- public policy on diversity at national and local levels;
- research on how innovations come about and how new ideas are disseminated through networks;
- the contribution of social psychology to understanding how individuals and groups behave in relation to each other.

The cosmopolitan city

Writers have long concerned themselves with the question of what the city is and how it works as an economic and social entity (Park et al, 1925; Mumford, 1938, 1961; Wirth, 1964) and this has included consideration of the value of variety. However, Jane Jacobs is perhaps the first writer on cities not simply to describe diversity but to make the case for it as a driving force for long-term urban prosperity (Jacobs, 1961). Although her take on diversity is less concerned with culture and ethnicity than with economics and land use, the principle remains the same. Writing way ahead of her time, when principles of order, zoning and homogeneity were radically reshaping Western cities, she presaged many of the concerns that now dominate our current city debates. She was one of the first people to conceive of the city, not as a machine but as an organism and thus to pursue a line of enquiry akin to our understanding of biodiversity. Just as we know that the greater the variety and diversity of an ecosystem, the greater will be its resistance to misfortunes brought on by disease, weather or the economy, so we should intervene to ensure cities retain the same qualities.

Peter Hall (1998) has reviewed cities through history that have left a mark on the world and asks what makes for a creative city and an innovative milieu. Looking at Athens, Rome, Florence, Paris, London and Berlin in the former category and Manchester, Glasgow, Berlin (again), Detroit, San Francisco/Silicon Valley and Tokyo-Kanagawa for the latter he finds some common themes. One of these, he reminds us, is that the city of diversity is not an invention of our current age. Dynamic cities have always attracted migrants to them and their greatness has often sprung from the tension created between the insider and the outsider. As he says:

> *A creative city will therefore be a place where outsiders can enter and feel that state of ambiguity: they must neither be excluded from opportunity, nor must they be so warmly embraced that the creative drive is lost.*

Richard Florida (2002a, 2002b, 2003) has attracted widespread interest by being the first in the field to establish a quantitative methodology to endorse the notion that diversity is a positive urban asset. His thesis is that the cities that compete most successfully in the modern world will, not surprisingly, have command of the most advanced technologies. More than this, though, they will also be able to attract and hold the most talented people ('the creative class') and that one of the main factors in making them 'talent magnets' will be the tolerance the cities demonstrate to people in all their diversity. Based on a study of 50 US cities he gathers a range of data to measure and compare levels of tolerance and diversity, to produce indexes that he claims as predictors of city competitiveness. The technique was more recently applied, in truncated form, to 50 UK cities, and also to the nations of Western Europe (Florida, 2003; Florida and Tinagli, 2004).

His work has undoubtedly raised the level of interest in issues of city diversity and stimulated a lively debate. The application of statistical data gives greater weight to the assertions, though it must be borne in mind that while Florida claims tolerant cities are the most successful cities, this is not a causal relationship but simply a correlation, for which he has been subject to scholarly critique (Malanga, 2004). It is also apparent from Florida's work that there are many different forms and impacts of diversity. While he can demonstrate the beneficial effects that highly skilled migrants from the Far East might have on American cities, he admits the creative economy does little to ameliorate the traditional divides between whites and non-whites in American society, and may even exacerbate them.

In a similar vein, Charles Landry (2000) is concerned with what are the sources of energy and ideas that drive the growth of cities, but is more concerned than Florida with practical implementation. Looking beyond the conventional explanations, he seeks to explain how the apparently intangible quality of creativity can be distilled into a resource and a methodology for use by the 'creative cities' of the future. He recommends cities move beyond the institutionalized separation of multiculturalism towards a new understanding of what it means to live interculturally. He acknowledges rapid people change can destabilize communities yet when mutual respect predominates, newcomers enrich and stimulate possibilities by creating hybrids, crossovers and boundary blurring. Second, he argues that cities must learn to value and work with the various visions of all their citizens in all their diversity and that inward-looking ethnic ghettoes are unlikely to contribute to solving the wider problems of cities. Creativity may happen in fragmented places, but certainly not in marginalized ones.

Meanwhile, some writers have attempted to move beyond Florida in understanding the relationship between diversity and city competitiveness (Alesina and La Ferrara, 2004). Ottaviano and Peri (2004, 2005) take the issue a stage further by testing the various theories against a piece of empirical research in US cities. They ask whether cultural diversity can be demonstrated to have an impact upon the economy in a way that is incontrovertible in economic theory. By comparing a range of both ethnically homogeneous and heterogeneous US cities and looking at patterns of wage levels over an extended period, they conclude that US-born citizens earn more and are more productive in cities that receive high numbers of immigrants than those that do not. They further establish that this is a causal relationship and not a mere correlation – that immigration makes cities more competitive, not that competitive cities attract more immigrants. Unfortunately, the same process of research could not be undertaken in the UK because, unlike the US, the relevant data are not collected at the city level. The nearest equivalent to this line of enquiry in the UK, typified by research conducted by Dustmann et al (2003) for the Home Office, found little evidence to support claims of some that immigrants either take away the jobs of the resident community or that they depress the wages of those in work.

This leads us into a deeper investigation of studies that have sought to understand the relationship between urban economies and cultural diversity. First, there is a considerable literature around immigrant and ethnic entrepreneurship, from which emerge differing approaches either side of the Atlantic. To simplify, the dominant school of thought in the US is that the main factor driving minorities and immigrants into small business is demand-side economics (Light and Gold, 2000; Light and Bhachu, 2004). Markets are there to be made and US society is open enough to enable entry to be quite feasible. European perspectives are rather different, suggesting that to a greater or lesser extent, the various national labour markets are much less open to outsiders either by culture or even statute (Kloosterman and Rath, 2003). As a consequence, immigrants are more likely to be driven into self-employment as the only viable alternative to unemployment. In the UK several scholars chart the trajectories of minority businesses arguing that while it has become commonplace to associate certain groups with particular forms of business and to identify 'ethnic economies' of groups largely trading with themselves, there is a need to enable ethnic businesses to 'break out' and enable them to achieve a 'mixed embeddedness' in both the culture that gave them succour and mainstream economy (Ram and Smallbone, 2001). There is some evidence from the Midlands (Henry et al, 2002) and London (CEEDR, 2003), for example, of Asian entrepreneurs moving out of traditional business sectors and into the creative industries. Related to this is research (Ram et al, 2002) into the potential for cities with a substantial ethnic business sector to improve competitiveness through supplier diversity initiatives, that is, the opportunity for larger companies to gain advantage through enriching their range of products and services through access to a more diverse range of local suppliers.

Trading connections are also the subject of a line of research concerned with potential advantages to be gained from the exploitation of 'diasporic links'. The Chinese are best known for maintaining close ties between communities across the world (Kee, 1994; Cheung, 2004) There is a suggestion that such networks can be fruitful sources of innovation, with particular reference to the Chinese in Silicon Valley (Sher, 2003). Saxenian (1999) describes a virtuous circle in which the best of the world's talent comes to the West Coast, forming hybrid innovation teams that maintain southern California's leading edge. They are responsible for bringing foreign direct investment into the region, and while they maintain networks they channel support and knowledge back to their countries of origin. The issue of whether a diverse population makes a city a more attractive proposition for foreign direct investment has recently been investigated in the case of London but remains difficult to quantify (DTZ Pieda Consulting, 2004).

Diversity in organizations

In a world of difference, race stills plays a significant part but the most important factor is culture. Culture is the sum of those things that define us as individuals and as members of our group and, therefore, that which distinguishes us from others. Alternatively, to think and behave with cultural awareness is to establish a means of understanding and interacting with others that may transcend perceived barriers. We may never fully know what it means to be someone other than ourselves, but if we can understand what factors and influences have made them see the world in the way they do, and we can also reflect upon how our own personal and group behaviours have been formed, we have the basis of a form of empathy upon which relationships can be built.

This idea has been the basis of a body of thought that has expanded rapidly over recent years in inverse proportion to the apparent shrinking of our world brought about by the jet engine, multinational corporations, global communications and migration. Acquiring the capacity to understand others, and be understood by them, may at one time have been thought to be all about language training but it is now recognized as far more than this. Cultural competence is now considered to be an essential skill in an increasing number of professional environments. One writer referring to health outcomes suggests that operationally defined cultural competence is the integration and transformation of knowledge about individuals and groups of people into specific standards, policies, practices and attitudes used in appropriate cultural settings to increase the quality of services, thereby producing better outcomes (Davis, 1997). While the public services in diverse communities have been an obvious interface at which these new competencies have been necessary, it has been in, and for, the world of international trade and commerce that the practice of intercultural communication has been developed most comprehensively. In most societies, trade has throughout history been the primary motivation for exploration and consequently encountering strangers and difference. So it is no surprise that the discipline has been driven in response to the demands of business people to know how they can open up new yet incomprehensible markets.

Rogers and Steinfatt (1999) chart the route by which our understanding of intercultural communication has evolved, explaining the derivation of terms we now take for granted such as social difference, cultural relativism and ethnocentrism. They argue that the greatest boost to the development of the discipline came in post-war America with the realization by the US government that it was too ignorant of other cultures to enable it to fulfil its role of global leadership.

There have been several attempts to produce a typology of cultures to explain to a business audience why different races, ethnicities and nations behave differently (Hofstede, 1991; Trompenaars and Hampden-Turner, 1997). Moving beyond the original need to understand how to sell things to others, these insights are now increasingly valued by those seeking to build multicultural management teams in order to give their corporation a competitive edge over rivals.

This has spurred a growing literature on the perception of a 'diversity advantage' to be claimed by organizations who embrace a diverse workforce and market place with positive strategies. Some of this has the boosterist or proselytizing tone of management self-help manuals (Jameson and O'Mara, 1991; Fernandez and Barr, 1993) while other texts are more reflective. Yet over the past decade diversity management has become a critical aspect of operating a business. Increasing globalization, the changing composition of the population and increasing reliance on non-traditional workforce talent provided a fundamental stimulus for diversity management (Montes, 2000). In other words, a proper business case for diversity has to be built. A review of the literature indicates that this is certainly possible (Cox and Blake, 1991). By focusing on the benefits of diversity and also highlighting the challenges, it is possible to present a very strong business case. However, developing a business case for diversity is made more difficult because of the failure to systematically measure and document the impact of diversity on the bottom line (Robinson and Dechant, 1997).

The new paradigm for diversity management transcends traditional moral arguments by seeking to connect diversity to business perspectives. The new model accepts the philosophies of former paradigms by promoting equality of opportunity for all employees while acknowledging cultural differences among people. It recognizes and respects the value of those differences. The new model for managing diversity lets the organization internalize differences among employees so that the organization learns and grows as a consequence (Coleman, 1995).

Building the business case for diversity has focused on the potential for increased company performance. Recent research into the link between cultural diversity and firm performance in the banking industry indicates that, within the proper context, cultural diversity does in fact add value to the firm (Richard, 2000). The findings of this study indicate that the relationship between racial diversity and a firm's performance is moderated by business strategy. When firms pursue a growth strategy, higher racial diversity is positively related to productivity, return on equity and market performance. Racial diversity enhances productivity and this relationship intensifies as strategic growth increases. Cultural diversity can provide firms with diverse experience and knowledge. These are beneficial qualities for firms with an orientation towards growth (Cox, 1994; Priem et al, 1995; McLeod et al, 1996)

The Australian government's Department of Immigration and Multiculturalism and Indigenous Affairs (DIMIA), in recognition of the business advantage of the country's culturally diverse workforce, has placed a policy focus on the concept of 'productive diversity'. The 2002 DIMIA report, *The Innovation and Learning Advantage from Diversity: A Business Model for Diversity Management*, identifies that in a diverse workplace there 'tends to be more friction, conflict and communication problems', but it also emphasizes that if properly managed, diverse workplaces 'produce more creative and effective outcomes'. According to the DIMIA report (2002):

> *The drivers for such innovation are inevitably the employees and managers of the organization – the human resources – who engage in the learning activity and bring with them unique knowledge sets. An organisation with a greater mix of employees of different cultural backgrounds, mental models, and experience and functional levels will, when appropriately managed generate more innovative products and services.*

Other countries such as New Zealand have recognized the links between diversity, innovation and learning and acknowledge that there have been many missed opportunities in the past. The report *The Integration of Highly Skilled Migrants into the Labour Market:*

Implications for New Zealand Business, prepared for the New Zealand Immigration Service by the University of Auckland (1998), notes that in 'New Zealand, however, the evidence from existing sources suggests that we underutilize skilled migrant labour'. Despite this positive approach to the diversity dividend it is not necessarily an acknowledgement of interculturalism. It asks companies to maximize the advantage of diverse cultural knowledge by a deeper understanding of global markets.

In addition, organizations that overcome resistance to change by accepting diversity appear to be well positioned to handle other types of change, so enabling improved flexibility (Iles and Hayers, 1997). However, in firms that have no growth or negative growth, human resource diversity may impede firm performance. This is because diversity can increase coordination and control costs, especially during downsizing (Williams and O'Reilly, 1998). Interestingly this echoes research conducted on the impact of diversity on the performance of nation states (Collier, 2001).

Another strand of literature is concerned with the potential for diverse teams to increase creativity and innovation. Cultural diversity enables employees to provide different perspectives for the performance of creative tasks. In addition, employees who feel valued and supported by their organization tend to be more innovative (Eisenberger et al, 1990). In another research study, the ideas produced by ethnically diverse groups were judged to be of higher quality than the ideas produced by homogeneous groups (McLeod et al, 1996). Adler (1997) draws on numerous international studies to highlight the superior performance benefits of culturally diverse teams, especially when they are engaged in complex tasks requiring innovation and creativity. The 'Higher Quality Problem-Solving in Teams Research' shows more diverse teams produce more innovative solutions to problems.

Culturally diverse members with different backgrounds and life experiences can see problems from a variety of perspectives. Multiple perspectives stimulate greater discussion and lead to higher quality solutions. Watson et al (1993) found that initially culturally homogeneous teams performed better than culturally diverse groups.

However, as time passed, between-group differences began to converge and ultimately culturally diverse groups performed better than homogeneous groups. The results of this research suggest that diversity in ethnic background may have negative effects on individual and group outcomes early in a group's life, because it takes time for group members to get over their interpersonal differences given that initially there are lower levels of attraction and social integration (O'Reilly et al, 1989). However, once a certain level of behavioural integration has been achieved, groups may obtain benefits from the greater variety of perspectives inherent within a diverse group (Hambrick, 1994). While diverse groups experience more conflict in agreeing on what is important and in working together at the outset, they ultimately outperform homogeneous groups in identifying problem perspectives and generating alternative solutions (Jackson et al, 1995).

The 'business case for diversity' remains a contentious issue. Critics point to the lack of empirical evidence to support assertions that diversity leads to greater creativity or productivity (Lynch, 1997; Grossman, 2000; Kochan et al, 2003). Instead, they claim, organizational context and situational factors moderate diversity-performance relationships. Thus Kochan et al suggest taking a more nuanced view of the business case for diversity focusing on the specific context (Kochan et al, 2003).

Some critics also argue that mainstream thinking on intercultural communication is taking the wrong track (Antal and Friedman, 2003). They criticize the impulse to categorize and reduce cultural differences to a series of typologies. They caricature cultural competence as the simple ability to amass knowledge of customs, rituals, facts and figures that give the Western traveller a fix on a foreign culture. True intercultural communication, they say, is less about content and more about process. In other words the minutiae of what makes two people different is less important than the way they respond towards each other's difference. If difference is seen simply as the barrier that is getting in the way of achieving one's primary objective, one is missing the point. Difference, they argue, is not a barrier but an opportunity and through the mutual exploration of these differences, individuals and groups may find things far more interesting and useful than the objective with which they originally set out. Difference is something we should neither seek to water down, nor to reduce to a catalogue of exotica, but something to be explored for its intrinsic value.

Finally, a bold marriage in the 'business case for diversity' argument links economics and the emerging literature on cultural hybridism. Here Zachary (2003) is in no doubt that diversity can and must be turned to creative advantage. In declaring that countries must 'mongrelize or die', he states cultural hybridism not only to be a fact of modern society but the guiding principle and engine for growth. Cities and nations, just like corporations, must attract the best talent wherever they can find it, and should thrive on the ensuing creative tension. Acknowledging that diversity is only an advantage in strong economies, he is scathing of powerful states such as Germany and Japan that believe they can compete in the world while keeping global migration and culture at bay.

Innovation, networks and knowledge diffusion

In testing the hypothesis that diversity is a source of innovation, we need first to understand what innovation is, how and why it happens and why it is important for cities. Then we need to understand how new ideas spread from the originator to become part of the fabric of our society.

Economic theory over the last few decades explains how innovation, cycles of creation, obsolescence, destruction and re-creation are a familiar path followed by successful economies and companies. 'Home grown' endogenous activity has come to be seen as equally influential as external macroeconomic trends. In this context, cities have started to gain awareness of themselves as actors (Lucas, 1988; Romer, 1990). There is an important debate over the extent to which cities and their component interest groups are able to influence their economic destiny; for instance, the extent to which ideas and knowledge 'spill over' from one group or firm to another within a confined environment so generating the process of competition and collaboration that characterizes the way value is created in the modern urban economy. This sharpens the debate on economic diversity. Should cities encourage the widest selection of economic activity (after Jane Jacobs) or specialize and cluster (after Michael Porter)? Which route is more effective in generating innovation (Duranton and Puga, 2001)? What can the discourse on the merits of economic diversity offer our understanding of cultural diversity? Pinelli et al (2003) apply these principles to the variable of 'the multicultural city' and ask how diversity can affect the economy and, with Lazear (1995), they conclude that diversity can be both a cost upon and a benefit to the urban economy.

There is a problem within the innovation debate as to what an innovation is and how to measure levels of innovativeness. To some it is quite simple: an innovation is a new technology or concept leading to new products and processes, and this can be measured by such things as investment in research and development and the registration of patents (Feldman and Audretsch, 1999). But how does one patent a cultural or social innovation or view and perspective that may have emerged from no one knows where deep within an urban community? New patterns of behaviour and working, fashions, images and brands, foods and languages are all now extremely important economic assets. They tend to emerge in cities, oblivious of research and development budget, knowledge transfer strategies and intellectual property law. If we are to get to the heart of whether urban cultural diversity really is a tangible force, we need a new way of understanding and expressing the process of innovation. Hall and Landry (1997) propose a new means of classifying and benchmarking a much wider range of innovations in the economic and technological field but also social, environmental and cultural innovations. It looks at projects and their capacity to push boundaries of technology, technique, procedure, process, implementation mechanism, problem redefinition, target audience, behavioural impact and professional context as well as creating a new end product. A fresh approach to innovation as the product of diversity is also proposed by Frans Johansson (2004) in *The Medici Effect*.

Welz (2003) approaches innovation from the standpoint of the urban anthropologist. She asks why certain times and places are more innovative than others and whether it is possible to identify and plan in advance the cultural conditions that produce innovative activity. She believes it is possible, that cultural diversity helps and that certain qualities are required within a city to maximize the benefit. Welz summarizes this as the capacity to be 'co-actional' and portrays modern cities as an economic and cultural vortex – a cultural swirl – in which all manner of new ideas and energies are being generated. These can only be realized, not through the insight of a single genius, but through proper structures and collective interaction. The successful innovative cities of the future will thrive on striking the right balance of order and disorder.

A new idea or innovation is of little value unless it is adopted. This process, known as diffusion, has been studied and codified to its most refined level by Everett Rogers (2003). By tracking real life examples of how innovations, ranging from the QWERTY keyboard to hybrid corn, have become adopted, he develops a typology of different social actors, such as early adopters and laggards, to explain how ideas spread through society. He also quotes cases of how perfectly good ideas fail to take hold due particularly to culture and the failure to understand it. This gives us an insight into how diverse and divergent groups within an urban setting might be the source of new and potentially valuable thinking, but also how easy it is to squander or suppress these energies through ignorance or misunderstanding. We also start to understand the roles of different kinds of social actors such as the innovators themselves, and the intermediary brokers, change-agents or opinion-leaders who disperse and connect.

This has been taken up by others, notably Malcolm Gladwell (2000) who is interested in 'how little things can make a big difference'. He identifies typologies of individuals who play crucial roles in the dissemination of knowledge and ideas: connectors, mavens and salesmen. This has echoes with our own interest in 'intercultural exchange agents'.

Culture shock: Absorbing difference and diversity

Every cross-cultural experience is a personal one with downstream emotional and psychological effects and usually an element of stress and even fear. It is a dynamic, though not necessarily positive, experience for both parties. It is better to acknowledge potential difficulties at the outset than to look at mixing through rose-tinted glasses. This is true whatever the reason for mixing: working abroad, visiting friends, tourism, taking the first step of moving to a country permanently, negotiating the mainstream culture as a second-generation immigrant, or hitting foreign shores as an asylum seeker.

Intercultural contact and the potential conflict of values and behaviours between cultures are as old as history. Whether contact results from a short visit or from a permanent stay, the effects of cultural accommodation and dealing with difference can linger on for generations as migrants become settlers and all but indistinguishable from the original host.

We considered earlier the demographic scale and scope of people movement around the globe but there is also an extensive literature on the psychological impacts when different groups and cultures come into contact. This is the literature of 'culture shock' (Ward et al, 2001), deriving from a concept originally proposed by Kalvero Oberg (1960). The simple increase in numbers creates overload and absorption problems. Change feels too fast. Contact with difference, the unfamiliar, the strange and the 'Other' on this scale can be and usually is unsettling in spite of the occasional speck of delight and surprise. The abrupt loss of the familiar and moving from an environment where one has learnt to function easily and successfully to one where one cannot is dramatic for both parties. In addition, being discriminated against can turn people inwards and cause a sense of isolation or diminished self-importance.

The case of the refugee brings most difficulty, having been 'pushed' rather than 'pulled' into a new environment. 'Cultural bereavement' is an apposite term here, expressing the sense of emptiness felt by being displaced, mourning over loss of identity, values, social structures, and even guilt over abandoning a homeland (Eisenbruch, 1991).

All groups have their own stresses and adjustment problems and this applies as much to the host as well as the 'guest'. Even tourism, mostly projected as desirable and pleasurable, can in reality be stressful as people ponder perceptions of safety, crime and the unusual (Pearce, 1982).

How much we learn of and from the 'Other' is much less than one would hope, which makes the challenge of interculturalism urgent and difficult. The summary of the literature suggests mass tourism is at best neutral with respect to increasing mutual understanding and intergroup harmony and in many instances has negative psychological consequences. The cross-cultural connections of students and foreign workers are far less than imagined and these semi-permanent residents make up increasing numbers in cities. The situation of permanent immigrants is little different.

There is overwhelming empirical evidence that interacting with culturally different individuals or functioning in changing, unfamiliar social or physical settings leads to outcomes from mild distress to anxiety and requires coping responses for both incoming groups and the host (Ward et al, 2001). People can adapt to these stresses and successful adaptation involves acquiring culturally relevant competences and skills and creating a positive setting that fosters cultural exchange. The intercultural challenge is that both sides need to adapt – adaptation is not one-way. This affects identity over time. Often, though, it is assumed that the outsider assimilates as the host essentially wants to stay the same.

In mixing or crossing cultures, different social attitudes, moral values and behavioural inclinations meet. This has been explored by several disciplines focusing on different issues. There is a vast array of research on how students adapt to foreign countries (Kagan and Cohen, 1990), how expatriates cope with working overseas (Aycan 1997), how immigrants cope with adjusting to a new country, particularly with a focus on mental health effects (Berry, 1990), or how tourism impacts, especially economically. There is far less research, however, on how hosts are affected by new arrivals and on the broader relationship between a migratory group and the host community and there is limited cross-referencing and cross-fertilization of the literature on immigrants, refugees, tourists, business people and hosts.

The range of research on cross-cultural contact includes: cognitive theorists who focus on how immigrants perceive and think about immigration (Zheng and Berry 1991); social psychologists looking at the attitudes and beliefs people adopt and at intergroup processes and dynamics (Bond, 1986); personality theorists measuring the feelings, states and traits of individuals and how they cope (Leong and Ward, 2000); and communication theorists on verbal and non-verbal messages (Neuliep and Ryan, 1998).

Briefly, they all note that in order to simplify, people stereotype other cultures and they fit reality into their preconceived notions. People cling to stereotypes because they lessen the threat of the unknown by making the world predictable. Anxious people need a familiar predictable world. But the trouble with blanket labelling is that it blocks any realistic or fair-minded appraisal of what people are like. While stereotypes may have a 'grain of truth' in them – 'English people drink lots of tea' – they tell but a fraction of what is there to be known about another culture.

Two theories help us to understand the barriers to successful intercultural engagement. The *culture–distance hypothesis* (Babiker et al, 1980) predicts that the greater the perceived gap between cultures, the more difficulties will be experienced in crossing cultural boundaries. The *similarity–attraction hypothesis* suggests that we are more likely to seek out, enjoy, understand, want to work with, play with, trust, believe, vote for and generally prefer people with whom we share salient characteristics. These include physical attributes like colour and complexion, interests, values, religion, group affiliation, behaviour, attitudes such as those towards women, skills, age, language and knowledge of the cultural zone (Byrne, 1969).

The success of cross-cultural communication therefore depends upon relative degrees of perceived difference, even if the person in question has been in a country for a very long time. Some cluster these differences into 'cultural syndromes' (Triandis, 1990): patterns of attitudes, beliefs, norms and behaviours used to distinguish cultures, such as how they relate to time, women, authority, and perhaps most importantly their view of individualism and collectives. This pattern of reciprocal relationships between the individual and the group sets an implicit contract regulating social life. It balances the freedom of the person and the kind of restrictions to achieve common goals. It affects how the family operates, the political system, industrial relations, the delivery of health, education and justice and even the creation and appreciation of art.

So an Australian or German businessperson is likely to find it easier to work in and adapt to Auckland, New Zealand or Los Angeles than Guangzhou, Yokohama or Manila, while a migrant from Italy or Poland is more likely to be able to adapt in Britain than someone from Somalia. The latter suffer in particular from the cultural distance syndrome – they are black, African and speak a completely different language. Equally, in the US a survey revealed that light skinned immigrants receive more acceptance than dark skinned ones (Espin, 1987).

Difference is exacerbated because of the tendency for cultural and social groups to show ingroup favouritism and to denigrate or disparage outgroups (Abrams and Hogg, 1990). There is a strong tendency to attribute desirable factors to one's own group and less desirable ones to others. These are strategies to maintain self-esteem, especially in the face of insecurity and anxiety. Incomers have strong preferences to retain their cultural identities while sustaining good relations with their hosts. But ingroup favouritism on the part of both parties suggests efforts at integrating are difficult to maintain given outgroup stereotyping, prejudice and discrimination. In fact Henri Tajfel's *social identity theory*, which is about how people see themselves in contrast to others, has rather negative implications for multicultural societies (Tajfel, 1978).

Studies of overseas students consistently show that in spite of being aware of the benefits of contact with the host community and the fact that students actually desire this contact, they report that their best friend comes from their own nationality, because they get socio-emotional support. In one study, 70 per cent had no close British friend after one year, even though when they had close contact they achieved a far better experience and results (Bochner et al, 1985). Our own study in Auckland confirmed these findings (Brecknock Consulting, 2006a).

This suggests that conflict, prejudice and discrimination are strong tendencies of intercultural contact and thus that cultural learning, which focuses on how we feel, behave, think and perceive, is key. What psychological analysis tells us is that perceived discrimination retrenches people and creates less willingness to adapt to the host culture or to understand another culture. When people become threatened increasing differentiation occurs.

Typically when cultures meet there are four responses, whether this is for a Briton moving to Spain, a Costa Rican to Canada or a Hong Kong Chinese to Australia:

- to stay monocultural and become chauvinist by rejecting new influences as alien so retreating and entrenching within one's own culture and at the extreme to become a militant nationalist;
- to assimilate to the host's culture and to 'pass off' as part of the new, so rejecting one's origins;
- to marginalize oneself by identifying with neither culture or to vacillate between the two and feel at home in neither;
- to synthesize elements of one's culture of origin and that of the host, which is the equivalent of integration at the personal level. The result is to acquire a genuine bicultural or multicultural personality. These people can code switch – they are like a hyphenated person. They have flexibility and a relatively high degree of resilience (Bochner, 1979).

What strategies exist to reduce ingroup favouritism and outgroup negativity? Social psychology tells us that contact is key for mutual understanding, but only under certain preconditions. Rather than expand upon Gordon Allport's 'contact hypothesis' here, we devote significant attention to it later in the book (Allport, 1954).

The best sense of psychological well-being, satisfaction and resilience occur where the culture of origin is respected and overlaid with that of the host. The culture change process then moves towards a bicultural identity. Acknowledging this biculturalism achieves better educational outcomes as studies of Korean-Americans (Gil et al, 1994) or Hispanic youth (Golden, 1987) in the US have shown. In a survey of two New York schools (Rotheram-Borus, 1993), one where most pupils from a variety of backgrounds identified themselves as bicultural was more integrated than a neighbouring tense school where 70 per cent identified themselves mono-ethnically. Donà and Berry's 1994 study of Latin American refugees to Canada found that 77 per cent adopted an integrationist/bicultural attitude and had fewer psychological problems than assimilationists and separatists or those who exhibited high or low cultural preservation. A Quebequois study with Africans showed that although they wanted to integrate biculturally, only 31 per cent could because of lack of openness in the host community (Dompierre and Lavallée, 1990). Such separatism creates ethnic enclaves that provide support yet also shield from communicating with other cultures.

Cultural learning, such as intercultural training, is a major strategy proposed. This can lead to greater understanding of one's own culture and a greater likelihood of thinking about other cultures in more complex terms; an increase in world-mindedness, helping people to be more biculturally competent; and the capacity to solve problems that require cultural understanding and more effective work performance in mixed teams (Brislin and Yoshida, 1994).

A final point. Writing with cross-cultural sensitivity is in itself difficult as there is a Eurocentric bias in setting out and analysing problems in the first place (Sue et al, 1996). For instance, there are major cross-cultural differences in the core values that govern business and industrial systems and often North American business attitudes are treated as if they were universal. Equally, how contemporary group and individual psychology is discussed has a Eurocentric and North American bias.

Cultural diversity and public policy

There is an extensive literature on the different policy models for diversity. The classic division stemming from the 19th century was between *jus soli* ('right of the soil') and *jus sanguinis* ('right of blood') (Brubaker, 1992). One is essentialist, the other not. In the former, nationality or citizenship could be given to any individual born in the territory of the specific state. In the latter, by contrast, an individual needed to be born to a parent who was a national or citizen of that state. Nation states commonly divided themselves between those granting nationality on the grounds of *jus soli* (France, for example) and those granting it on the grounds of *jus sanguinis* (Germany, for example). Most European countries then chose the German conception of an 'objective nationality', based on 'blood', 'race' or language opposing themselves to the republican 'subjective nationality', a notion based on belonging to a land. Today's massive increase in people movement has made countries reassess where to line up between these two antagonistic sources of right.

The initial study that provided us the opportunity to think through ideas around *The Intercultural City* was produced within a UK context in which the policy consensus for over 30 years was multiculturalism. This approach has come under intense scrutiny in Britain (less so in countries like Australia or Canada) and challenged us to explore an alternative approach.

This clarification is, we believe, necessary because even a brief review of only the larger nations of the Western world will reveal a wide variety of policy approaches to cultural diversity. In an earlier book, our colleagues Bloomfield and Bianchini (2004) identified in some detail a range of national approaches to immigration, integration and citizenship. They are briefly summarized and updated below.

International approaches

Civic cultural integration, as practised in France. This approach has evolved as a response to the colonial past influenced by the strong tradition of civic republicanism and state secularism of the French state. Basically all French citizens, regardless of ethnicity, are considered equal under the law. This requires a strict loyalty and adherence to French cultural norms within the public sphere. While, for example an Algerian- or Caribbean-origin citizen is allowed private rights of cultural or religious practice, these are not recognized in any official capacity (Castro, 1994; Favell, 1998). Increasingly this approach has been challenged, particularly by the descendents of migrants who have become clustered in the isolated and desolate *banlieue* housing estates on the periphery of French cities. First, there were high profile legal challenges in which, for example, students demanded the right to wear culturally specific clothing such as headscarves in school. Second, the remarkable success of the French football team drawn largely from people of African stock emphasized just how absent people of colour were from most other aspects of French public life, politics and the media. And most recently, the whole world had the issues of French diversity policy brought dramatically into their living room by the nightly dramas played out as the *banlieues* erupted in insurrection in autumn 2005. It will be interesting to see whether, in the aftermath of this shock, the French state will review its approach (Lichfield, 2005).

Ethnic nationalism, as practised in Germany, became better known in recent decades as the *Gastarbeiter* system. The basis of nationality in Germany (and Austria) has been founded on *jus sanguinis*, the 'right of blood', which made it impossible for anyone other than an ethnic German to attain full rights of citizenship (Brubaker, 1992). Like other Western economies, however, Germany required overseas labour in the 1960s and 1970s and invited large numbers or workers and their families, predominantly from Turkey and the former Yugoslavia, but conferred on them no rights of permanent settlement or full participation in civic affairs. Over several decades, these groups have put down roots, built communities and acquired the German language, making their continued tenuous citizenship seem increasingly anomalous (Soysal, 1996). The issue was brought into even sharper relief when, following the break up of the Warsaw Pact and the Soviet Union, large numbers of 'ethnic Germans', from communities often resident in the East for scores if not hundreds of years and often with little command of the German language, were allowed to settle in the West and given full rights of citizenship. This anomaly has now become the source of open political debate and, in certain parts of the federal state, experiments are now taking place to encourage greater social integration and political participation for minority ethnic groups (Vertovec, 1995; Sandercock, 1998; Bloomfield, 2003).

The southern European approach, particularly Italy, Spain and Portugal, has been characterized by a rapid reappraisal of policy on immigration and integration in recent years. For decades, these were countries of emigration and if immigration was considered by policy makers at all, it was treated in a highly laissez-faire fashion. There was no regulation or monitoring of and fairly relaxed procedures for naturalization. More recently, however, as these countries have joined the EU and the Schengen Agreement, they have built up their economies and started to consider themselves as the southern flank of a 'fortress Europe' and a radical policy shift has taken place. Highly restrictive immigration regimes have been introduced, punctuated by periodic clampdowns on illegal migrants (King and Black, 1997). With regard to integration, the picture is now very patchy, often depending on the political colour of the local authority. So, for example, while Rome and Turin have taken a very explicit approach to encouraging intercultural expression and engagement, the city of Milan has sought to discourage and downplay any sense that it might be comfortable with the fact that is it becoming a multiethnic city (Foot, 2001).

The 'melting pot' is the common analogy to describe the approach of the US. With some similarities to the French approach, the US has insisted upon integration of immigrants under a common language and constitutional rights. In some ways, by encouraging adherence to cultural uniformity, national values and the market-driven 'American way', it might be said to be more assimilationist than any other model considered (Isbister, 1996; Kurthen et al, 1998). Alternatively, the US is a migrant nation *par excellence* and continues to take a very proactive stance in its encouragement of immigration, although entry restrictions have become more robust since 9/11. What is clear is that the US is a far from culturally homo-genous society on the ground. US cities are clearly distinguished by ethnically defined districts. The general conclusion seems to be that while the US workplace is becoming highly diverse, many Americans still choose to live in communities made up people of the same ethnic background as themselves. And, while it seems that most newly arrived minority groups are finding little difficulty in finding a niche in the US economy, there is evidence that a large proportion of indigenous black people (perhaps up to one third) are locked into spatial and economic ghettoes from which there is little hope of escape. The recent catastrophe affecting the mainly black population of New Orleans and the speculation that the city may be repopulated in a very different ethnic configuration is an illustration of the fact that 'the melting pot' is perhaps an unhelpful metaphor for the current state of US cultural integration (Niman, 2005).

The cultural mosaic is the analogy that has come to describe the approach taken by Canada and, to a lesser extent, Australia and New Zealand. Canada has probably gone further than any other state to institutionalize and celebrate the diversity of its population. Canada is an enthusiastic proponent of immigration – there are now over 200 languages spoken and 44 per cent identify themselves as being other than English or French Canadian in origin. The principle of cultural pluralism was established in law with the 1988 Multiculturalism Act, which sought to assist in the preservation of culture and language, to reduce discrimination, to enhance cultural awareness and understanding, and to promote culturally sensitive institutional change at the federal level (Kelley and Trebilcock, 1998). Perhaps the alacrity with which Canada has adopted a pluralist approach is understandable in relation to its history in which there has been a clear need to accommodate both the bipolarity of Anglophone and Francophone peoples and more recently the rehabilitation of aboriginal groups. Canada is also perhaps the most obvious example of a state-inspired attempt to bring an intercultural approach to its multiculturalism. Cities have brought in policies not only to guarantee the rights of groups to celebrate their distinctiveness but also to encourage the active interplay of different groups, proclaiming it not only a moral imperative but an economic opportunity. 'Diversity, Our Strength' is the motto of Toronto. Furthermore, the federal government has gone further than any other to bring in programmes to properly integrate immigrants into the small towns and rural communities as well as the teeming metropolises (DeVoretz, 2003), although it is not without its critics (Li, 2003).

Australia, a highly diverse, culturally complex and largely tolerant multicultural nation has been following a similar trajectory to Canada (Jayasuriya, 1997). However, since the ascendance of the Howard government, a more sceptical public face has been turned on the value of immigration and cultural pluralism and, since 9/11 in particular, the government has been strident in its position. At a time when the current government is supporting a high level of skilled immigrants, it is also proposing stricter citizenship requirements and shifting the terminology away from multiculturalism to integration. Even though there is a high degree of harmony and interculturalism, there are unresolved issues within Australian society regarding diversity and integration, as demonstrated by the 2005 communal disturbances in Sydney (Marks, 2005).

It is also worth noting that Canada and New Zealand are officially bicultural nations. Canada, New Zealand and Australia all are seeking to resolve their relationships with their indigenous, aboriginal cultures but Australia has found the reconciliation process most difficult.

Corporate multiculturalism best describes an approach taken by The Netherlands and the UK between the 1970s and the 1990s. The Netherlands took a *jus soli* approach, recognizing that anyone born in the state had the right to opt for Dutch citizenship. This was backed by strong equality legislation and extensive social programmes to ensure access to education, welfare and housing for migrants. Historic Dutch approaches to the protection of Protestant, Catholic and secular rights also provided for the easy establishment of Muslim and other denominational schools, while a quota system was established to ensure minorities found work and representation in the media and politics (Entzinger, 1994; Vermeulen and Penninx, 2000). However, Dutch multiculturalism has faced major challenges in recent years. First, from the populist and openly gay politician Pim Fortuyn, later murdered, who challenged Dutch society to its core by criticizing elements of the minority population for holding views that were anti-gay and, as such, inimical to the Dutch tradition of tolerance. Second, one of the most troubling chapters in recent Dutch history was brought about by the ritualized murder of filmmaker and controversialist Theo van Gogh by Moroccan-born Islamic extremist Mohammed Bouyeri, after he had made a film critical of the abusive treatment of women in Islam. Clearly the Dutch people's own self-image as a society in which all can flourish together has been rocked to the core and it remains to be seen how they will deal with this (Hylarides, 2005).

The UK approach

The UK approach to postcolonial cultural diversity was distinct from, for example, the French model in being concerned less with assimilation and more with 'managing public order and relations between majority and minority populations ... allowing ethnic cultures and practices to mediate the process' (Favell, 1998). A virtual 'open door' policy to immigration was increasingly restricted through immigration legislation in 1962, 1971 and finally the 1981 Nationality Act that largely stopped black migration to Britain, beyond family reunion. Meanwhile Race Relations Acts in 1968 and 1976 introduced a legal framework to outlaw discrimination as well as to encourage public institutions to acknowledge distinct religious and cultural identities.

This approach echoed that of The Netherlands, but the UK diverged from the Dutch in not matching its commitment to cultural distinctiveness with welfare support for the integration of minorities into the labour and housing markets. It might be argued that this led to the emergence of enclaves characterized by high unemployment and deprivation, which were sporadically torn by rioting throughout the 1980s. Nevertheless, there was a dominant consensus throughout the 1990s that not only had the UK created a successful multicultural society in which the life chances of minorities were increasingly aligning with those of the majority, but that the UK model was probably superior to any other around the world (Favell, 2001). For some it seemed that race and ethnicity might even be becoming a non-issue.

The UK was shocked out of its state of complacency by a series of seismic events. The first, in February 1999, was the Macpherson Enquiry into the circumstances surrounding the death, and subsequent police enquiry into, the murder of the black London teenager Stephen Lawrence six years earlier. The report found that there was widespread and deep-seated 'institutional racism' in the police force and the criminal justice system, and that other public institutions, not least educational services, also needed to seriously rethink their approach (Macpherson of Cluny, 1999). Two years later in the spring and summer of 2001, the northern industrial towns of Oldham, Burnley and Bradford were traumatized by the most violent civil disturbances for over a decade. Subsequent independent enquiries into all three found that while there were several potential causes including severe economic decline, there was no doubt that race was the dominant factor. In particular, there was concern that the towns were divided spatially into ethnic enclaves in which groups lived parallel lives rarely meeting or interacting, leading to mutual ignorance, suspicion and rivalry that were susceptible to exploitation by extremist politics (Cantle, 2001). This lead to a major review of policy regarding local government and neighbourhoods that has become known as the 'community cohesion' agenda.

Meanwhile, the latter part of 1990s saw a growing interest in a public debate that had not been aired, it seemed, for centuries. The question of 'what does it mean to be English?' emerged through a raft of TV programmes, press articles and scholarly texts (Kumar, 2003). Perhaps the devolution of power to the Celtic nations and the growth of European Union powers spurred this bout of self-analysis from this previously unselfconscious nation. It raised further questions of what was the meaning of multiethnic Britain at the turn of the 21st century. Capturing this mood was the Runnymede Trust, which commissioned a group of prominent intellectuals to go further than anyone before to answer this question. Their report questioned the liberal orthodoxy of the previous generation, finding evidence of the failure to achieve a multicultural society of equal opportunity (Parekh, 2000). More than this, they questioned the old framework of 'majority' and 'minority' cultures, of 'migrant' and 'host' culture and of assimilation and integration. They also questioned approaches elsewhere such as the multicultural 'community of communities' model in Canada as it prioritized communal above individual rights.

In seeking to avoid favouring either a liberal rights-based individualist approach to diversity or the conservative corporatism of community cohesion, the Commission called for a future Britain that would be both 'a community of citizens and of communities'. It also called for recognition that the dominant character of the UK was now of cultural hybridism – a place of citizens with multiple identities. Ultimately, most of the subtleties of the Commission's case were unfortunately ignored amidst the political and media storm brought about by its claim that the concept of Britishness itself was racially tainted and should therefore be abandoned.

The prevalent discourse over recent years has been the open questioning of multiculturalism as a creed still being able to provide a basis for UK cultural policy and national identity (Alibhai-Brown, 2000; Malik, 2002; Goodhart, 2004; Phillips, 2004, 2005) pre-eminent of these has been Commission for Racial Equality chief Trevor Phillips who, in 2005, declared:

> *there has to be a balance struck between an 'anything goes' multiculturalism on the one hand, which leads to deeper division and inequality; and on the other, an intolerant, repressive uniformity. We need a kind of integration that binds us together without stifling us. We need to be a nation of many colours that combine to create a single rainbow. Yes, that does mean recognizing diversity and rejecting assimilation. But I believe we are in danger of throwing out the integrationist baby along with the assimilationist bathwater. In recent years we've focused far too much on the 'multi' and not enough on the common culture. We've emphasized what divides us over what unites us. We have allowed tolerance of diversity to harden into the effective isolation of communities, in which some people think special separate values ought to apply.*

Alibhai-Brown (1999, 2000, 2001) argues that over the last 20 years in the UK there has been a dominant ideology at play, up-held by a marriage of convenience of the liberal intelligentsia and a self-appointed cadre of ethnic community leaders. 'Multiculturalism' is now past its prime though and is becoming a hindrance to creating a more dynamic and interdependent society. Difference has become a fetish to be defended unquestioningly and group identity is reinforced primarily as the route to political and financial influence on the state. Alibhai-Brown has taken much criticism for her iconoclasm, but she has refreshed and added to the discourse. Importantly for our purpose, she has opened the way for an exploration of intercultural approaches, a better understanding of the emergence of groups and individuals with hybrid and multiple identities, and a recognition that the UK is moving beyond Commonwealth diversity to becoming a truly globalized society. This questioning has been taken up by voices from the right to signify an admission on the part of the liberal consensus that its policies over 30 years have failed (Liddle, 2004). Other voices have sought to retain the core values of multiculturalism while seeking to modernize it and make it relevant to new conditions (Modood, 2005).

One powerful voice has argued against the growing communitarian trajectory of the government towards 'cohesion' based upon spatial neighbourhoods, proposing that the distinctive feature of mixed neighbourhoods is that they are 'communities without community', each marked by multiple and hybrid affiliations of varying geographical reach' (Amin, 2002). This suggests a society in diverse cities based upon local accommodation to difference: 'a vocabulary of rights of presence, bridging difference, getting along' (Amin, 2002). Amin's piece from 2002 and subsequent writings (Amin and Thrift, 2002; Amin, 2006) have been a major source of inspiration for this book and have opened up our interest in another broad field of literature concerned with contact, interaction and the public (which we consider separately in Chapter 5) and an interest in the nature of local political engagement and citizenship (which we look at in Chapter 7).

Managing the city of difference

One final area of policy we have reviewed is concerned with the governance and management of the city of difference, for which there is now an emerging literature (Allen and Cars, 2001; Andersen and Van Kempen, 2001; Jones-Correa, 2001; Amin and Thrift, 2002; Tatjer, 2003).

How can city leaders and officials possibly cope with a situation in which 'the world in microcosm' appears to have sprung up in their jurisdiction? They have to cope as globalization's effects refract into a myriad small, mundane, street corner issues that need sorting on a daily basis. The underlying attitudes they adopt to these mundane issues will ultimately determine whether they succeed or are overwhelmed. At what point do cities start to see diversity as less of a cost, a drag on scarce resources and a mind-numbing complexity and start to see it as a force, a resource and an opportunity?

The urban planning literature also features an increasingly intense debate on how the planning profession can modify its practice in response to rapidly changing cities (Qadeer, 1997; Burayidi, 2000; Friedmann, 2002). Sandercock has probably gone further than anyone, however, to explore what diversity really means for the planning and running of the city of the future or, as she names it, *cosmopolis* (Sandercock, 1998, 2003a, 2003b). She dissects the principles upon which the established wisdom of town planning is based, demonstrating that, in general, statutes and by-laws will be framed in favour of the majority, imposing uniformity on the diffuse needs of minorities. When these are aggravated by cultural misunderstanding or even antagonism they can clearly lead to serious problems that can be far more costly to solve than they would have been to get right in the first place. She also describes how an added level of complexity arises when market mechanisms impinge on the planning process in multicultural cities. She offers seven proposals for the reform of urban planning and management systems (Sandercock, 2003a).

Sandercock has also declared she is prepared to re-theorize multiculturalism 'which I prefer to rename as interculturalism'. She proposes the basis of a theory of interculturalism as follows (Sandercock, 2004):

- *The cultural embeddedness of humans is inescapable. We grow up in a culturally structured world, are deeply shaped by it, and necessarily view the world from within a specific culture. We are capable of critically evaluating our own culture's beliefs and practices, and of understanding and appreciating as well as criticizing those of other cultures. But some form of cultural identity and belonging seems unavoidable.*

- *'Culture' cannot be understood as static, eternally given, essentialist. It is always evolving, dynamic and hybrid of necessity. All cultures, even allegedly conservative or traditional ones, contain multiple differences within themselves that are continually being re-negotiated.*

- *Cultural diversity as a positive and intercultural dialogue is a necessary element of culturally diverse societies. No culture is perfect or can be perfected, but all cultures have something to learn from and contribute to others. Cultures grow through the everyday practices of social interaction.*

- *The political contestation of interculturalism is inevitable, as diverse publics debate the merits of multiple identity/difference claims for rights.*

- *At the core of interculturalism as a daily political practice are two rights: the right to difference and the right to the city. The right to difference means recognizing the legitimacy and specific needs of minority or subaltern cultures. The right to the city is the right to presence, to occupy public space, and to participate as an equal in public affairs.*

- *The 'right to difference' at the heart of interculturalism must be perpetually contested against other rights (for example, human rights) and redefined according to new formulations and considerations.*

- *The notion of the perpetual contestation of interculturalism implies an agonistic democratic politics that demands active citizenship and daily negotiations of difference in all of the banal sites of intercultural interaction.*

- *A sense of belonging in an intercultural society cannot be based on race, religion, or ethnicity but needs to be based on a shared commitment to political community. Such a commitment requires an empowered citizenry.*
- *Reducing fear and intolerance can only be achieved by addressing the material as well as cultural dimensions of 'recognition'. This means addressing the prevailing inequalities of political and economic power as well as developing new stories about and symbols of national and local identity and belonging.*

We think it appropriate to end this section with Sandercock's principles. In much of the remainder of this book we will be seeking to explore, test, substantiate and extend upon them.

NOTES

1   Statistics Canada (2006) www.statcan.ca/ accessed 10 June 2007.
2   Australian Bureau of Statistics (2006) www.abs.gov.au/ accessed 10 June 2007.
3   UNHCR (2005) Statistical Yearbook, UNHCR, www.unhcr.org/cgi-bin/texis/vtx/statistics.
4   WTO cited in Vellas and Becherel (1995).
5   Fraser, A. (2006) 'Clean bowled: Why cricket has double standards over cheating', *The Independent*, 22 August.
6   http://en.wikipedia.org/wiki/House_music.

3

Living Apart: Segregation

A growing concern about the direction many European towns and cities are going in has emerged in recent years. Most Europeans, as the cliché goes, commonly like to consider themselves as a quint-essentially tolerant and egalitarian people. A series of incidents – local and international – over recent years have shaken that self-understanding: 9/11 in New York and 7/7 in London, the murder of Dutch film-maker Theo van Gogh in Amsterdam, protests about cartoons portraying the prophet Mohammed in Denmark's *Jyllands-Posten*, and civil disturbances in the *banlieues* of France and the mill towns of England. Now some stark and not easily answered questions are on the agenda about what European society means and, more pertinently, who is in and who might be outside it.

In crude terms people began to talk about the emergence of 'ghettoes' that effectively keep minorities in and the majority out, breeding ignorance and mistrust on all sides and harbouring poverty and disadvantage, crime and, more latterly, extremist and terrorist sentiments. In more measured terms, there has been the concern that in significant sections of urban Europe there may be little or no contact of any sort between different groups such that, in the words of Cantle (2001):

> *Separate educational arrangements, community and voluntary bodies, employment, places of worship, language, social and cultural networks, mean that many communities*

operate on the basis of a series of parallel lives, [which] often do not seem to touch at any point, let alone promote any meaningful interchanges.

This chapter starts from this re-emergent concern to examine in greater detail what is actually meant by concepts such as segregation, integration and social mixing. It will look back into history and across a breadth of different contemporary situations to try to understand why we are all now so exercised by these things.

The default position of contemporary debate seems to derive from an assumption that a strong correlation exists between three distinct factors: ethnicity, spatial location and socio-economic integration. The logic goes that where people of one race or religion are disproportionately concentrated in a defined space, they are more likely to experience social and economic exclusion and are less likely to share the value system or the sense of civic commitment of the broader population. Whatever political interpretation people may subsequently apply, there is a tendency to assume these three characteristics are linked.

A HISTORY OF SEGREGATION

In this section we aim to test this and related assumptions by asking a series of questions:

- What are the factors that create segregation? Is it about exercise of choice or denial of choice?
- Is segregation always a negative or can there be good and bad forms of segregation?
- Are there important social, cultural or economic factors that determine that segregation may be tolerated in one place while not in another?
- Is it possible for different ethnicities to live spatially separate while being socially, economically and culturally integrated?

First, throughout history cities have been divided and partitioned. Segregation has always existed, albeit in many different forms and for different reasons.

Hippodamus of Miletus, considered by Aristotle to be the founder of town planning and a resident of 5th century BC Athens, argued that cities should be divided into three parts for artisans, farmers and soldiers and that land should further be divided into sacred, public and private space.

Peter Marcuse (2002) has reasoned that a clear pattern of partition can be discerned through history based upon three distinct influences:

- *Cultural divisions* whereby parts of cities can be identified according to the language, ethnicity, religion, national descent or lifestyle of the inhabitants.
- *Divisions by functional role*, for example for the use by specific guilds, or processes such as retail or manufacturing, or residential areas located in relation to the industrial activities of residents.
- Finally, there are divisions according to *differences in status* reflecting differential power relations by virtue of ethnicity such as colonial or South African townships, or by class such as elite residential areas or slums.

Clearly these factors may work in conflict, in combination or overlap. So, for example, cultural difference may be used to reinforce status as is the case in black/white or Arab/Israeli dichotomies. Or, status and function may conflict with employers wanting to be close to their staff at the workplace but not as residential neighbours. The defined enclaves of past imperial cities probably combined function, status and culture and some argue that this trend is reappearing in the post-industrial city in which the division of labour and status is increasingly defined along ethnic lines (Cross and Waldinger, 1992).

It is also clear that social relations correlate with spatial relations, albeit fluid and subject to change and conflict so that, for example, while in one era or economic phase a downtown industrial zone or river frontage may be low status, in another it may become the height of desirability. Finally, it seems division by culture and functions are generally voluntary, but no one deliberately chooses to have themselves defined as low status. The divisions by status have the suggestion, albeit implicit, that they are enforced – ultimately by the state.

THE CLASSIC GHETTO

The classic historical case where functional, cultural and status division have been enforced is the ghetto. The word is sure to arise in reviewing any literature on the state of our cities, often in terms far from its original meaning with descriptions of Monte Carlo as a 'rich man's ghetto', BBC concern over a possible 'Muslim digital ghetto'[1] and, bizarrely, even the 'ghetto latte'!

It is well to remind ourselves what the original ghetto was, how it has been legitimately ascribed elsewhere, and what it is not. The world's first ghetto was a quarter of Venice in which the city's Jewish population were required to reside, as well as wearing distinctive clothing by which they could be identified. The word derives from the Italian word for slag as the area in question, *Cannaregio sestiere*, was the place where a local foundry left its by-product to cool. Although Venice was more tolerant of Jews than many Christian or Muslim cities of the Middle Ages, the ghetto was enclosed and a night time curfew imposed. While conditions were undoubtedly overcrowded and unsanitary, the occupants were encouraged to engage in a wide range of trades and were prosperous, enabling them to establish many fine institutions. Other ghettoes (or the *Judengasse* in Germanic states) emerged throughout Europe between the 15th and 18th centuries, but during the 19th century they were progressively abolished and eventually eradicated completely by 1870. Tragically they were to re-emerge in far more sinister form in Eastern Europe during the Second World War as part of the Nazi Final Solution programme. Far from being economically integrated into the life of the surrounding cities, they were no more than extended jails and transit camps.

GHETTOS, ENCLAVES AND CITADELS

Subsequently, ghetto found its most popular usage in the US to describe the ethnic concentrations that emerged, particularly in immigrant-receiving cities in the 19th and early 20th centuries including the Irish and Poles, Little Italys, Chinatowns and Spanish Harlem. As these have dissipated with time, the tag of ghetto has stuck most adhesively to the concentrations of poor urban blacks in many US cities. Meanwhile, the term has 'escaped' and can now be used liberally to describe any clustering of people who are in some way distinctive from their surroundings.

Marcuse (2001) helps to clear up the current ambiguity with a typology of urban spatial separation. He defines a ghetto as:

> *an area of spatial concentration used by forces within the dominant society to separate and to limit a particular population group, externally defined as racial or ethnic or foreign, held to be, and treated as, inferior by the dominant society.*

Whereas the *classic ghetto* is integrated economically with the surrounding area, a modern phenomenon, the *outcast ghetto*, contains only those with little or no connection to the mainstream economy.

Many of the places casually referred to as ghettoes should, more correctly, be called *enclaves*:

> *an area of spatial concentration in which members of a particular population group, self-defined by ethnicity or religion or otherwise, congregate as a means of protecting and enhancing their economic, social, political and/or cultural development.* (Marcuse, 2001)

A development on this is the *exclusionary enclave* or:

> *an area in which members of a particular population group, defined by its position of superiority in power, wealth*

or status in relation to its neighbors, cluster as a means of
protecting its position. (Marcuse, 2001)

Marcuse further identifies a *citadel* as a variation on an exclusionary
enclave in which the members are also concerned not only to protect
its position but also to enhance and display it.

With this lexicon we can with greater clarity express the various
ways in which people now segregate themselves or are segregated
from the rest of society, be they the fast emerging gated communities
of US and South African elites, the congregation of newly-arrived
migrants in point-of-arrival and portal cities around the world, the
branded little India of Toronto or the Chinatown of London, the
people who live on the wrong side of the via Agnelli wall in Padua,
or the generations of blacks who have lived in black ghettoes of
Compton, Los Angeles or the south side of Chicago.

THE ASSIMILATIONIST CITY

How has segregation been understood in the process of city development? It is perhaps not surprising that the first attempts to
formulate a place for the ghetto in the modern sense were made
in Chicago. This great transport hub and industrial powerhouse
received and transported multiple waves of internal and foreign
migrants over the years and provided the inspiration for the Chicago
school of urban theorists including Robert Park and Louis Wirth.
They developed models for understanding the growth of cities based
upon the rise and fall of neighbourhoods and the outward expansion
of cities creating concentric rings of settlement. Observations of the
settlement of minorities suggested a pattern, as illustrated in Figure
3.1.

Shortly after their arrival in a new city, ethnic groups would tend
to cluster. The graphs indicate, for instance, that in 1890, 60 per cent
of Italians living in Chicago lived within two miles of the city centre
but 50 years later only 20 per cent lived there. This indicates both
a dispersal of the concentration and a suburbanizing of population.

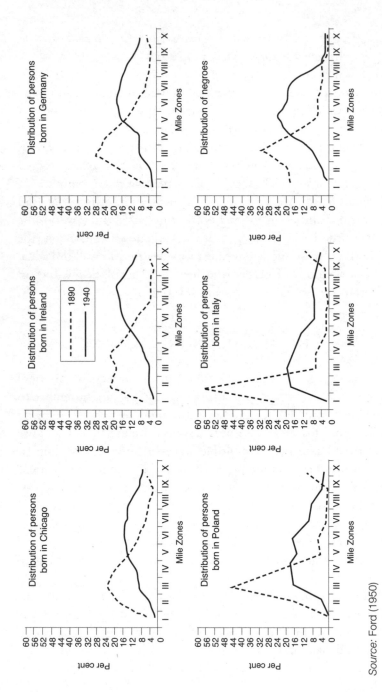

Figure 3.1 Transects showing the zonal distribution of minority groups in Chicago, 1890–1940[2]

Source: Ford (1950)

From this the theorists claimed to identify a continuum whereby migrants would naturally congregate, disperse and assimilate into the background of US society over a period of three generations.

> *The Chinatowns, the Little Sicilys, and the other so-called 'ghettos' with which students of urban life are familiar are special types of a more general species of natural area which the conditions and tendencies of city life inevitably produce ... the keener, the more energetic and the more ambitious very soon emerge from their ghettos and immigrant colonies and move into an area of second immigrant settlement, or perhaps into a cosmopolitan area in which the members of several immigrant and racial groups live side by side.* (Park, 1926)

This became the received (US and international) opinion on urban development for many years, but it became apparent in the 1980s that the reality was not entirely shaping up. While thousands of third generation Irish, Italians and Poles clearly were marrying out, moving out and moving up, handing their inner-city houses over to succeeding waves of Latinos or Vietnamese, and leaving behind symbolic ethnic retail and restaurant enclaves, one group was bucking the trend. A large proportion of blacks were not only staying put from one generation to the next but also they were becoming more concentrated and, alarmingly, spatial concentrations were becoming closely aligned with indicators of poverty and deprivation.

What became apparent was the difference between the dynamic, voluntarily adopted ethnic enclave in a process of assimilation and the involuntary, externally imposed and stagnating ghetto from which there seemed no escape. Whereas some forms of segregation are necessary and positive (the ethnic enclave as a place where new arrivals can find their feet in familiar circumstances, but also as a launch pad for full socio-economic integration), there is also a form of segregation in contemporary cities that is destructive, not only of the individuals within it but of the prospects for a better society as a whole (Peach, 1996).

Expected Relationship between
Segregation and Social Assimilation;
Assimilation Model

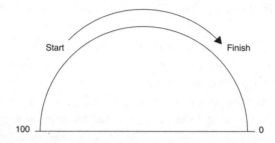

Start   Finish

100   0

City of Chicago, 1930, 1950 and 1960
Indices of Dissimilarity for Foreign-born Whites
born in Poland

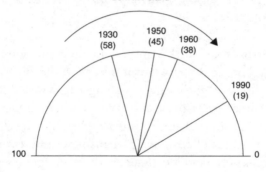

1930   1950
(58)   (45)   1960
                    (38)

1990
(19)

100   0

Black–White Segregation Chicago 1930–1990
(Ward/tract level)

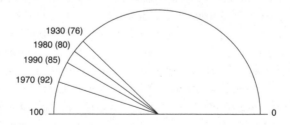

1930 (76)
1980 (80)
1990 (85)
1970 (92)

100   0

Source: Peach (2001)

*Figures 3.2 to 3.4 Hypothesized relationship between segregation
(index of dissimilarity) and assimilation over time*

Adopting a technique for measuring segregation called the Index of Dissimilarity, Peach (2001) presents an ideal model of development according to the Chicago School in Figure 3.2 with evidence of one ethnic group (the Poles) following this track in Figure 3.3, but with a stark picture of escalating black–white segregation in Figure 3.4.

It is now generally accepted that the black ghetto has bucked the trend so confidently predicted by Park and others. This is due not primarily to poverty but to the particular form of racial discrimination practised and institutionalized through housing policy and 'red lining' over decades in the US. This was exacerbated substantially by flight – not only of whites but of middle-class blacks too – to the suburbs, with insufficient numbers from other sections of the population to replace them. This has lead to a large-scale abandonment of sections of cities such as Detroit, where 60,000 lots are empty in what is now an urban prairie, and St Louis. Clearly both the causes and effects of ethnic segregation are more complex than first imagined.

THE UNDERCLASS

By the 1980s this led some to identify an 'underclass' in some Western societies by making direct connections between spatial and cultural concentration and aspects of poverty and deprivation. The negative 'neighbourhood effects' were working to magnify problems making it even harder for residents to leave. For example, 'this concentration of poverty generates attitudes, behaviours and values that impede the ability of residents to grasp whatever opportunities exist for social mobility' (Schill, 1994).

Such ideas were initially dismissed in Europe as peculiar to the US context, but the impact of economic restructuring and globalization during the 1990s has forced people to think again (Castells, 1994). Large numbers of unskilled migrants who travelled to European cities to take up jobs in manufacturing have found themselves marooned as their jobs disappeared and have travelled in the opposite direction to the developing world. Whether it was Pakistanis in Lancashire, Turks in the Ruhrgebiet or Algerians around Lille, there is often now a cruel mismatch between the requirements of the economy and the skills many of them can offer.

There is now a rich field of enquiry into what the effects of differing forms of urban policy, migration policy and attitudes to the welfare state might have upon ethnic segregation around the world. This includes assessing the relationship between spatial separation, ethnic segregation and differential measures of deprivation. The assumption now is that segregation in many cities is substantial enough to produce negative effects. This in turn has created a debate on whether current integration policies are adequate or whether some groups are lagging behind, through either social or self-exclusion; and whether it is inevitable that a high level of segregation or a strong spatial concentration will have a negative impact on integration and upward mobility.

INTERNATIONAL VARIATIONS

Some societies have a greater tolerance for inequalities of income than others. Of 124 countries measured according to income inequality, for example, the three most egalitarian were Denmark, Japan and Sweden, while Norway was 6th, Germany 14th, The Netherlands 24th and France 34th. The UK was placed at 51 and the US at 92 (United Nations, 2005). This has inevitably had an influence on the ways in which different states have responded in policy terms to the prospects of ethnic segregation.

Some countries, particularly ones that have only more recently begun to take in high numbers of migrants, such as Norway, have sought to avoid concentrations ever developing by operating an active policy of dispersing people to all parts of the country, although in a free society and market economy it proves very difficult to maintain this. Germany, while having received high migrant levels for many years, based its policy on an assumption that these 'guest workers' would eventually return to their countries of origin. When it finally accepted this would not be the case, the state engaged in a fierce policy of attempted integration, including dispersal.

France, by contrast, pursued a vigorous policy of assimilation from the outset, to the extent that no demographic statistics were taken according to ethnicity or religion. Perhaps this compounded its difficulty in perceiving the emergence of enclaves verging on ghettoes in the *banlieues*.

Some countries, for example The Netherlands, support state intervention to ensure diversity of housing type and tenure in cities, while neighbouring Belgium has devolved almost all housing provision to the free market. This has been used to explain why two states with broadly similar levels of welfare provision and relatively low levels of income inequality experience notable differences in the level of ethnic and social inequality and separation.

One writer has even suggested that the cities with the liveliest debates about acceptable levels of ethnic and social separation tend to be those with the lowest level of spatial inequality (Musterd, 2005).

GOOD AND BAD SEGREGATION?

To counteract the contentious notion of the underclass and neighbourhood effects, there has been a line of enquiry that seeks to highlight the positive effects of ethnic concentration. It is argued that the persistence of spatial proximity enhances contacts and the retention of family and social networks around places of worship, shops and clubs (Portes and Sensenbrenner, 1993). This in turn enables ethnic entrepreneurs to access both employees and markets and to establish a firm financial base (Alesina and La Ferrara, 2005). Particularly with the loss of low skill employment, small businesses, sheltered within a supportive ethnic milieu, can provide ways into work through self-employment.

In most continental European countries, the only group that seems to be significantly segregated from the rest of society appears to be the very rich, leading significantly more separate lives than people with low income, of whatever ethnicity. This opens up the issue of gated communities, lifestyle ghettoes and voluntary ghettoes, which we do not intend to discuss in detail but need to note.

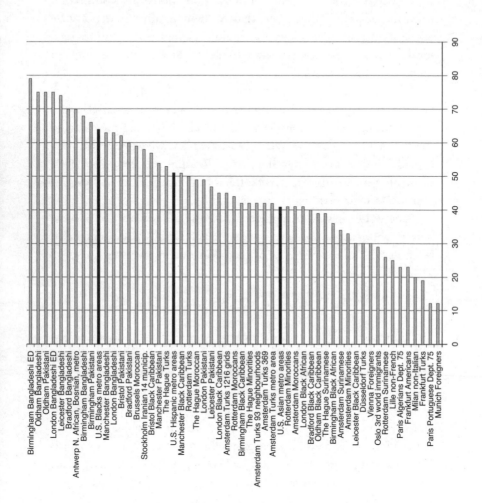

Note: The axis on a scale of 1 to 100 is a relative measure of segregation, whereby a score of 100 would indicate a group lived completely separately from others in the city, while 0 would indicate the ethnic group was distributed evenly throughout the city.

Source: Musterd (2005)

Figure 3.5 Index of segregation, ethnic minorities

It is now possible to make accurate international comparisons according to levels of income inequality, but the calculation of ethnic segregation is a much less exact science. One researcher, Sako Musterd (2005), has attempted this by drawing upon data from eight different sources to compare the proportion of certain ethnic groups making up specific enumeration units in international cities. As the units vary in size from a UK enumeration district to, in the case of the US, an average across the whole metropolitan area, the author advises caution. Nevertheless certain patterns can be discerned.

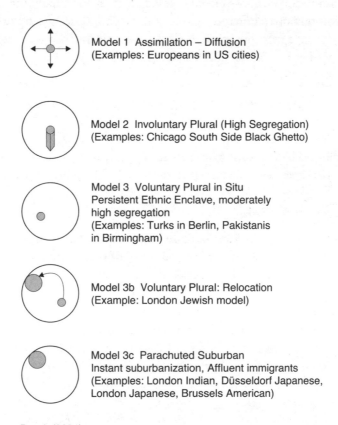

Model 1 Assimilation – Diffusion
(Examples: Europeans in US cities)

Model 2 Involuntary Plural (High Segregation)
(Examples: Chicago South Side Black Ghetto)

Model 3 Voluntary Plural in Situ
Persistent Ethnic Enclave, moderately
high segregation
(Examples: Turks in Berlin, Pakistanis
in Birmingham)

Model 3b Voluntary Plural: Relocation
(Example: London Jewish model)

Model 3c Parachuted Suburban
Instant suburbanization, Affluent immigrants
(Examples: London Indian, Düsseldorf Japanese,
London Japanese, Brussels American)

Source: Peach (2001)

Figure 3.6 Diagrammatic representation of different spatial models of assimilation and multiculturalism[3]

Clearly, though, it is not all down to state policy, at national, city or neighbourhood levels, whether people agglomerate or not. Studies, particularly outside the US, have now formulated variations to the classic model based particularly upon the differing behaviour of various ethnic groups. For example, there are the orthodox Muslim communities who choose to remain in one location in spite of rising prosperity in order to stay close to places of worship or specialist shops; or communities who move en masse from one enclave to another such as the Jews who have transferred from the East End of London to the north of the city; and also enclaves of highly mobile and autonomous ethnicities who are able to 'parachute' into suburban or high status locations, such as the Japanese or Americans in several European cities. Figure 3.6 illustrates this typology.

EMERGING FORMS OF SEGREGATION

Humans are ever the innovators, not least in the ways we find of avoiding each other's company. There are many new forms of segregation appearing. We take but three to illustrate the point in depth.

A place in the sun?

The following is a description (based upon empirical research) of life for members of a specific ethnic minority of substantial size (in the tens of thousands) currently resident in the EU:

> *migrants working in the informal economy, paying no income tax or national insurance contributions, relying on emergency state health provision or inadequate private insurance, who are confused about what they are supposed to do to be legal residents, who are neither registered with their town hall nor have residence permits, who do not know who to turn to in times of difficulty, who cannot speak the language adequately and come unstuck when they need to call the police or an ambulance.*

78 percent ... were living in [the country] all year, yet one-third ... never meet [a local] family, friends or work colleagues; 60 percent only 'get by' or 'speak a few words', while only 2 in 10 can hold a conversation (and this does not necessarily mean they are fluent). Only 9 percent have ever voted in an election ... with half of those not voting either not having the right papers or enough information. Eleven percent admit they have worked informally or casually ... Most of the 25 percent who are currently working are self employed.

Many of these are informal (unregistered) businesses. Half of the respondents do not have residence cards and a third are not registered at the town hall (this figure is probably an under-estimation since those who are legal are more likely to complete survey questionnaires). The head teacher of [a private school for foreigners] explained how fees have to be kept as low as possible as many of her pupils are from lower-income families. Many of the pupils in this school had attended [local schools] but were not able to settle. All the children interviewed had experienced racist taunts or abuse from [local] children or knew another child who had... All knew of other [migrant] children who were not even attending school.

Some find creative ways of dealing with ... switching place of residence to best suit immediate individual needs. Other migrants simply do not know the best way to weave through the myriad rules, do not know who to turn to (and cannot afford to pay) for advice. Given the existence of a confusing array of frightening rules and regulations on the one hand, and the possibility to simply stay quiet and hidden on the other, many opt to retain an ambiguous status between states – the status of the excluded. Because they want to avoid doing the wrong thing, they avoid doing anything. (O'Reilly, 2007)

Who might these unfortunate people be? Somalis in Milan, Bangla-deshis in Stepney, Chinese in Dortmund, or Poles in Lincolnshire? In fact, it is none of these. They are British people resident in the Costa del Sol. This is drawn from an excellent piece of research by Karen O'Reilly into one of Europe's fastest growing ethnic minorities – people who have left the UK in search of a new life in Spain.

There is a reason for choosing this example. We suspect that most people reading our book, while caring deeply about the issues of migrants and their interrelationship with host communities, may not themselves have experienced the life of a migrant firsthand. However, much as one might empathize with migrants, it is almost impossible for the settled person – particularly from the developed world – to put themselves into the shoes of a migrant. Indeed, there may well be an all too easy assumption that the migrant is generally someone with origins in the developing world trying to find a way into the opportunities of North America, Europe or Australasia.

Not so. What O'Reilly's research demonstrates is that migration, and the consequent issues of whether or how to integrate, are be-coming facts of life for people of many countries, rich and poor. Of course, the British have always left home generally in larger numbers than those moving in the other direction, but their destinations have tended to be other 'Anglo' communities such as Canada, South Africa, Australia and New Zealand. In charting the recent history of British migration to Spain, O'Reilly tells a different story (one that repays recounting at a little length here) that should give us an insight into where the future might lie and what the consequences for intercultural exchange might be.

British people first started taking holidays in numbers in Spain during the 1960s and 1970s when the price of air travel fell but at that stage only a few chose to make it a partial or permanent home, for example ex-colonialists unable to reconnect with the British homeland after the end of Empire (King et al, 2000). As familiarity grew, and with the financial confidence arising from the boom in UK property prices in the 1980s, ever more people started to look to extend their annual fortnight's stay into an ongoing relationship through the purchase of timeshares and property. Some of these we might describe as transnational elites, taking advantage of increased health, wealth and easier international mobility opportunities within the EU and investment opportunities to blur the old distinction between tourism and migration (Gustafson, 2001; Williams and Hall, 2002). Of course the British were not the only newcomers, with many Germans and Scandinavians also investing heavily, and nor was Spain the only destination (Rodriquez and Salva-Tomas, 2001). The majority of settlers however were people of less substantial means, looking to live out their final years in a warmer climate but surrounded by people similar to them and with the familiar trappings of 'back home'. In a sense, they tried to recreate in Spain a romanticized corner of the old country that retained the virtues of community spirit and reciprocity they felt had been lost in Britain (O'Reilly, 2002). Hence the emergence of 'little England' enclaves that have become a familiar feature of many Spanish coastal resorts. For example, one research study found that only a quarter of Britons resident on the Costa del Sol described themselves as either quite or very fluent in Spanish (King et al, 2000).

None of this should particularly surprise us. Indeed it has almost become a cliché of liberal UK and elsewhere that, whenever there is a periodic media outcry about the failure of some migrants to learn English, we are reminded of the apparent wilful refusal of most of our compatriots to bother with the local language in Spain. The same charge is made against the Germans or the Scandinavians in Spain.

What is more interesting is the 'new wave' of British migration to Spain and the picture presented is of a new type of migrant with very different motivations. They are younger, sometimes single but often in partnerships and often with children of school age. They are disenchanted with a UK that they see as failing them and are looking to make a fresh start. They may be looking to draw a line under some unfortunate or unhappy episode in their life. They perhaps already know someone 'out there' and may have been enticed and emboldened by exposure to such TV programmes as the UK's Channel 4 programme *Get a New Life*. In many ways this is an update of the classic model of the economic migrant throughout history – but are we also seeing something new here?

When questioned by O'Reilly, some of them say they are very keen to integrate socially and economically into Spanish life as soon as they can, although others suggest they have little desire to move outside the ethnic economy of the enclave. Some may indeed be leaving behind the UK in disdain of its growing multicultural society and may have little regard for Spanish culture. Spain, for its part, still harbours many people of its own with prejudices against foreigners (Solé and Parella, 2002).

It is no surprise to find different attitudes towards integration on all sides, and these can be expected to moderate with time. What seems new is the awareness of large numbers of people, originating from one of the world's leading economies, finding themselves unwillingly segregated and victims of social exclusion in another EU state. Large numbers of people seem condemned to live precarious lives in which they neither seek nor are given basic rights of citizenship, suffrage, property or employment.

Why should we be particularly interested in this? Is it not simply the time-honoured story of migrants leaving home for a better life, finding it tough on arrival but as they 'learn the ropes' finding opportunities to integrate and achieve their ambitions? Time may prove this is so, but there is one phenomenon we can see with the 'Costa British' that is echoing the experiences of contemporary migrants elsewhere. In our increasingly complex but functionally differentiated societies people find that if they are unable to secure a place in one part of the system (say the labour market), they are often excluded from others (such as the health, education and electoral systems) (Halfmann, 1998).

Let us take another angle. Are we showing alarm at this case because these are misfortunes that are only supposed to befall 'them', yet now they are befalling 'us' with whom we can more closely identify? Is this just a British phenomenon or is it transferable to other advanced economies. There are no reports of impoverished Swedes, Germans, Dutch or French selling up and shipping out, to our knowledge. One reason may be that those countries have not seen the neoliberal challenge to the welfare state to anything like the extent that Britain has over the last quarter century. Certainly they all have growing populations of people who experience some form of social exclusion but these are generally recently migrated groups. Only in Germany, in the case of citizens of the former DDR, do we find large numbers of indigenous people who are alienated within their own land. 'Costa British' might be a harbinger of things to come, with increasing pressure placed by globalization on local forms of economic and social solidarity in nation states.

Segregation in cyberspace?

One thing that is certain is that new forms of segregation are always being created whether the examples of past and current segregation are creations of compulsion or choice. It had been widely thought that the expansion of information technology and opening up of cyberspace would create a new world, free from the iniquities and antipathies of the past. In cyberspace, it was argued, we could return to a level playing field based on merit. Others say the reality is that the digital age has created its own divides. Is there a specifically ethnic digital divide? The most obvious place to look is for possible disparities in the use of IT.

Research in the US found that blacks and Latinos are much less likely to have access to home computers than are white, non-Latinos (50.6 and 48.7 per cent compared to 74.6 per cent); and they are also less likely to have Internet access at home (40.5 and 38.1 per cent compared to 67.3 per cent). Alternatively, Asians have home computer and Internet access rates that are higher than white, non-Latino rates (77.7 and 70.3 per cent respectively) (Fairlie, 2005). It suggests income differences were partly but not wholly responsible, because even blacks and Latinos with incomes over US$60,000 had less usage than whites. Language was also a causal factor, particularly in the case of Mexicans.

Similar research in Britain found that being from a black ethnic group was a significant factor in lack of ownership of a PC and not using the Internet at home, even after economic factors were accounted for. While many of the differences in levels of information technology access could be accounted for by age, household structure and income, ethnic group was a factor in its own right in the case of black and Asian groups and particularly South Asian women. The study found that black and minority ethnic (BME) respondents who owned a PC were more likely to use it for educational purposes than the white group (Owen et al, 2003).

Beyond the bland statistics of ownership and usage, there is a less visible but far more insidious and influential process taking place. It is no revelation that our lives are increasingly mediated by IT. In many aspects of our working and non-working lives we are confronted with processes of selective access. This may be as humdrum as the electronically surveyed access to our office or car park, our online purchasing of this year's Christmas presents, or password access to our banking or medical records. Selective access inevitably means that some are let in while others are kept out. The process of sorting people into those who are in and those who are out is as old as human society itself, but some argue we are now seeing a qualitative and quantitative change of major proportions. The vast quantity of data gathered about us and the enormous process power available to those who wish to make use of it is leading to a new reality of 'publics that are often prioritized, enacted and kept apart by hidden worlds of software sorting' (Graham, 2005).

True, its proponents would argue, but so what? Is not technology neutral and colour-blind? Far from discriminating on ethnic grounds and creating divisions, they say, technology enables people to override the old distinctions and discriminations, to lift themselves out of externally imposed boxes, to reach out to and engage with others of the same or vastly different characters – indeed to be anyone they want. As the saying goes, 'On the Internet nobody knows you're a dog'.[4]

How does this affect the way we lead our lives at a local level? Take as an instance where we choose to live and who we choose to live alongside. Up until recently our choices of where to live would have been drawn primarily from verbal advice from friends and relatives, or filtered through a range of local professionals such as estate agents or journalists. Most people with regular access to the Internet will have in recent years come across Internet-based Neighbourhood

Information Systems (IBNIS) that have taken over this function. A fascinating recent study has looked into their implications (Burrows et al, 2005). Websites such as www.upmystreet.co.uk or www.homecheck.co.uk ask us about our preference in relation to people and places and on the basis of this tell us about places that we might or might not like, drawing upon vast amounts of official, commercial and personal data. This could be seen as quite positive in several respects. Access to a detailed but accessible profile of a neighbourhood could be the tool that many residents need to meet neighbours, join clubs and networks and become more active citizens. It could also lead to a form of 'online local tourism' that could result in enhanced commercial and social activity for businesses and organizations in the neighbourhood. These sites could even be used by neighbourhood activists to compare their places with other similar places, enabling them to learn and institute improvements.

Alternatively, IBNIS could provide a massively powerful tool for confirming and exacerbating prejudices and segregational tendencies, particularly when combined with the new facility for socio-spatial classification provided by the emergent disciplines of geo-spatial analysis and geodemographics.[5] Whereas many of us may have been born into a society that was neatly packaged into upper, middle and working classes, the Acorn classification system now divides British society into 56 types within five categories, based upon data on our housing type, lifestyle and spending habits.[6] Type 08, for example, describes 'Mature couples in smaller detached houses' who are part of a larger group of 'Affluent Greys' within the category of 'Wealthy Achievers'. Their place of abode, lifestyle, opinions and preferences are expected to be significantly different from Type 18 'Young Educated Urbanites' in flats and Type 49 'Hard-pressed' and struggling families with many poorly-educated children. CAMEO Germany divides the 82 million Germans into 50 groups and CAMEO Italy has just come on stream. PRIZM NE, as one of many, does the same for the North American market with 66 segments.

This may merely acknowledge that we are now a society that judges itself as much by its personal consumption and values as it does by its labour market. But it could be argued that IBNIS, Acorn and other systems provide the basis upon which people can choose to avoid anyone who is different from themselves while making it much easier for them to live in a homogeneous neighbourhood of people who think and behave just like they do. Most of the categories are not ethnic-specific, but it is easy for the seasoned eye to assess the whiteness of each category and, in some cases, Acorn does the job for us. For example, category 18 is multiethnic, young, converted flats, 31 is home-owning Asian families, and 37 is crowded Asian terraces.

The pessimistic assessment of IBNIS says its logical outcome is to create a mosaic of socially and ethnically distinguished enclaves and to create a hierarchy of reputation driving up the desirability of the 'citadels' while locking in the ghetto-like tendencies of the least desirable places. Once having created a perfect homogenized enclave, it is only a short step for its members to protect and defend it from those who do not belong.

Whatever the prognosis, one thing is certain. Information technology will play a far from neutral and passive role in the future of integration and segregation in our communities.

The ecology of micro-segregation

So far, much of our understanding of segregation has been drawn from macro-level datasets generated from residential locations of large numbers of people. But increasingly it has become apparent that such information can only tell us a limited story of how people behave with each other. Segregation is actually played out at the micro level in the thousands of small and mundane interactions or avoidances we all practise in our daily lives. Only by close observation of how individuals and small groups behave can we really appreciate whether people are simply sharing the same physical space or other aspects of each other's lives.

This research has taken off with scattered and revealing examples over the last four decades. Public transport is one area of public space people are obliged to share with each other. The chance of encounter with a stranger of a different race is ever-present on the bus, tram or train. Anyone observing his or her fellow travellers in transit will know that all too often this is an environment of studied avoidance – although by no means exclusively along racial lines. It seems clear these often short-term but often highly intense encounters in frequently crowded and stressful conditions might serve merely to reinforce already-held prejudices or fears. Such was the conclusion of one of the very few pieces of research into social interaction in transport. Davis et al (1966) looked at the way in which black and white travellers chose to seat themselves on the bus in New Orleans, six years after transport in the city was desegregated. What they found was that most passengers were maintaining separation with very few people prepared to break with convention. They noticed that even where a black person and a white person were in conversation at the bus stop, they would invariably choose to sit apart on the bus. When the bus became more crowded, people showed a greater tendency to seek out co-ethnics. The authors concluded that greater numbers of people tended to increase the individuals' perception of 'racial threat' and heightened their need to seek the security of a co-ethnic.

The queue is another semi-formal aspect of the public domain where people exercise a certain amount of autonomy. Here too observers have noted the default tendency to avoid contact with another race. A study in the US cities of Cincinattti and Richmond found a significant association between the race of a customer approaching a shopping queue and the race of the last customer in that queue: in simple terms, customers tended to avoid queuing behind a person of another race (Kaplan and Fugate, 1972). The study attempted to find whether there was any difference in behaviour between a city in the north and one in the south. It found that whites practised avoidance in both cities but that blacks only did so in the north. This is perhaps not quite the form of racial equality that civil rights reformers had been hoping for!

In recent years, the social psychologist John Dixon has led various fascinating pieces of research attempting to understand how people really behave with each other in public (Dixon and Durrheim, 2003; Dixon et al, 2005a, 2005b). There is a flaw, Dixon argues, in contemporary academic understanding of ethnic interaction because it fails to appreciate what he describes as the 'ecology of micro-segregation'. Most studies, he says, tend to draw upon 'macro-level' data at street, neighbourhood or institutional level to determine the extent to which people are living or schooling together or separately. A statistical index of exposure might suggest a particular neighbourhood is actually very mixed in terms of the ethnicity of its residents. We might then draw the conclusion that the level of interracial interaction will be higher than surrounding areas. Dixon argues that this assumption is unsustainable without actually observing the way in which individuals behave with each other when they occupy the same 'everyday life spaces' (Schnell and Yoav, 2001).

To prove it, Dixon and his team have spent thousands of hours surreptitiously observing semi-clothed South Africans with cameras and notebooks to come up with a very sobering conclusion. By plotting where people chose to settle on a beach near Durban, with whom and at what time of the day, Dixon has been able to demonstrate that at their most relaxed and leisured, South Africans of different races retain a subtle but very definite distance from one another and are able to 'holiday together apart' (Dixon and Durrheim, 2003).

Three clear factors emerged from Dixon's painstaking work:

- Almost 100 per cent of groupings on the beach were racially homogeneous.
- Blacks and whites used different parts of the beach.
- Blacks and whites used the beach on different days and at different times of the day.

This confirms that while South Africa's beaches and other public spaces are now formally desegregated, the different races are employing a strategy of avoidance.

Dixon calls this the 'micro-ecology of racial division' (Dixon et al, 2005b) and argues that it is a better guide to the true level of interaction than the other indicators currently in usage. He has gone to even greater lengths to prove this with a study of how people use a public space within a racially mixed educational institution. The Jameson

Steps are where students of the University of Cape Town habitually gather to chat and eat their lunch between classes. The University's enrolment statistics at a macro-level indicate a high degree of racial integration, and one would expect higher education students to be one of the groups in South African society most relaxed about ethnic interaction. By taking high-resolution photographs at 30-second intervals in sessions spread over five days, Dixon's team were able to measure who was sitting with whom on the Jameson Steps (Tredoux et al, 2005). They found that black, white and coloured students, travelling between classes in which they were highly likely to be sitting next to students of a different race, chose almost exclusively to sit with their co-ethnics on the steps. Each group also occupied specific areas of the steps – a pattern that was repeated throughout the five days.

The advantage of Dixon's methodology is that he is not simply taking a slice in time but is able to gauge the response of his subjects to different situations they encounter at different times of day. For example, he found that students were more likely to join groups of their own race when the steps were sparsely populated but when there was competition for space the seating pattern became less segregated.

Of course we can draw the conclusion that even 15 years after the dismantling of apartheid, old habits die hard and it is not surprising that people still behave in this way. This is probably why the team has extended its study to the northwest of England to observe how multiracial undergraduates behave in the cafeteria of one of the universities in Manchester (Clack et al, 2005). Once again, there was scant evidence of social interaction but rather multiple processes of segregation. The majority of whites sat with other whites and the majority of Asians sat with other Asians, and particular areas of the cafeteria were favoured by different ethnic groups. In particular, all-female groups were found to be half as likely as all male or mixed gender groups to engage in interethnic interaction. Interestingly, one finding of the study does appear to contradict observations made in the South African university. When the cafeteria became more crowded (over 40 people) students showed a greater rather than a lesser tendency to gravitate towards groups of their own ethnicity.

In conclusion, Dixon acknowledges his findings are sobering for those who would seek greater interethnic engagement in the public spaces of our cities. His revelation that the apparent closeness of people of different races in public space may be no more than 'illusory contact' is a difficult but important truth.

NOTES

1   See http://news.bbc.co.uk/1/hi/uk/4798813.stm.
2   See Ford, 1950.
3   See Peach, 2001.
4   From a cartoon by Peter Steiner that appeared in the *New Yorker*, 5 July 1993.
5   See http://geodemographics.org.uk/.
6   www.caci.co.uk/acorn/acornmap.asp.

4

Living Together Then: A Short History of Urban Encounter

Intercultural Cities in History

The risk inherent in calling for interculturalism in contemporary life is that we assume it is the next and inevitable stage in a long historical march of progress. This may be the case, but human history is far more episodic, characterized as much by discontinuities as by natural progressions. This chapter attempts to identify other episodes in history when intercultural engagement has been consciously espoused and practised.

In searching for interculturalism in the past, our reliance is upon a much older terminology – we are in fact in search of cosmopolitanism. The term *cosmopolitan*, meaning 'citizen of the world', refers to a capacity to recognize and engage with cultures other than one's own and to describe a universal love of humankind as a whole, regardless of nation. It derives from the Greek κόσμος (cosmos) meaning world, and πολις (polis) meaning city, people, citizenry, and was widely used as a concept by ancient philosophers, such as the Stoics and Cynics.

These ideas were subsequently taken up by Immanuel Kant in his *Idea for a Universal History from a Cosmopolitan Point of View* in 1785, in which he called for a cosmopolitan order based upon a lawful external relation among states and a universal civic society. Kant's was a powerful and enlightened voice against the increasingly fractious atmosphere of late 18th century Europe when emergent nation states jostled for supremacy. He was arguing in effect for a framework of international law and universal human rights.

Given this intellectual lineage, it is generally assumed cosmopolitanism derives from, and belongs exclusively to, the Classical and Judaeo-Christian traditions and has been refined for contemporary consumption through the Age of Enlightenment. This assumption is wrong. First, while cosmopolitanism was widely discussed in Ancient Greek society, it was mostly propounded by outsiders, such as the Semite Zeno and Diogenes from Sinope in Asia Minor. In fact it jarred with the Greeks' sense of themselves as separate from and superior to the world of barbarians. Second, Kant's abstractions are somewhat undermined by his less than lofty views on race such as 'Humanity achieves its greatest perfection with the White race. The yellow Indians have somewhat less talent. The Negroes are much inferior and some of the peoples of the Americas are well below them' (cited in Fine and Cohen, 2002).

In looking for the roots of a modern spirit of cosmopolitanism we should cast our net wider. Below we briefly explore six episodes in which elements of intercultural or cosmopolitan thought or behaviour were in evidence. None is a paragon, except perhaps when juxtaposed with the brutality that often surrounded them, but each has something to tell us. What is significant is that all six occurred before the Enlightenment, one of them before Ancient Greece and at least one other beyond the influence of classical philosophy. What this should tell those brought up in the Classical/Enlightenment/ Judaeo-Christian tradition is that they should not easily assume that pluralism, universalism and a cosmopolitan and intercultural openness to others are a birthright exclusive to them.

PERSEPOLIS

The Achaemenid Empire, centred upon Persepolis in Persia, ruled large tracts from North Africa and the Balkans through to the edges of China and India between 550 BC and 330 BC (Weisehofer, 2001).

Then it was conquered by Alexander the Great. The empire's founder, Cyrus the Great, came to power after a period of anarchy and, with great political shrewdness, continued the Assyrian and Babylonian policy of transferring large populations between areas, in effect mixing disparate groups together and diluting any nationalism they may otherwise have had. Intended as a calming measure, it resulted in the Achaemenid era being known as a relatively peaceful period in Middle Eastern history. The Achaemenids were enlightened despots who allowed a certain amount of regional autonomy in the form of the satrapy system. The empire's 20 satrapies were administrative units, organized on a geographical basis, and ruled by a governor or satrap, and a high level of interaction and trading was encouraged. Zoroastrianism, which became the predominant religion of the empire, derived from many sources and influences throughout the empire, but the rulers never enforced its adherence at the expense of other localized doctrines and beliefs. Just as the Achaemenids were tolerant in matters of local government and custom, as long as Persians controlled the general policy and administration of the empire, so were they also tolerant in art so long as the finished and total effect was Persian.

The empire then fell to Alexander and subsequently, memory of its achievements appears to have been belittled and overlain by propaganda generated by the Ancient Greeks. This in turn helped form preconceptions in the West that some argue have widespread significance even today:

> *[In their recording of the Persian Empire] the Greeks helped create the division between Europe and Asia, those stereotypes of the freedom-loving, tough European versus the servile, luxurious, effeminate, despotic Asian. We have gone on living with those stereotypes in an extraordinary way, because of the way Greek literature was absorbed into the mainstream.*[1]

One needs only to consider the combination of two events in early 2007 to see this age-old cultural anxiety continuing to be played out, albeit in new forms: the arrest of 15 members of the Royal Navy in the Shatt-al-Arab by the Iranian military and the latest screen blockbuster from Hollywood, *300*, the story of how a small band of valiant Spartans (dressed, according to Philip French of *The Observer*, as if they were responding to an invitation to a fancy dress party at a New York gay club!) defended Western civilization from the Persian hordes at the battle of Thermopylae.

ROME

The only other empire of the ancient world to match the size and ethnic diversity of the Achaemenids was Rome. By the 2nd century AD, the Roman Empire had reached the limits of its expansion and contained a rich variety of conquered peoples. The way in which it maintained order exhibits extreme pragmatism, particularly with regard to the rights of citizenship (Huskinson, 1999). Anyone, regardless of ethnicity or ancestry, could in effect become a fully fledged Roman citizen if they could be educated and trained to be so. Roman society was rigidly structured in terms of class and status and effectively 'colour-blind', particularly through the great 'Romanizing' institution of the army. At the heart of this multicultural empire was perhaps the world's first great cosmopolitan metropolis, the city of Rome itself. Furthermore, it was a city that was self-conscious and proud in its diversity, as illustrated in Aristedes' *Laudation of Rome* (cited in Briggs, 2004):

> *To you there comes from all lands and seas what seasons bring forth and what climates produce, what rivers and lakes and handicraft of Hellene or barbarian make. Whoever, therefore, wishes to view all this, must either journey through the whole world or stay in this city.*

Records suggest that, with the exception of the ruling elite, the inhabitants of the city itself were not spatially segregated, and there were plentiful opportunities for people of all races, incomes and occupations to mix freely (Dupont, 1992). Roman society was also highly tolerant of different customs and religious practices (apart from, that is, its problems with a sect called the Christians!).

Of course, the dark underbelly of Rome is that all of its achievements in culture, politics and economics were built upon a vast foundation of human misery through the conquest, enslavement and exploitation of subject nations. While it was entirely possible for a slave of any background to achieve freedman status and even rise through society, the vast majority did not.

In Ancient Rome, therefore, we have the enormous paradox of a quintessentially vibrant, open and cosmopolitan society, but one that drew upon these very qualities as by-products of its drive to conquer, enslave, economically exploit and assimilate. When it could no longer continue to do this, it dissolved.

T'ANG DYNASTY CHINA

The period 618 to 907, under the rule of the T'ang dynasty, is considered by historians to be the zenith in Chinese civilization. Also, in the case of a culture that has often been considered by outsiders as enigmatic, insular and closed, the T'ang period is seen to be a period of greatest interaction with the outside world.

During this time there was extensive contact with India and the Middle East, and Buddhism was widely adopted by the Chinese, including the imperial family. The introduction of block printing made the written word available to many for the first time and a system of government administration that lasted until the 20th century was established, based upon the *jinshi*, or the 'presented scholar' exam. It was also during the T'ang dynasty that Empress Wu Zetian made her mark, her rule being one of only a handful of examples in which women seized power and ruled China, and the only example of a woman who ruled in her own right. T'ang influence reached into Korea, Japan and Indochina and as far west as the Caspian Sea, and the free flow of goods along the Silk Route established the T'ang capital of Chang'an (modern day Xi'an) as the most populous and cosmopolitan city on earth. The southern port cities of Canton, Quanzhou and Fuzhou grew in size as maritime trade along the coast and throughout Southeast Asia expanded greatly, with much of it in the hands of Arab merchants.

The T'ang period was one of a flowering of new ideas that grew out of one of China's bloodiest and most anarchic periods, the Three Kingdoms. During this time the agrarian, quiescent, homogeneous and rather decadent Han culture had been invaded by 'barbarians' from north and west, introducing new qualities of adventurousness, mutual aid and openness to outsiders. It is considered to be a booming collision of cultures followed by a much-needed blood transfusion to an ailing body (Chen Yinke, 1996).

Under the T'ang, China developed a new concept of the outside world. This meant that for the first time all known kingdoms and peoples should be accorded a place within the Chinese scheme of things – 'that no-one was left out' (Terrill, 2003). The phrase 'tian di zhi dao' was coined, meaning literally 'approach the Barbarians from the positions of Heaven and Earth'. In other words, benevolence to non-Chinese people should be practised and outsiders were to be received and nurtured, so long as they did not reject the Emperor's authority.

More than any other epoch in Chinese history before the 20th century, it seems the Chinese in the early and mid T'ang had the self-confidence to be open to the new and different. Perhaps because a universal religion and foreign origin gave China links to all the other countries of Asia, east of Persia; or perhaps because the elite included many families of non-Chinese descent; or because China had the military might to garrison the Silk Road and keep it open for trade, the Chinese in this period were more than happy to gather about them the best of what the rest of their world had to offer.

UMAYYID CÓRDOBA

Any visitor to the Spanish city of Córdoba will be struck by discovering what seems to be one of the most bizarre buildings in the world.

The Mezquita is a vast mosque that contains at its centre a baroque cathedral. At one time there were many mosques in Spain but most were torn down during the *reconquista*. However, when they came to require their own cathedral, the Catholic citizens of Córdoba could not bring themselves to destroy their mosque. Although it symbolized a history of subjugation by the Moors and jarred with the fundamentalist mood of the Inquisition, the mosque and the decision to retain it represented a residue of the tradition of tolerance and cosmopolitanism that had been bred into the culture of the city over many centuries.

Córdoba was the capital of the emirate, and later caliphate, of Al-Andalus that, between 756 and 1031, was the site of one of the greatest flowerings of Islamic culture (Mann and Glick, 1992) When the Umayyad caliphs of Damascus were overthrown in the 8th century, they took refuge in Córdoba while the remainder of the Islamic world fell under the much more severe regime of the Abbasid caliphs based in Baghdad. Over the next 200 years they constructed a 'culture of tolerance' in which Jews and Christians were encouraged to practise and thrive alongside Muslims. This was based partly, in the early years, upon a pragmatic need to survive but was also founded upon a particular reading of the Qur'an and those sections of it that prescribed tolerance of non-believers within the broader context of Sharia law.

At its height, in the early 10th century, Córdoba was a remarkably rich and vibrant place in which scientific, medical and cultural innovation flourished and all faiths were not only tolerated but also celebrated. During this time, for example, Hebrew was reinvented as a living language for both poetry and daily discourse and it is no coincidence that Moses Maimonides – one of the greatest of all Jewish philosophers – was born in Córdoba in 1135. His great Muslim contemporary, Ibn Rushd (also known as Averroes), was responsible for translating Aristotle for the first time into Latin, thereby opening up a whole strand of Greek classical thought to the Islamic world and Christendom alike. Jews and Christians were also very active in government through their appointment as viziers to the caliph.

Even after the caliphate went into relative decline and the Christian *reconquista* of the Iberian peninsula began, a long period of *convivencia* ensued in which many local Spanish nobles came to realize that it was in their best interests not to forcefully expel Jews and Muslims but to retain them for the benefits they could offer.

Remarkable as mediaeval Córdoba was, it was far from a liberal paradise by contemporary standards. The caliph was an absolute ruler who enforced his authority through military might and a system of slavery. Non-Muslims were also undoubtedly second-class citizens before the law and were subject to special taxes and restrictions. The city itself was quite specifically segmented in spatial and ethnic terms. While market and civic spaces explicitly encouraged interaction, living quarters were very clearly separated along ethnic as well as clan lines. Indeed, the enclosed and inward-facing style of the Andalusian housing plans, which modern tourists find so beguiling, was an expression of the clannish and exclusive tendency of the city's rulers.

Nevertheless, in the modern era when it is almost a commonplace for the three 'religions of the book' or monotheistic religions to be at odds with each other, the flowering of Umayyid Córdoba is not only an inspiration but also a reassurance that intercultural exchange leading to urban advantage is achievable.

CONSTANTINOPLE

Córdoba was not the only example of a functioning multicultural society in the mediaeval world. Many of its qualities – military and political power, cultural and scientific exploration, religious tolerance – appear to have been inherited by the Ottoman Empire. The Seljuk Turks were an obscure central Asian clan who conquered the Middle East, North Africa and the Balkans, establishing their capital in modern day Istanbul and founding in 1299 the Ottoman dynasty named after an early ruler, Osman I. The 'golden age' of the empire from 1453 to 1566 culminated in the reign of Suleyman the Magnificent. Not only was this a period of great strategic power but also of a flourishing of science, technology, mathematics and geography (Imber, 2002).

Underlying this was a strong commitment to religious tolerance and openness to the outside world. Echoing Córdoba, non-Muslims, or the *Dhimmi*, were accorded a limited status under the law (Arbabzadeh, 2004). This meant, for example, that Jews or Christians were required to build houses lower than Muslim neighbours, and to ride on inferior animals such as mules, and had to perform the less pleasant duties in society (such as the castration of eunuchs).

The *Dhimmi* were governed according to the *milet* system. In effect, the non-Muslim population of the empire was divided into five *milets* or self-governing communities (Jewish, Greek Orthodox, Armenian Orthodox, Catholic and Protestant). Each was led by a high-ranking religious leader and had widespread law-making capacities, although no territorial jurisdiction.

It is not surprising, therefore, that when the *convivencia* finally broke down and the Jews were expelled from Spain in 1492, many of them headed for Constantinople. Indeed one Jewish physician, Hekim Jacub Pasha, became so highly revered that a whole district of the city was named in his honour.

One thing we can deduce from the restrictions on the height of houses is that Muslims and *Dhimmi* were living together as neighbours and that Constantinople was not a particularly segregated city. However, there were strict regulations on intergroup relations and the marriage of Muslim and *Dhimmi* was not approved. There were also questionable practices, notably *Devşirme,* whereby *Dhimmi* nations conquered by the empire were required to give up a proportion of young boys as a 'blood tax'. They would be trained and assimilated into Turkish customs and groomed to become civil or military officials in far-flung parts of the empire. While some have portrayed this as a form of slavery, others have seen it as a subtle means of broadening the scope and outlook of the empire and preventing a narrow Turkish Muslim elite from gaining control of all the levers of power.

The slow and long decline of the Ottoman Empire in the face of, first, other empires and, later, the rise of the nation state needs no repeating here. However, it is argued that the root cause of the decline was the empire's conquest of Mecca and Medina and its leaders' hubristic assumption of pan-Islamic leadership, which ushered a retreat from cosmopolitanism to dogmatic conservatism. Be that as it may, the spirit of tolerance and coexistence the Ottomans inspired could be said to have survived long after the final disappearance of the empire in the form of multiethnic cities such as Sarajevo. It will be recalled that it was not fundamentalist Islam that sought to put an end to cities like Sarajevo, but other forces.

THE DUTCH GOLDEN AGE

For all that the liberal West portrays itself as the fount of tolerance and cosmopolitanism, it is ironic that there are many notorious examples of quite the opposite in the history of Christian civilizations. Expulsion, Inquisition, ghetto development, pogroms and the Final Solution are, after all, manifestations of a Christian society's rejection of the Jews and other religious and ethnic minorities.

Perhaps the first Christian state to expressly espouse toleration was the Dutch Republic in the period 1584 to 1702. The mercantile wealth, backed by major cultural and scientific achievements, led the period to be dubbed the Dutch Golden Age. Yet it is widely believed that the defining factor in its flowering was the willingness of the community to accept outsiders of (virtually) all backgrounds and confessions (Po-Chia Hsia and van Nierop, 2002)

During the last third of the 16th century, the Dutch were fighting for independence from Spain. The drivers of the struggle were demands for political and economic independence but also for freedom to practise their Calvinist faith. This third issue in particular, a rejection of *gewetensdwang* or 'forcing of conscience', was the source of inspiration for many – a belief, in effect, that not only was it wrong for them to be denied freedom of conscience but for them to deny it to anyone else. As such, in the founding document of the independent Dutch Republic, the Union of Utrecht (1579), it was stated that 'everybody shall remain free in his religion, and nobody shall be examined because of his religion'. The policy of the Dutch government towards religion henceforth became one of tolerance and detachment.

Independence enabled Dutch merchants to rapidly create trading networks across the world that for a period made Amsterdam the richest city and market in the world, and established the model of mercantile capitalism that would influence world development for many centuries to come. In 1602 the world's first multinational – the Dutch East India Company – was founded, based upon hugely profitable trade in spices, jewels and slaves. This explorative impulse also encouraged innovations in the sciences, with Huygens inventing the pendulum clock and Leeuwenhoek the microscope, and the perfecting of land reclamation with polders. A greater openness, expressed by a boom in book publishing, enabled ideas to spread more quickly. Most significantly, perhaps, the university became the home of philosopher Rene Descartes, driven from France by religious persecution, along with many other intellectual migrants of conscience. Jewish thought and culture in particular underwent a renaissance, as exemplified by Benedict Spinoza.

There were limits to the tolerance of the Dutch. The practice of Catholicism was formally banned (though in most cases a blind eye was turned) and there was repression of atheists and agnostics, and attitudes outside Amsterdam were generally less accommodating. Nevertheless, the 17th century saw nothing less than the founding of a national identity and polity in which the tolerance of difference and, in modern parlance, the notion of diversity advantage were central. Nothing like it had been seen before (and very little since). Only in the last few years, with the debates surrounding Pim Fortuyn and Theo van Gogh, has the place of pluralism at the heart of Dutch life been called into question.

CONCLUSION

Much of our understanding of history has been defined in relation to the achievements of clans, tribes and latterly nation states – and their leaders – and in this regard, homogeneity and cohesion has often been attributed to powerful influence. In seeking historical episodes in which ethnic and cultural diversity were important factors, we were inevitably drawn to some of the great empires of history in which peoples of many cultures have been brought within the scope of one polity.

We have to be prepared to accept that historic intercultural contact may often begin with the will to conquer and dominate, territorially, economically or culturally. Further, the subsequent emergence of a more cosmopolitan climate may be due less to a great philosophical or philanthropic urge and more to do with the pragmatic requirement to maintain social order within a heterogeneous situation. Finally, cosmopolitan periods are often episodic in as much as they appear to have a prelude, a zenith and a decline in which, through hubris or complacency, more attention is given to reaping the benefits of cosmopolitanism than attending to its maintenance.

We could have included many other examples, particularly of trading city states ranging from mediaeval Venice to contemporary Singapore; of imperial capitals such as *fin de siècle* Vienna, London and Berlin; contemporary global hubs such as London, New York and Los Angeles; and bustling cultural entrepôts such as Beirut, Buenos Aires, Sarajevo and Johannesburg.

NOTE

1   Neil McGregor, director of the British Museum, quoted in 'Enlightened Empire', by Peter Aspden, *Financial Times*, 2 September 2005.

5

Living Together Now: Modern Zones of Encounter

WHY INTERACT?

The case for social mixing

There is a long tradition of interest in the question of whether social homogeneity has a connection with social deprivation, stretching back via Mumford to Engels, Rowntree, Booth and Ebenezer Howard. Varying reasons have been proposed to support the creation of social heterogeneity as a priority of public policy and it is worth reviewing these (Sarkissian, 1976).

Strong in the minds of Victorian society was a belief that if the lower orders were exposed to their class superiors, they would be motivated to aspire to be more like them, and thus social mixing would raise standards by *nurturing a spirit of emulation*. Related to this was a concern that, if there were diversity of buildings in residential areas occupied by different social classes, it would stimulate inhabitants to keep their housing up to an *aesthetic standard* worthy of the whole.

More in tune with current thinking has been the belief that socially mixed residential areas could promote intellectual and cultural advances through *cultural cross-fertilization* among social groups, and that this in turn will lead to greater *tolerance of difference*.

Also that mixed communities give *greater opportunity* for (particularly underprivileged) people to exercise choice (for example in education), to move up occupational and social ladders, and to participate fully in economic and political life.

Mix has been said to promote *social harmony* by reducing social and racial tensions, by reopening channels of communication and interaction, decreasing mistrust and hostility, and promoting a better understanding between groups. Paradoxically, heterogeneity is also claimed to promote *social conflict* in order to foster individual and social maturity. Disharmony is thought by some to be essential to individual psychological growth and that by recognizing the *vitalizing challenge of dissonance*, varieties and antagonisms can be reconciled by emphasizing them.

Some people point to *improved physical functioning* of the city and its inhabitants, because in order to support even the most elementary civic infrastructure such as roads, sewers, fire departments, public transport, police services and schools, a mix of income groups is essential, particularly where local taxes still account for a significant proportion of expenditure on local services.

Because a high degree of residential mobility might undermine social and kinship networks, a mix of housing types, sizes, costs and tenures, appealing to varying age groups, ethnicities and family sizes, permits existing residents the choice of staying within their own area as their housing requirements change, thus maintaining *social stability*.

A more *globally holistic* approach suggests that residential areas should reflect in themselves and their immediate surroundings the variety and mix of the wider physical and social world, enabling contact with different sorts of people. Finally, mix is thought to provide freedom of choice in housing, particularly in aid of minority and disadvantaged groups who have traditionally been denied access to 'open housing'.

Social homogeneity, by contrast, particularly when it is connected to monotone housing tenure such as the sprawling council estate, has been generally vilified over recent years and the priority of public policy has been to attack it through area-based initiatives.

Let us now explore the different arenas in which social and cultural mixing may be possible in a modern society.

Contact hypothesis

Concerns with mixing have extended far beyond the matter of where and how people should live. In the US of the 1950s there was an increasingly heated debate over the pros and cons of racial segregation. A powerful lobby held with the status quo, arguing that while segregation might not be ideal, its dissolution might lead to social instability, conflict and chaos. The challenge for liberals was to find a theory, backed by a body of evidence, to justify desegregation. Among those to rise to the challenge was psychologist Gordon Allport who in 1954 proposed his 'contact hypothesis' (Allport, 1954).

Although the theory was largely developed to explain anti-black prejudice, it has achieved much wider application and remains today the theoretical basis of much work concerned with social mixing and desegregation. In essence it suggests that as majority group members come into contact with other minorities, they will be progressively less likely to hold prejudicial attitudes towards them. By exposing majority group members to new information about minority groups, contact helps majority group members question negative stereotypes and develop more favourable views of minority groups. However, Allport argues that the effects of contact on prejudice vary, depending on the quality and quantity of contact, whether contact is voluntary, the extent to which the contact is between majority and minority members of 'equal status', whether contact occurs in a competitive or collaborative environment, and the area – or the 'interactive setting' – in which contact occurs.

With these key theoretical points established, we now embark on an extensive review of all the potential zones within which positive intercultural contact and engagement might feasibly take place. We take a critical look at these, seeking evidence where available to substantiate our proposals, but also to demolish some common misconceptions about the nature of sociability.

Allport's work has been particularly influential in the field of education and the movement to desegregate US schools, and has led to the formulation of an 'opportunity hypothesis' that proposes that the occurrence of cross-race friendships increases as the opportunities for them increase. Therefore, children in mixed race schools should have more cross-race friendships than children in single race schools. Studies have found that minority students report a greater proportion of cross-race friendships than majority students (Hallinan and Smith, 1985). In addition, when the proportions achieve greater equilibrium, or where there are several groups present, the opportunity for children to form cross-racial friendships increases greatly.

Contact and opportunity theory now represents the mainstream view, particularly in the US. It has focused the attention of policy-makers on modifying structures and practices to enhance the opportunity for contact. In some cases this has led to notoriously unpopular and unsuccessful initiatives such as the US school bussing experiment (Rossell, 1990), but there are many examples of successful application too, particularly in education (Pettigrew and Tropp, 2000). It has been followed by other theories such as the 'similarity-attraction hypothesis' (Byrne, 1969) that predicts that individuals are more likely to prefer and seek out people with whom they share salient characteristics, and the 'culture-distance hypothesis' (Ward et al, 2001) that predicts that the greater the cultural gap between actors, the more difficulties they will experience.

However, the contact hypothesis is not without its sceptics. Dixon et al (2005a) argue that in setting optimal conditions for interethnic contact, social scientists have created an abstraction that is only meaningful in the most controlled environments such as schools or colleges, and that real life just is not like that. Contact means different things to different people depending upon their background and the wider context.

This school of thought argues that a theory based on rehabilitating prejudiced individuals is inherently limited because society is not formed solely by individual interaction but also by the interplay of larger socio-political forces and cultural groups (Forbes, 1997). In other words, people who might be well disposed following one-to-one contact with someone of a different ethnicity might feel and behave differently when they are responding as part of their particular group in interaction with another group.

According to some, contact theory also ignores deeper power relations that form the context in which individual contact takes place. In a study of friendships between black and white American girls, Scott (2004) argues that desegregation is played out in a normative environment that accepts white values and cultural reference points as the ideal, and therefore requires a greater level of accommodation from the minority group member.

Feminists like Mary Jackman and Marie Crane (1986) argue that within contact theory there is a tendency to accept prejudice and discrimination as an emotional response based mainly on ignorance, rather than as the protection and reinforcement of one group's privilege over another. They argue that it is quite possible for two individuals to lose their suspicion of each other through contact, develop an affectionate relationship and even love for one other, even while the underlying inequality might remain between them. They cite as their evidence the case of marriages in which love and sexism can coexist.

One attempt to ground contact in more of a social context has been made by Ted Cantle (2005), building on ideas developed by Ashutosh Varshney (2002) in his study of Hindu/Muslim conflict in India and of 'The Troubles' in Northern Ireland. Cantle also draws upon earlier work by Putnam (2000) in distinguishing different forms of social capital. He identifies that *bonding capital* (among members of a family or close ethnic group) is different from *bridging capital* (between different groups), and that high levels of the former may inhibit development of the latter. Cantle offers a new typology of cross-cultural relationships and argues that those concerned with building greater inter-communal exchange need to structure their thinking around five different forms of engagement:

- Intra-associational – integrated and multiple identity: *Associations are open to people of different backgrounds and facilitate interchange and cooperation within the organization.*

- Inter-associational – networked single identity bodies: *Associations represent separate and distinct interests on an exclusive and single identity basis, with associations formed by networks of separate bodies.*
- Social incidental – arising from everyday activity: *Interaction by individuals meeting through shopping, travelling or leisure activities, at an individual level, without organization.*
- Social organizational – arising from planned and organized activity: *Interaction by participating in sporting, music, drama and arts, which involves group activities, generally organized through clubs and societies.*
- Structural Cross-cultural Contact: *This will depend upon the extent to which schools and housing are segregated, employment opportunities are linked to particular groups and market factors create divisions, which militate against cross-cultural engagement.* (Cantle, 2005, p177)

Cantle stresses the practical applicability of the typology for local agencies. It could become the basis, for example, on which a local authority might conduct an audit of community relations. If it then found a high number of inter-associational bodies but comparatively few intra-associational ones, this might be a sign that action needs to be taken.

The interaction cycle

A different account of ethnic contact and interaction, which takes into account both individual and group, as well as emotional and political factors, has emerged from research recently commissioned by the Commission for Racial Equality from SHM Ltd, 'Promoting Interaction Between People from Different Ethnic Backgrounds.' (SHM Ltd, forthcoming).

The report seeks to establish the different forms of social inter-action and why we interact. It first distinguishes between two different forms of interaction: *familiar* interactions that aim to *consolidate* something, and *unfamiliar* that aim to *broaden* something. It then makes a second distinction based upon what that 'something' means to the person interacting: whether it is internal to the individual's world, relating to their *identity and values,* or *external* to them, relating to the wider environment. This gives us four possible permutations on why a person might interact:

- *Grounding.* These are interactions with close and familiar people (such as family or friends with whom we share a common history) that help confirm and consolidate our existing inner identity and values, for example a relative's birthday party or being part of a religious congregation.
- *Strokes.* Interactions with familiar but less close people (such as neighbours or acquaintances with whom we share a common community) that consolidate our confidence as a member of the wider group, for example nodding to and being acknowledged by people in the street.
- *Opportunity.* Interactions that open one up to new people and that might lead to benefit for oneself and for them (such as fellow professionals with whom one has individual benefits in common), for example by joining a work or business related network or, dare we suggest, a work-based affair.
- *Growth.* Interactions that open one up to new people (from a different background or culture with whom one has a mutual curiosity in common) and that, through discussion, debate and learning, lead to one achieving a new and enhanced understanding of the world to the extent that one's identity and values are changed, for example through doing voluntary work in another country, or perhaps marrying someone from another culture.

This can be summarized by Figure 5.1.

Our concern is to seek encouragement for greater ethnic interaction and a more intercultural society, so it might then seem obvious to suggest we would prioritize 'growth interactions' above all others. But it is not as simple as that.

	Grounding	Strokes	Opportunity	Growth
Description	Consolidate identity and values	Consolidate external environment	Broaden external environment	Broaden identity and values
Typical motivations	Link to your past or roots / Feeling that other people understand you / Being able to rely on others / Passing on your experience to others	Being recognized or known in a community / Feeling popular / Identification with other people	Identifying new possibilities / Self-promotion / Professional or amateur networking	Learning from others / Expanding your perspective / Sharing ambition and common goals / Curiosity
Typically with	People you have history in common with	People you have community in common with	People you have benefits in common with	People you have curiosity in common with
Impact on individuals	Builds self-confidence	Develops a sense of belonging	Opens up new opportunities	Expands perspective
Impact on inter-ethnic interactions — Positive	Pride and identity	Good community relations	Mixing	Understanding and integration
Impact on inter-ethnic interactions — Risk	May accentuate differences and distinctions between ethnic groups	May create complacency	May reinforce inequality if opportunity networks are not fully open	May alienate or dilute identity / Efforts to engineer growth interaction can seem false

Figure 5.1 Four types of interaction

Source: SHM Ltd (forthcoming)

There are both positive attributes and potential risks in each form of interaction. Communities formed primarily around grounding interactions will be internally cohesive and self-confident. They may be unable to find common ground with other communities. Alternatively, communities formed primarily upon growth interactions will very readily form new relationships but run the risk of feeling transitory and superficial. If growth interactions were too blatantly promoted, perhaps as part of a policy initiative, they could appear forced or insincere. There is no right or wrong form of interaction. A healthy and vibrant society requires all four in relatively equal measures. Judgement as to what is right in given circumstances is key. It will dictate that at times there may be a greater need for people to consolidate and at other times for them to reach out. SHM has devised the diagram below to suggest the dynamic relationship between the four types and how an individual or group may move from one to another.

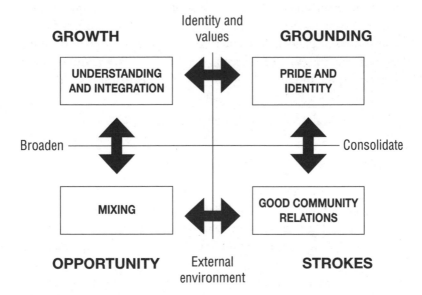

SHM Ltd (forthcoming)

Figure 5.2 The interaction cycle: How interactions can change from one type to another

To imagine how this might work, think of a situation of a new ethnic population migrating into a small town. They experience initial mistrust and prejudice and so turn inwards, reinforcing relationships with each other and emphasizing internal pride and identity. This builds self-confidence and provides the basis for establishing casual relationships with other townspeople. Through this they begin to identify opportunities for business or learning that embolden them to reach across the ethnic divide, and some of these interactions lead to more profound change and growth. Gradually a new form of shared community pride and identity is developed with other townspeople, for example through support of a local sports club or in joint opposition to some common threat such as a motorway proposal.

SHM acknowledges this is a simplistic schema that cannot do justice to the complexity of diverse societies and we should avoid falling into the trap of assuming that communities all move with one mind or in one direction, or that people solely inhabit the one community. Nor does it take full account of other cross-cutting factors such as class or gender. Nevertheless, this is a useful way of thinking about interaction as a process, the possible barriers to, and enablers of, interaction, and likely forms of effective policy intervention.

ZONES OF ENCOUNTER

Housing and neighbourhoods

The inquiries into the reasons for the swathe of civil disturbances that hit northern English cities in 2001 all came to a clear and definite conclusion. These places, they said, were characterized by extreme spatial separation of certain ethnic communities, namely Pakistanis and Bangladeshis, and, because people lived in different parts of town, their educational, recreational, working and shopping activities were also largely separate from those of the majority community. Further, it was said that not only were they living 'parallel lives' but many had chosen a life of 'self-segregation' (Home Office, 2001; Independent Review Team, 2001).

These reports coined a new term – *community cohesion* – the pursuit of which has subsequently become a major priority of the British government and that it in turn has made the duty of all municipalities and other local agencies to engender. One of the most significant aspects of this new policy direction is the extent to which housing has been brought to the forefront. In Britain over the last 20 years or so, housing had been falling steadily down the policy agenda as council house sales and the breaking up of local state monopolies undermined its coherence and salience. However, for a society that prided itself on social mobility, it came as something of a shock in 2001 to find that, for example, a boy of Bangladeshi heritage born into a stone, private rented terrace in the valley bottom of an English town and a white boy born in a brick social rented housing estate on top of the hill seemed destined to grow up leading lives that, at the very best, were indifferently separate, but also with the potential for mistrust and violent conflict. In looking for explanations, commentators homed in where people were living – or not living – and why.

Superficially the explanations were straightforward. Early patterns of settlement of migrants to Britain in the 1950s and 1960s were shaped by the availability of low-cost housing at a time of otherwise acute national housing shortage. In the absence of a supply of public housing, the accessible property was primarily private rented or privately owned 19th century terraced housing in areas due for clearance and redevelopment. Such housing was located in inner urban locations that became the focus for concentrated BME settlement. With the establishment of small communities, the 'path dependency' factor ensured they were followed by fellow countrymen from the same or similar regions, thus heralding the emergence of ethnic clusters.

In research we conducted in the London Borough of Lewisham (Comedia, 2007) we were told by members of the Somali and Vietnamese communities that clustering was both a result of the need for access to social housing and a desire for community support systems and social capital. We also found that clustering can be an arbitrary result of recent arrivals being allocated available social housing. In our Auckland study (Brecknock Consulting, 2006a) we were told that a number of recent migrant communities had been dispersed into small clusters as a result of limited social housing and that this had created mutual support problems due to the limited public transport connectivity.

Demographic factors, such as a higher than average birth rate, added to their growth, but it is claimed their emergence as ethnically distinct enclaves has been particularly exacerbated by the phenomenon of 'white flight'.[1] Whether white families were leaving inner-city locations because they were too racially bigoted to accept a black neighbour or because of more innocent factors of social mobility and suburbanization, the effect has been to emphasize the emergence of enclaves. In some towns this has inevitably led to the 'racialization' of territory and the identification, real or imagined, of 'no-go areas' (Phillips et al, 2002). This has led to the creation of a second or parallel housing market in which householders select or discount potential properties to buy or rent on the basis of whether they would feel comfortable in their ethnicity in relation to their likely neighbours.

Another profound factor has been the policies and practices of housing allocation agencies over the years. It is no longer in dispute that the single most important factor in the creation of black ghettoes in the US was the deliberate policy of many local authorities and estate agents to restrict access by black residents to only certain parts of the city through a range of both statutory and more underhand means. As far back as the 1960s such practices were identified in Britain too (Rex and Moore, 1967), and (very presciently as it turned out) it was revealed that the local council in Oldham was systematically seg-regating South Asian applicants for social housing eight years before the riots erupted (Commission for Racial Equality, 1993). The complex interplay of official manipulation, fear of real or imagined threat and then the emergence of (sometimes politically motivated) forms of resistance has led to the creation in some British towns of white and BME enclaves defined by specific types of housing and tenure.

The official interpretation is well summed up by Sir Herman Ouseley (2001) in his report on the Bradford riots:

Different ethnic groups are increasingly segregating them-
selves from each other and retreating into 'comfort zones'
made up of people like themselves ... self-segregation is
driven by the fear of others, the need for safety from harass-
ment and violent crime and the belief that it is the only way
to promote, retain and protect faith and cultural identity
and affiliation.

It is therefore perhaps unsurprising that the post-riot explanations
should have pointed to a change in housing policy as a route to
a solution – but does it stack up? The proponents of community
cohesion have argued that if people do not live in proximity they
are unlikely to do other things together. For example, according to
Cantle (2005):

Provision of new [housing] developments and renewal
activity is therefore of critical importance as it shapes so
much of our formal and informal social interaction. It
is particularly closely related to the education agenda, as
housing patterns will often determine school catchment
areas and, therefore, the social interaction beyond the school
gate. Housing patterns will also determine other aspects of
social interaction and access to services, such as health and
sporting and leisure activities.

This emphasis on the importance of achieving residential diversity
actually predates the recent interest in ethnicity and echoes earlier
debates in the UK and other parts of Europe about the value of creating neighbourhoods that are variegated in terms of housing tenure
and the social class and income levels of their occupants.

Despite quite high concentrations of ethnic groups in its major
cities, Australia has successfully avoided many of the serious segregation problems of the UK, Europe and North America. In our research
in Logan, Australia (Brecknock Consulting, 2006b), it was found
that there was a high degree of dispersed residential diversity as a
result of housing policy based on rental support for recent arrivals

moving into the private rental sector rather than being clustered into traditional social housing developments.

Herbert Gans (1961) was one of the first to suggest that a balanced or heterogeneous community would produce manifold social benefits, such as open-mindedness and tolerance, the broadening of educational aspirations and opportunities, and exposure to alternative ways of life. This did not, however, prevent most cities of the Western world constructing vast monotypic housing estates for several decades afterwards and it was not until the 1990s that authorities began to conclude that there might be a connection between housing type and tenure and some of the social and economic difficulties that many tenants were experiencing. The Netherlands government, for example, launched *De Gedifferentieerde Stad* ('The Differentiated City') white paper in 1996, setting out the case for re-engineering housing construction programmes and tenure, and dispersing residents from poorer to more mixed areas. France introduced the *modele republicain d'integration*, imposing financial penalties for local authorities that did not attain targets for construction of social housing in mixed areas. In Sweden, meanwhile, the goal of social mixture has been enshrined in housing policy since the 1970s (Musterd and Andersson, 2005). In Canada, social diversity has been seen as a guarantor of neighbourhood vitality to the extent that many cities have explicitly sought to attract higher income 'gentrifiers' to settle in traditionally working class areas (Dansereau, 2003). In the UK too the government has unambiguously endorsed measures to break up the social homogeneity of many areas in the process of neighbourhood renewal:

> *The Government believes that it is important to create mixed and inclusive communities... Local planning authorities should encourage the development of mixed and balanced communities; they should ensure that new housing developments help to secure a better social mix by avoiding creation of large areas of housing of similar characteristics.*[2]

In the US, while the means may be different, federal policy is also wedded to the achievement of greater diversity. However, given its closer cultural attachment to spatial mobility, US policy is not for social mixing to be imposed upon struggling communities but for them to uproot and seek a better life, for example through the Moving to Opportunity and the HOPE VI programmes (Popkin et al, 2004).

Clearly there is widespread consensus among policy-makers and this has been taken up enthusiastically by planners, demolition contractors, property developers and letting agents as Europe and North America's most notorious and stigmatized neighbourhoods have been knocked down, reconstituted, tarted up, rebranded or even erased completely. There is only one problem, as far as large numbers of both academics and social activists would claim – there is precious little evidence that any of this will actually achieve the desired outcome and may, indeed, lead to even greater problems caused by the tearing up of established social networks. '[T]here is not a majority in the UK in favour of mixing communities by income, class or housing tenure' (Kearns and Parkes, 2003). And in respect of Dutch cities:

> *it is most likely that there are no or virtually no neighbourhood effects on the social mobility of those who are in a relatively weak social position. Therefore, targeting neighbourhoods with the objective of affecting their social composition is not a very productive strategy.* (Musterd, 2003)

What also seems to be absent from most of the arguments in favour of social mixing is any sense that responsibility for achieving it should fall equally upon all sections of society. In most cases it is only the homogeneity of poor areas that is held up for opprobrium, carefully ignoring the fact that many middle- and upper-income areas are equally monocultural (Atkinson, 2006). Therefore, when changes and sacrifices are to be made, it is always the poor who have to make them, and that is not an unimaginably large step from saying

BEING INTERCULTURAL

Box 5.1 City Safari, Rotterdam

'Sometimes it feels like I am keeping this community going single-handedly', says Claudette de Agua Rosada as she serves tea and sandwiches to the strangers who have just walked into her house in the Pendrecht district of south Rotterdam. 'But the support we get through City Safari helps to keep the children's activities going and meeting new people and making friends gives me a real lift.'

Claudette is originally from Curaçao and is now known as the 'mother of the neighbourhood' in this mainly Antillean community of the Dutch city. As well as bringing up four children of her own she runs activities for most of her neighbours' children, and is also actively involved in the local school and in a carnival drum band. 'Some of them take me for granted – take liberties. My husband says I should pack it all in and just care for my own family. But if everyone took that attitude what would become of the community?'.

The strangers privileged with a brief insight into this real life drama are the author (PW) and his family – part of our Rotterdam City Safari. We had already been to visit Mr Ali for a tour of the Shane Moustafa Mosque that serves the Surinamese Muslim community. After lunch with Claudette we headed on the metro back across the river to Oostplein to meet Nigerian musician Amancio, where we worked up a sweat attempting some Yoruba rhythms on his collection of djembe drums. We concluded the day by dropping in at the house of Mr and Mrs Van 't Hof in Oude Westen. They were both born and brought up in the area in the 1930s and lived through the total devastation of Rotterdam by the Luftwaffe in the Second World War. Subsequently they have seen this traditional working class district become populated by migrants from all of The Netherlands' former colonies and now many other parts of the world too. It is fascinating to listen as they describe the changes they have seen in the city. It seems that perhaps the one point of continuity in their lives are the extended family of Koi carp (numbering hundreds) that they keep in the pond at the back of their terraced house.

In our seven hour safari we visited just four Rotterdam households, but the organisers have over 300 addresses on their books reflecting many aspects of this city's life. It could be someone who takes you for a walk through the history of their neighbourhood, any number of different religious faiths (including a shaman), a local police officer or public official, or someone with an unusual lifestyle.

City Safari was founded in 1996 by Marjolijn Masselink with the intention of raising the profile and reputation of the run-down district of Feijenoord within the wider city. The message was that everywhere has something of interest and it is not necessary to artificially create an attraction to make a place attractive. The other message was that people can become tourists in their own city, because City Safari was aimed primarily at Rotterdammers themselves.

While City Safari was not created explicitly to become a zone of intercultural encounter and engagement, in a city as diverse as Rotterdam this is what it has become. It is not promoted as being something that is 'good for you' but rather as entertainment and therefore attracts a lot of parties with something to celebrate or colleagues on a team-building exercise or staff outing. This seems to us the best way to be intercultural.

The one question remains, if this is such a good idea, why hasn't it been taken up elsewhere? Perhaps it requires a specifically Dutch sensibility towards openness to make it work on such a large scale. It certainly requires a level of trust and tolerance that is not found everywhere. One can imagine, for example, the tabloid press in England (where the home is a castle) cynically writing it off as an opportunity for burglars to 'case the joint' of future victims.

Whatever, for the 3500 people who each year undergo this brief insight into the lives of their fellow citizens, City Safari offers otherwise unavailable opportunities to forge connections from which the very fabric of an intercultural city can be built.[3]

that being poor and homogeneous is probably mainly their own fault anyway.

So, while there endures such a division of opinion over the efficacy of social mixing, what should we make of arguments in favour of engineering ethnically heterogeneous neighbourhoods? The point to make is that it is a much more difficult issue to address for two main reasons. First, the differential treatment of applicants for housing on the grounds of race or ethnicity is prohibited under race relations legislation and so any policy set on the redistribution of population and housing tenure on ethnic lines needs not only to be more subtle but also within the law (Robinson, 2005). Second, housing tenure has been used as a proxy for class, but it cannot be used as a proxy for ethnicity (Goodchild and Cole, 2001).

So while the proponents of community cohesion have been explicit in targeting ethnic housing enclaves with the blame for many of society's ills, it has not been so easy for government and its allies to make prescriptions for change. There are of course other potential contradictions in the policies of the UK and other neo-liberal governments. The 'choice agenda' in housing (and also in education) offers individuals the right to make decisions about their housing needs that, while working best for them as individuals, may be antithetical to the creation or maintenance of a mixed community. Also, while the current trend towards 'place-making' and 'place-shaping' as the basis of 'sustainable communities' assumes among other things more settled and less transient populations and the forging or maintenance of strong social bonds, the achievement of more ethnically mixed neighbourhoods would require not only much greater mobility but also the breaking down of some existing social frameworks. It is perhaps too glib to call this the need to adequately balance bonding capital with bridging capital, but this certainly is one of the challenges of our age. In which case, should we be expecting public and private sector housing providers to be at the forefront of providing a solution?

Well, in many cases it seems that we do just this. In Frankfurt am Main in 1994, for example, the city council's housing department drew up a 'treaty' with local property developers and building contractors (the Frankfurter Vertrag) to ensure a greater spatial distribution of immigrants, guest workers and welfare recipients, through adherence to quotas.

In Singapore there has been a strong policy imperative to achieve a 'balanced' ethnic mix, avoiding in particular the emergence of exclusively Chinese or Malay enclaves. As such, Singapore has been implementing an ethnic quota policy on public housing since 1989. With 86 per cent of the population living in public housing, the state

BEING INTERCULTURAL

BOX 5.2 INTERCULTURAL HOUSING IN ROCHDALE

Social landlords operating in the Newbold area of Rochdale are working together to promote the neighbourhood as a safe and desirable place, breaking down historic barriers to particular ethnic groups. The Community Induction Project (CIP) was launched to tackle three challenges:

- limited housing opportunities and poor living conditions experienced by the South Asian population;
- limited interaction and integration between three different ethnic groups;
- sustainability of local estates and the wider community.

Six project workers are managed by a steering group of landlord representatives. Early achievements include:

- a programme of events and daytrips to draw residents together;
- boosting the housing choice for South Asian families by opening up what had previously been 'no-go' areas;
- underpinning sustainability – landlords now report live waiting lists for local housing;
- lessons learned, including the importance of landlords working together to achieve common goals and the importance of core management tasks to support community cohesion.

Significant gains can be made by actively engaging with housing applicants about what is or is not available, talking through their options and explaining the consequences of holding out for a popular area. However, gains can only be sustained through continued attention that points to the importance of ongoing funding and mainstreaming of community cohesion principles within core management tasks (Robinson et al, 2004) has a powerful influence and it also reserves the right to dictate who a private flatowner may sell their property to according to ethnicity. Clearly, in terms of social control, Singapore bears little resemblance to Western states, but even here there is evidence of clusters emerging. The conclusion is that:

> *Blanket policies designed to remedy the ills of observed spatial separation are doomed to fail without detailed understanding of how spatial forms have been mediated by particular sets of social, cultural, economic and political factors. Instead, public policy relating to ethnic dispersal must look beyond the confines of the public housing arena and embrace wider forces at work in the cultural and socioeconomic spheres, some of which may be operating in opposing fashions.* (Chih Hoong Sin, 2002)

More sophisticated policy instruments are now beginning to emerge. There is, for example, a recognized difficulty in accessing social housing arising from a lack of knowledge about what is available and how to get it, a problem that in turn is matched by a lack of cultural awareness among social housing providers and inadequate procedures for assessing potential demand. As a result, low demand from ethnic minorities is read by providers to indicate that their services are not required.

This particular impediment has been recognized and successfully addressed by a choice-based letting initiative in Bradford called Homehunter.[4] Through a dynamic campaign to disseminate information, dispel myths and fears, streamline procedures and put applications on a 'first come first served' rather than a 'heard it through the grapevine' basis, the scheme has vastly increased applications from BME clients for social housing in the city from about 300 per annum to over 4000.

Despite these historic obstacles, and while there remains a strong commitment to owner occupation, especially among Asian communities, there is a growing recognition that high housing costs and a lack of availability of suitable properties may inhibit access to home

BEING INTERCULTURAL

Box 5.3 Intercultural housing in Bradford

National housing provider William Sutton Trust and Bradford-based Manningham Housing Association launched a joint community initiative to boost multicultural understanding in the Tyersal area of Bradford. A partnership between the two housing associations allows William Sutton to tap into the local knowledge and networks of BME-led Manningham. In return, William Sutton's experiences support Manningham's development of tenant involvement strategies. The joint initiative, which seeks to develop racial and cultural awareness and help to boost choice in rehousing, was named Best Partnership Project in an annual awards event organized by the Federation of Black Housing Organizations. William Sutton and Manningham jointly employed Soyful Islam as the community initiatives officer to the project. His role has involved organizing cultural activities including dance and cookery classes, holding meetings and training sessions for tenants of both associations as well as leading development work on issues of racial and cultural awareness. According to Soyful:

> *A lot of our early work has been to dispel myths and challenge people's preconceptions about racial and ethnic identity. We are trying to find the best way of delivering community cohesion through activities which people can enjoy as well as learn from. Both William Sutton and Manningham are very committed to developing understanding between communities and we are now starting to look at how housing management practices can make a positive contribution.* (Cited in Robinson et al, 2004)

---

ownership. There is a growing interest in social housing and shared ownership among minority communities, and greater flexibility in terms of preferred location. There are also increasing problems of disrepair in older properties in traditional neighbourhoods that also support the pursuit of new options.

This inevitably will increase the opportunities for people of different ethnicities to live alongside each other in cities. In itself this is not a guarantee of intercultural exchange, and in the short term might even create the potential for conflict. But this must be considered a desirable step towards the intercultural city.

It is also important to consider the impacts of the lack of diversity in housing stock. In our research in Lewisham (Comedia, 2007), this lack was raised as a significant barrier to meeting the accommodation needs of large families and to their leading fulfilling cultural lives at home. This was especially true for Muslim families who traditionally lead very home-based lives where family, community and faith-based celebrations brought together large numbers of people.

The housing issue is a classic case of social consequences flowing from a built environment problem. Cramped housing conditions for large families lead to a range of social problems that then impact on other aspects of the city. For example, the impact on children and teenagers of living in a crowded household include poor educational outcomes and an increased likelihood of ending up in the juvenile justice system. Imagine how difficult it would be to concentrate on homework when there are, say, six or more siblings vying for space in a two-bedroom flat. The resulting low educational performances have impacts such as limited employment options or, worst still, a decline into crime. Likewise we were told that the cramped home conditions result in teenagers, especially the boys, spending a lot of time out on the streets with their friends. In some cases this leads to antisocial behaviour or inter-gang rivalry and violence.

In our Auckland study (Brecknock Consulting, 2006b), Samoan participants discussed their frustration in trying to find or build housing stock that is suitable for their large extended family units. This highlights the fact that in order for a city to plan interculturally, new forms of *cultural needs analysis* are required to ensure the urban planning process and handling of development applications are culturally sensitive and relevant.

The planning and design issues associated with the provision of flexible housing options for culturally diverse families is an issue that the Commission for Architecture and the Built Environment (CABE) has considered. Their report, *Creating Successful Neighbourhoods*, provides a number of relevant case studies of providing successful outcomes for cultural groups such as Jewish, Muslim and Asian communities (CABE, 2005).

Notwithstanding the dominant influence of choice and the market, those responsible for development and management of housing should accept a responsibility for the impact of their actions upon community cohesion and interculturalism. The principal aims should be the development of policy instruments to tackle the factors that create and exacerbate monocultural housing areas. In particular, policy should break out of stereotypes that assume that monoculturalism is due to the failure of one ethnicity (black) or one class (working class) to integrate. Choice-based letting schemes that aid mixing should be encouraged and backed up with long-term welcoming and settlement programmes provided to tackle harassment. Private sector partners should be encouraged to participate through accreditation schemes and the intervention of professional bodies in the case of unacceptable performance.

Ultimately, however, we would argue strongly against housing policy being seen as the only, or even the primary, tool in dealing with ethnic segregation. We require a more comprehensive policy mix as a more productive and cost-effective means of achieving intercultural contact.

Education

It is a common belief that the place in which lifelong social attitudes are formed is childhood and early adolescence. We should look here for the influences that will determine whether people are more or less inclined to mix across ethnic boundaries in later life. There are many studies on this theme and in particular on the effect of schooling.

It may seem obvious but if a child attends a school at which all children are of one ethnicity, through lack of contact their chances of making friends with a child of another ethnicity will be limited. Their chances of forming

Box 5.4 Collingwood Neighbourhood House, Vancouver

Satinder Singh grew up to a life of wealth, privilege and exclusivity in India and Bahrain until the mid-1980s, when violence erupted between Sikhs and the Indian government. Concerned about their two children, her engineer husband suggested they seek a safe future in Canada and reluctantly she agreed to move. The Singhs landed in 1990 on Vancouver's East Side with no friends or family, far less money than they were accustomed to, and in a place Ms Singh recalls tearfully as 'cold': 'We came to Canada with our backpacks, and not knowing a single soul... It was a really hard transition'.

The family's struggle changed the day Ms Singh walked into Collingwood Neighbourhood House, a non-profit community agency in Vancouver's southeast corner, looking for daycare for her young son and daughter, then aged 10 and 7. The children found a place – and so did their mother. Over time, Ms Singh says, Collingwood House changed all of their lives. Immigration and multicultural experts elsewhere in the world are now taking note of Collingwood's ability to integrate immigrants into local society. This spring in Germany, the charitable arm of BMW Group awarded the top international prizes for intercultural work to Collingwood House and to Leonie Sandercock, director of the University of British Columbia's school of community and regional planning. The BMW awards are aimed at fostering peaceful intercultural coexistence and building bridges between cultures. Dr Sandercock won for her work on cosmopolitan urbanism and her hands-on work at the House, as well as for a documentary, *Where Strangers Become Neighbours: The Story of Collingwood Neighbourhood House and the Integration of Immigrants in Vancouver*, created with University of Rome's Giovanni Attilli.

Collingwood House, a non-profit organization with an independent board of directors and diverse funding – from government to donations to fees – is housed in a two-storey complex of gymnasiums, meeting rooms, rooftop gardens and playgrounds, daycare and parent-tot centres. At its heart is a large industrial-style kitchen. The House, on Joyce Street, is attached to an elementary school that lies within a block of a public health centre and community police station. The House serves a multicultural neighbourhood of 48,000. About 70 per cent of residents come from other countries, and only 27 per cent speak English as a first language. Mandarin, Cantonese, Punjabi, Vietnamese and Spanish are more commonly heard on the streets than the English spoken by old-timers, who include Aboriginal residents. About 30 per cent of the population lives below the poverty line. Dr Sandercock declares:

> *I've looked at a lot of negative examples of how [people] don't live together, all the problems of negative cultural differences and diversity, [and] at the challenges of how urban and social policy are not coming to grips with the challenges of multiculturalism.*

Collingwood's demographic mix is in some ways typical of any mixed neighbourhood in Vancouver, Toronto, Montreal, Sydney, Melbourne or Los Angeles, but:

> *Vancouver is doing remarkably well compared to most places... in part because it's had specific initiatives since the 1980s to embrace the idea of the multicultural city and to do outreach, to try and develop inclusive policies.* (Dr Sandercock)

For Ms Singh, the house was an entry point to a life in Canada she now describes as 'my spot under the sun'. She arrived in Canada with a university degree but no work skills. After her children started attending daycare at Collingwood House, she offered to help out. With English as her first language and fluency in Hindi, Punjabi and Urdu, she was soon helping new immigrants settle in the city. Eventually, she said, she decided to take a degree in early-childhood education and work full time at the House. Her husband supported her dream by moving his engineering business into their home, and he looked after the children while she worked at Collingwood and attended university. Today, Ms Singh is the coordinator of the family programme at the house, helping new immigrants. Her husband runs his own import business, and their children – who would have attended elite private schools in India – graduated from public schools and later from Simon Fraser University. Their son, 27, is a banker and their daughter, 23, works on international development in

Ottawa for the Canadian government. Ms Singh credits Collingwood House for helping her children thrive because from daycare they moved into volunteering and youth jobs, and took leadership training programmes provided by the organization. 'For the first 10 years, I was questioning our move', said Ms Singh, who argues that her daughter especially benefited from growing up in Canada:

in her thinking, her feminism. She's a very strong girl. What I find in Canadians is that by and large they're willing to teach you. People talk about racism, or not being given opportunities. But for me, maybe I'm lucky and maybe it's the neighbourhood house, but it's a giving place.[5]

inaccurate or antipathetic attitudes towards other groups may be heightened. This in turn will reduce the likelihood that they will make friends with adults of another ethnicity in later life. It has also been suggested that in cases where a school mainly comprises two ethnicities, but with one in an overwhelming majority, the chances of cross-racial friendship are also limited (Hallinan and Smith, 1985).

This finding derives from the aforementioned work in the 1950s by Gordon Allport (1954). He held that not only was contact important but that the context in which it took place was key. The positive effects of intergroup contact were likely to occur only in situations marked by four key conditions: equal group status within the situation; common goals; intergroup cooperation; and the support of authorities, law or custom. In addition, when the proportions achieve greater equilibrium, or where there are several different groups present, the opportunity for children to form cross-racial friendship increases greatly. This 'opportunity hypothesis', which proposes that cross-race friendships increase as the opportunities for cross-race friendships increase, is now the mainstream view.

Not surprisingly, studies such as these began in the US and originally concerned themselves with the Caucasian/black polarity.

However, more recent studies have taken account of the richer diversity in many schools in the US and elsewhere.

One study (Joyner and Kao, 2000) was interested in how school composition affects high school students, finding that the percentage of students of other races can be used as a measure of opportunity to have interracial friendships. When opportunity for interracial friendships was controlled, Hispanic Americans and Native Americans were more likely than Caucasians to have interracial friendships, but African-Americans and Asian Americans were less likely than Caucasians to have an interracial friendship. In terms of school racial composition, students' likelihood of having a cross-race friendship increased as the proportion of other-race students increased.

A recent study in the UK (Bruegel, 2006) confirmed many of the earlier US findings, concluding that:

- *Friendship at primary schools can, and does, cross ethnic and faith divides wherever children have the opportunity to make friends from different backgrounds.*
- *At that age, in such schools, children are not highly conscious of racial differences and are largely unaware of the religion of their friends.*
- *The positive benefits of mixed primary schooling particularly for White children, extend into the early years of secondary school.*
- *There was some evidence that parents learned to respect people from other backgrounds as a result of their children's experiences in mixed schools.*
- *The process of secondary school transfer affects behaviour and interracial relations as children react to a sense of rejection.*
- *Secondary school transfer processes also tended to disrupt pre-existing interethnic friendships more than others.*

The classroom environment

Raw numbers, proportions and physical co-presence have a powerful impact, but there are other influencing factors (as Allport first

BOX 5.5 NOITARGETNI: COMBATING EDUCATION
WHITE FLIGHT IN COPENHAGEN

In the late 1980s the Danish government passed legislation giving parents the right to choose any school within the city border for their children. In practice this resulted in parents with Danish origins opting for schools with a majority of white pupils, generating a polarizing effect and resulting in other schools with 80 per cent or more pupils of foreign origin.

A group of parents in the Indre Norrebro district of Copenhagen set up a network with the aim of convincing white parents to stay loyal to their local public schools. They called it Noitargetni (integration spelled backwards). The group's main activities are organizing debates in schools and neighbourhood centres, visiting kindergartens to lobby parents and publicity campaigns. Within two years the network started to show results as more and more white parents decided to allow their children to enrol at local schools.

The network is now supported by both the government and by the local council, and their idea is for it to be spread all over the city of Copenhagen. Unfortunately, the national government has now introduced new legislation that now makes it possible for parents to choose schools beyond the city limits – so the struggle continues.[6]

suggested), not least the environment that is created within a school. Research has found that small class sizes and an ethos of cooperation within small groups leads to greater cross-cultural friendship (Slavin and Cooper, 1999).

The formation of mixed-race 'cooperative learning teams' in which students remain for up to three years has been seen as particularly useful in building understanding based upon equality and a common purpose. As students talk and work with each other they are not only gaining academic knowledge and skill but are also building up a shared cultural paradigm for defining the group, its work and the social identities of the participants. They are establishing a group culture that sets the social context in which relationships among students are given value and meaning. The hope is that they can carry this cultural paradigm with them into adulthood.

One initiative in the US in recent years has been National Mix It Up At Lunch Day.[7] Based on the belief that school cafeterias have become the stage upon which all (not only racial) forms of cliquishness and exclusion are now played out, the campaign set out with the modest aim of encouraging students on one day a year to have their lunch with someone they don't know. In November 2006 this involved over 4 million students at 10,000 schools.

A study commissioned by Comedia (Coles and Vincent, 2006) assessed the impact of an experiment in building cultural integration within and between schools in the city of Leicester. The principal finding from studying the Beacon Community Cohesion Pathfinder programme was that creativity lies at the heart of building intercultural understanding in schools. The arts and creativity were seen as central to the work of developing interculturalism and improving community cohesion because they dealt with the deep issues of both personal and communal identity. At their best, they helped young people to see the world from another person's point of view, to stand in their shoes, as well as to work together with others to achieve a common purpose. It was found that the intensity of young people's experience was such that, even during the course of a single day, they could establish valuable connections with those from different communities that, in many cases, then developed into more long-lasting relationships.

School twinning

An initiative with growing currency around the world is schools twinning or linking. The principle is that pairs of schools within the same borough but with very different ethnic profiles should be encouraged to establish long-term relationships involving joint activities and exchanges of students. This generally involves a class, or several classes across different year groups, being bussed alternatively to each other's schools for periods of a day or half-day per week over a term or a year, to share in activities. This might include curricular activities such as science or geography, but will often also involve a supplementary input of creative activity, joint visits to external locations such as a mosque, church or gurdwara and possibly some non-competitive sport. It often culminates in a final presentation or performance to which the whole school and, sometimes, parents may be invited.

Oldham was one of the first places to try the idea in 2000 and following the riots of 2001. Ted Cantle, who was appointed by the British Government to report upon various civil disturbances of 2001, returned to Oldham in 2006 and produced a five-year report on progress in overcoming separation and mistrust between white, Pakistani and Bangladeshi groups (Cantle, 2006). He included in his report a study of the Oldham School Linking Project. Starting with six primary schools in 2000, the project now involves 50 of Oldham's 95 primary schools, and seven secondary schools. It has given nearly 4000 children opportunities to meet and mix with those of a different social and cultural background. Cantle (2006) quotes the findings of an Ofsted inspection (Limeside Primary School Ofsted Report, February 2004) of one of the participating primary schools, which he says is typical of many others:

> *The Linking Schools Project has given pupils a close link with a local primary school which has a high multi-ethnic intake. This relationship has given pupils from both schools the opportunity to be involved in joint ... activities which have greatly helped in raising pupils' awareness of the cultural diversity of the local community and is helping to break down barriers.*

Cantle adds, however, that it is as yet too early to tell what impact the project is having in influencing the attitudes of Oldham's children and young people.

The one school linking project that has so far been subjected to rigorous evaluation identifies a significant beneficial effect. Bradford has a BME population of almost 22 per cent. Fifty-nine per cent of primary school children attend schools in which 90 per cent or more

% of children	Before	After
With no cross-cultural friendships	39	11
With 2 or more cross-cultural friendships	4	38
With 4 or more cross-cultural friendships	0	16
With no interest at all in mixed friendships	28	9
With enthusiasm to develop more mixed friendships	19	32

Source: Raw (2006)

Figure 5.3 Cross-cultural friendships

of the children are of one ethnicity, indicating a disproportionately low level of mix. The city launched its Schools Linking Project in 2001, which grew rapidly to involve 61 primary and 12 secondary schools, involving 1880 pupils by the time it was evaluated in 2005–2006 by Anni Raw (2006). It was found that (starting from an admittedly low base) the project had made a notable impact upon the level of interaction between children of different cultures with participating children making an average of 2.6 new cross-cultural relationships through the project. Figure 5.3 demonstrates the wider impact of the project.

Other significant findings of the study were that:

- there were generally greater impacts amongst BME children than white children;
- years 4 and 5 children showed the greatest impact;
- children in urban schools react more actively than those in rural settings;
- longer time spent linking leads to greater impact;
- socio-economic background appeared to have no influence;
- there was no difference in impact between children in faith-based or secular schools.

A small number of children demonstrated adverse reactions with a hardening of their aversion to cultural mixing. This finding may be due in part to the general raising of confidence levels among all children, and therefore the confidence of some to express prejudiced views. There was also a correlation of the prejudiced views of children and those of parents and family friends and also with the activity levels of extremist political groups in certain areas. In general, though, the Schools Linking Project is seen to be having a particularly positive effect on community cohesion in Bradford, and there is an intention to continue and extend it.[8]

In neighbouring Kirklees, the education authority has attempted to extend the community cohesion potential of twinning through the involvement of adults other than teachers, not only parents but also non-teaching assistants and playtime assistants who are often people with significant networks and influence in a locality (Herrick, 2006). This has been well received by the (albeit small numbers of) parents who have participated.[9] What was also notable in Kirklees was the high level of investment in the arts and creative activity as a means of engaging and stimulating the children to think beyond their normal space.[10] This echoes findings from previous research commissioned by Comedia into education and community cohesion in Leicester schools (Coles and Vincent, 2006).

Not everyone is so enthusiastic about school twinning, though. Irene Bruegel (2006) argues that schemes that only afford infrequent engagement, however well-meaning, are of limited value. Commenting on the Oldham project, she observes that:

> *One school governor noted that the children in the Moorside village would otherwise not see an Asian until, and unless, they went to the town's sixth form college. He felt that the mixed race children in the school benefited from the contact – 'they came alive', because people were 'talking about things that were meaningful to them'. But the children from the village referred to the twin school, as 'the brown school', 'down there'; they couldn't remember any of the children's names because they were 'difficult to pronounce' and the visits of the children did little if anything to assuage the sense of grievance of the White parents that the outer areas were losing out in funding to 'Banglatown', for example in*

the closure of the sixth form in the all-White semi-rural secondary school. The children from the White community envied the resources of the inner city school, but treated their days out as external to them and their concerns. The twinning earned the school 'brownie points', but appeared to make only a very superficial difference to attitudes.

Bruegel (2006) believes that day-to-day contact between children has far more chance of breaking down barriers between communities than school twinning and sporting encounters. She argues for concentrating not only on the schools that are already polarized, but also on the far greater number that are mixed now but could become polarized in the future.

If the aim of government is to defuse potential flashpoints and to create a new generation of interculturally confident and competent children, it should focus on the many schools where a balanced ethnic mix could be turned into ethnic polarization by the spatial politics of parental choice over coming years. This is a real concern because the evidence already shows that segregation in schools is more pronounced than in their surrounding neighbourhoods (Burgess et al, 2005). Furthermore, the all-white schools of suburban and rural Britain should also be part of a general uplifting in the priority given to the inculcating of intercultural skills and awareness.

In some respects, in places such as Oldham, Burnley and Bradford (Ward, 2003), the process of segregation has gone too far for contact theory to be effective but they stand as a warning of what might happen if it is not applied rigorously in other less divided parts of the country. There remains the vexed question of how to encourage inter-group relationship when groups are so physically and institutionally separate that their paths never cross. Perhaps the most controversial attempt to answer this arose in 1970s US with the experiment in 'desegregation bussing'.

Carrot or stick?

The gradual breakdown of segregation in education in the US,[11] the civil rights movement and onset of progressive urban policies in the

1960s brought about sweeping changes in the racial composition of schools and with it greater equality of access to opportunity. In many areas, schools had been so rigidly separated as to be monocultural so there was no prospect of contact without radical action. Among the methods communities used to desegregate schools was bussing of black students to predominantly white schools. Since the black schools tended to be in poorer neighbourhoods and had fewer resources, it seemed to make sense to bus black students to white schools until a balance of black and white students was attained. Beginning in Charlotte, Virginia, in 1969, court orders eventually spread the practice to many areas across the country.

Bussing is one illustration of how difficult it is to achieve true desegregation. The sense that it was being enforced by legislation was not particularly well received by either blacks or whites. In many large urban cities, whites who could afford to move to the suburbs, where the population (and consequently the schools) were predominantly white, left inner-city schools with dwindling white student populations.

The 1974 case of *Milliken v. Bradley* addressed the issue of 'white flight' to the suburbs by proposing to bus suburban children into the inner-city schools in which whites were the minority. Yet the US Supreme Court ruled that suburban students could not be used to desegregate inner-city schools. White flight continued and, because most of the people left behind were poor or working class, cities lost much of their tax base. Cities became poorer, spending less on education, and blacks and other minorities who could afford to move did so, and the inner-city populations became statistically poorer. By the end of the 20th century, many of the largest cities in the US had public schools that remained as racially imbalanced as ever but also in much greater need of funding for maintenance, basic supplies and more teachers. The general mood had moved on to believing that equality would be better achieved through raising standards and widening choice rather than through compulsion (Rossell, 1990).

The debate continues over what to do about the most extreme forms of educational segregation, but there is mounting evidence that where schools are mixed in composition, there are multifaceted benefits to be gained from achieving greater interaction. Studies have found that both African-American and Caucasian students with cross-race friends had higher educational aspirations and outcomes than those with only same-race friends (Hallinan and Williams, 1990); and also that in girls in particular a high number of interracial friendships was also associated with greater social competence (Hunter and Elias, 1999).

Another study (Holme et al, 2005) looked at the long-term impact of school desegregation on adult graduates of racially mixed high schools, capturing what they said about the impact of their schooling experiences on their current understandings about race, and on their lives in a racially diverse society. Of the 242 interviewees, nearly all said that their high school experiences left them more prepared for life in a racially diverse society than they otherwise would be, and every one said their experiences left them with a deeper understanding of people of other backgrounds and an increased sense of comfort in interracial settings. Many stressed the importance of experiences of negotiating race in high school as one of the most challenging yet rewarding aspects of their education and these lessons. They observed this could not be gained through multicultural curricula or student exchange programmes. Rather, such insights could only be learned by the daily experience of attending racially diverse schools. In the light of these experiences, the authors observe the need to reconsider the current retreat from policies designed to foster diversity in public schools.

The workplace

Most of the interest and the policy activity concerned with segregation and integration have focused upon two areas: the neighbourhood and the classroom. While colossal amounts of resources and pious hope have been invested in attempting to build a more harmonious society outwards from these two sites, the results have been largely disappointing.

One major area of life has, almost unnoticed, been demonstrating significantly growing levels of ethnic contact and integration: the workplace. In *Working Together: Crossing Color Lines at Work*, Cynthia Estlund (2005) poses two propositions:

> *First, the typical workplace is a hotbed of sociability and cooperation, of constructive and mostly friendly interactions among co-workers day after day, and often year after year. Second, of all the places where adults interact with others, the workplace is likely to be the most demographically diverse. In a society that is still largely segregated, the workplace is where working adults are most likely to associate regularly with someone of another race.*

She follows Putnam (2000)[12] in arguing that various forms of civic engagement may have gone into decline in many developed countries. She points out that many neighbourhood and school integration programmes may have been overwhelmed by more powerful countervailing social forces. Ironically, perhaps the most powerful of all – individual freedom of choice – has been vigorously pioneered by the very same governments that have wrung their hands impotently over segregation. The labour market has in the past exhibited all the hallmarks of segregation, but in recent years has become a much more ethnically diverse place. She quotes findings that when asked to think about people who they immediately work with, 63 per cent of white Americans reported having at least one black co-worker, and this rose to over 90 per cent in companies with more than 250 employees (Hellerstein and Neumark, 2003). This is also confirmed by research in Australia that found that 56 per cent of Australians had a lot of contact with people from different backgrounds at work (Ang et al, 2002). This is unsurprising given the growing diversity of all advanced countries but also the increasing importance of work in people's lives, not only in terms of the sheer amount of time it takes up but its role in identity formation. Yet the research remains underdeveloped in this area, especially in Europe.

There is evidence that in some workplaces, contact on the job can lead to relationships outside of work (Houston et al, 2005). For example, white men in the US military are eight times more likely to marry a black woman than white men in civilian life (Heaton and Jacobson, 2000), while female white military personnel are seven times more likely to marry a black man than a civilian (Farley, 1999). It is significant the military should be singled out. More than most walks of life it is an area characterized by intense processes of collective endeavour and interdependence, but also formal and quite rigid regulation and enforcement. This, says Estlund (2005), may be the clue as to why integration is apparently working at work:

> *Most people have little choice about whether to work and, once on the job, about with whom they work on a daily basis. Interaction among co-workers is often compelled by managers, constrained by rules, job duties, and the threat of discipline, and shaped by economic power and necessity. Moreover, the law regulates many aspects of the composition, organization, and treatment of the workforce.*

Several decades of labour market and workplace legislation has outlawed discrimination and discouraged prejudice. Mutual aversion may still be the norm in the US neighbourhood and school, but in the office, shop or warehouse, managers (pursuing a 'business case for diversity' agenda) have either demanded or incentivized cooperation and, what is more, this has been largely welcomed by all parties.

Segregation in the US might make integrated workplaces seem remarkable, but there is evidence from elsewhere that it is a factor of some substance. We have noted that Singapore has gone to great lengths to enforce ethnic integration through neighbourhood and housing policies and this has resulted in very low levels of group separation. Yet recent research into the formation of social networks found that 60 per cent of interethnic friendships between Chinese, Malays and others originated in the workplace and only 12 per cent in the neighbourhood (Appold and Chua, 2006).

There are also promising signs that even in places where interethnic suspicion has boiled over into violence and warfare, the workplace may have healing properties. A study of the aftermath of the Bosnian civil war in Sarajevo (Pickering, 2006) found many examples of individuals from all three sides of the vicious conflict rebuilding familiarity and trust through working together. The researcher (Pickering, 2006) even quotes the case of a Serb woman, Ana, who had rebuilt connections with Bosniaks (Muslims) through working together:

> *Though she did not describe her Bosniak colleague Anisa as a friend, Ana occasionally saw movies with Anisa and confided in her about her children. They established inclusive identifications based on professionalism and mothering. To express solidarity with her colleagues, Ana displayed in her office a 1994 newspaper photo of her and Anisa peering out from the window of their mortar-pocked office during the war, suggesting also the unifying experience of working together during war. Ana's connections at work provide psychological support and help her to solve practical problems. The mutual confiding, the time spent together outside the office, and perhaps also the photo indicate that Ana and Anisa have ties of moderate strength.*

Work is clearly important to people around the world as a place in which to cross racial barriers, yet it is not necessarily important for the same reasons. In a fascinating study of working class men in France and the US who identified themselves as not being racially prejudiced, it becomes apparent that while people may arrive at the same endpoint of agreeing that 'we should all get along', they justify this for very different reasons, including the importance of work (Lamont and Aksartova, 2002). In general, both black and white Americans thought the workplace had a positive role in racial equalization because it allowed them to earn equivalent amounts – which translated into respect – and gave them money to go out and spend it in similar ways. Work also enabled people of different ethnic backgrounds to demonstrate equivalent levels of competence and this also garnered mutual respect. Alternatively, French workers, both white and Maghrebi, had no concern with earning and consumer power as a signifier of equality. The French were far more likely to refer to the solidarity of the labour movement that transcended racial or cultural difference. Muslims also had a different take, seeing work as means of demonstrating one's moral character as a good, hard-working fellow human. If one thing did characterize these working class cosmopolitans of different national, religious and racial backgrounds, it was that none had any time for a multiculturalist world of celebrating difference, but grounded their anti-racist views in what they saw as fundamental elements of human sameness.

It would be naïve, perhaps wrong, to make too many claims for the workplace as an ideal of harmony and equality or as a model for the rest of society. First, even if people are getting on on a one-to-one basis over the office water cooler, they are only individuals and it takes a rather large leap of imagination to see this influencing group attitudes and behaviour across very large and sophisticated societies. Second, although there are positive stories emerging even from among the deskilled and deregularized world of the fast food outlets (Newman, 1999), the evidence suggests that greater proclivity for intercultural mixing exists in employees associated with higher levels of education and professionalism, and in larger organizations. Swathes of the labour market remain, and may even be becoming more, segregated. Contrary to the experience in the US, in Western Europe 'ethnic economies' such as Pakistani taxi drivers or Bangladeshi restaurants owe their existence less to the fulfilment of latent entrepreneurial urges and more to exclusion from the mainstream labour market (see Rath and Kloosterman, 2000; Wrench and Modood, 2000). Since the enlargement of the EU, many thousands of workers from Eastern Europe have moved west to fill jobs that are vacant because the British, Dutch and French do not want to do them. However, there seems little or no opportunity for a Pole to make friends with a British worker in the carrot fields of Cambridgeshire!

There is an emerging argument that the workplace is not so much a meeting place where differences can interact on an equal basis, but rather one in which everyone is expected to accommodate to the dominant cultural values of white people. The critique of 'whiteness' has tried to turn the focus of attention away from the segregation of minorities and towards the silent and much less understood ways in which white majorities retain and reproduce their own way of doing things. It has become commonplace to regard the high-tech and creative industries as part of a new cosmopolitan wave in which difference is not just tolerated but welcomed, and many have argued that diversity is at the foundation of its success (Saxenian, 1999). However, one study takes the archetypical post-ethnic world of the software industry in west coast US (Reitman, 2006) and holds it up to scrutiny. Meredith Retman argues that the vaunted multiculturalism of these 'creative class' businesses is based upon the laid back and very liberal, but nevertheless unyielding, assumption that the accepted codes of behaviour and cultural values for all the black, brown, yellow and white colleagues will be those of the boys who have been brought up in all white schools and who live in all white neighbourhoods. She argues that claims of 'colour-blindness' in such workplaces are based upon the 'whitewashing' out of racial politics of inequality leaving behind a shallow and exotic multiculturalism of food or music.

The workplace is likely to be a more effective location for inter-group affiliation when there is an adequate supply of paid employment. There is a lingering concern that in times of shortage or when wages are driven down, the labour market may be a site of potential conflict or segregation. It is no coincidence that the UK race riots of 2001 took place in three northern towns – Bradford, Burnley and Oldham – all of which had been founded upon a textile industry that had gone into terminal decline. During the 1960s and 1970s, when the industry was in its death throes, Pakistani and Bangladeshi migrants had been enticed to the UK to work in the mills. Paradoxical as it might seem, such was the flight of traditional white working-class mill workers from the industry that job vacancies were growing faster than the industry was shrinking (Law, 1999). When white workers remained in the industry, a diurnal workplace segregation began to happen with immigrants largely taking on the night shift and whites the day. This arrangement did little to foster workplace interaction and, when job cuts and closures continued to bite, competition for scarce resources eventually led to inter-communal rancour and strife.

In general, there has been extraordinarily little attention played to the role of the workplace in communal relations in the UK or Europe in comparison to the US, Australia and Singapore, but there was a notable reference to it in one of the 2001 post-riot reviews. The Bradford Review (Ouseley, 2001) referred specifically to the workplace as one of the prime locations in which to rebuild community cohesion. It recommended the establishment of the (rather inelegantly phrased) 'Behavioural Competency Framework for the Workplace', the role of which would be:

- *To give due recognition to the relevant skills and experiences derived from knowledge and understanding of the different cultures, faiths, needs, contributions, achievements and aspirations of multicultural communities in the UK.*
- *To apply a generic competency of demonstrable 'knowledge and experience of multicultural communities' to specifications for employment and test this competency through interviews, evidence production, assessments, exercises and other selection processes.*
- *To secure competent multicultural workforces at all levels in organisations, who are capable of working with each other in healthy, competitive and team-working environments, with dignity and respect, producing high quality, performance related operational objectives and standards.*
- *To set behavioural standards in line with best occupational practices and encourage and enhance people's knowledge, more tolerant attitudes and mutual respect across communities.*
- *To eliminate discriminatory, oppressive and unacceptable workplace practices which deny equal opportunities and fair treatment for people of all backgrounds.*

The labour market in most developed economies is much less ethnically segregated than the housing market. Some recent research has suggested that time factors need greater consideration, observing that many Americans are now living lives based upon daily shifts between integration and segregation. They interact in multiethnic work environments during the day before returning to monocultural residential areas at night (Ellis et al, 2004). Ellis et al (2004) conclude that:

> *If, as we suspect, interracial contact at work, and in other spaces outside segregated neighbourhoods, has helped stimulate the recent surge in rates of interracial partnership, it may also lay the foundations for the eventual desegregation of residential space. For interracial families must live somewhere, and as their numbers grow, they will become a substantial force in desegregating neighbourhoods because of mixing within families.*

One factor should not be overlooked: the discrepancy between different groups with regard to participation in the labour market. In 2003–2004 the employment rate amongst whites in the UK was 75.6 per cent while for non-whites it was only 58.4 per cent. This will be not too dissimilar for the rest of Europe. There are a variety of economic, cultural and demographic reasons to explain this but the discrepancy does have an influence upon the degree to which people can mix in the workplace. There are some significant regional variations. In the London Borough of Sutton, non-whites are actually more likely to be in the labour market than whites (80.6 to 79.6 per cent). In contrast, in the London Borough of Tower Hamlets, the employment rate for whites is 52.5 per cent and only 33.4 per cent for non-whites, equating to a discrepancy of 19.1 percentage points. However, outside the capital the discrepancy is even higher in some places, notably Bradford (22.6) and Blackburn (26.4) (Turok et al, 2006).

There can be no doubt that in the workplace we have a proven, dynamic and growing phenomenon of intercultural engagement and it should give us clues as to how we might progress towards greater engagement across society. From our discussion of the military we might draw the conclusion that people will only genuinely mix when there is a hierarchically imposed regulatory regime and the threat of individual punishment, or even of collective failure leading to potential loss of life in combat situations from failing to pull together. While legal compulsion undoubtedly has played a role in removing prejudice and aversion from the workplace in general, one should also highlight the positive power of collective endeavour and common goals as a driver of mutual learning, respect and trust. The workplace has a powerful role to play in retaining and rebuilding intercultural cohesion and therefore it is all the more a mystery and a concern that there appears to be so little focus upon it in the UK and other parts of Europe. The following is one of the very few references in the literature (and is an appropriate call to arms):

> *We would argue that the workplace is in fact critical as an environment where people develop informal networks and relationships, and where they are exposed to the values and norms of working communities and society more broadly. It is therefore an important place where social capital is formed, shaped and maintained. We would suggest that the workplace should be taken more seriously when considering levels of social capital in research, policy, and practices.* (Grenier and Wright, 2006)

The market place

A history of intercultural trade

The first movements of human migration in prehistory were in-fluenced by the need for tribes to seek out new lands and resources and to separate themselves from the rivalry and competition of other tribes. As cultures consolidated and agricultural and artisan economies established themselves, it become far more likely that they would begin to seek out other communities different from themselves with which to trade. This might be to source mundane essentials such as salt and flint or to enhance the lifestyles of their elites with exotic goods and services. Civilizations were attracted to trade. What we now understand as long-distance commerce substantially predates currency and may well have been going on for as long as 150,000 years (Watson, 2005).

The levels and types of intercultural trade varied in intensity throughout history. The Phoenician, Greek and Roman periods saw extensive activity around the Mediterranean, and the Vikings are credited with establishing ambitious intercontinental trade routes. This trend to reach out to strange and unfamiliar cultures became more systematic with the rise of mercantile city-states, notably those comprising the Hanseatic League based on Lübeck, and also Venice. Indeed, if any historic example of intercultural encounter is lodged in the popular imagination it must be the journeys of Niccolo and Marco Polo to China and the court of the Mongol emperor Kublai Khan (Larner, 1999). While this famous journey is told from a Eurocentric perspective, many cultures share inspiration from foreign exchange. Take, for example, Zheng He, imperial admiral of the Chinese Ming dynasty who is reputed by some to have circumnavigated the globe (Menzies, 2002), or the great 14th century Islamic explorer, Ibn Battutah (Mackintosh-Smith, 2003).

This is a pretext to saying that the market – both as a concept and a physical location – is central to any understanding of intercultural exchange. Indeed, one might say that the urge to seek profit and novelty through trade is the primary motivation for people of different ethnicities to seek each other out and establish meaningful contact. Becoming cross-cultural friends and lovers might point to other instincts and motivations but trade is a crucial zone of encounter on many levels.

The market place for many throughout history – and still today – is the place where, for the first time, people physically encounter someone who is visibly distinct from them, who speaks and dresses differently and who offers unusual cultural goods and experiences. Our notion of the market now extends far beyond gathering together a few stalls on a set day each week. Markets now operate spatially and temporally through the extension of mass media and communications technology.

We explore some manifestations by extending our inquiry to explore 'the market' beyond a 'place', as the overarching economic and cultural concept of our current stage of advanced global capitalism. Essentially we are interested in the time-honoured tradition of the physical encounter between a buyer and a seller and the exchange of goods and currency as well as other possible social or cultural transactions.

There is a vast amount of research into why people part with their money and how they might be persuaded to part with even more. Social science has also observed in detail the psychological and cultural factors influencing this, as well the intimate interactions that take place between buyer and seller (or in the professional vernacular, the nature of the 'service encounter'). There has been rather less thought given to the relationship of race and ethnicity and even less to the 'intercultural service encounter'. We review what exists and then draw some conclusions.

The reason this matters is that while people of different ethnicities may not live together or even go to school together, at least in urban settings they are likely to encounter the 'Other' through some form of commercial or service transaction, from buying their morning news-paper to any number of other regular or occasional experiences. This may seem trivial but for many it may be the only encounter across cultures they have. As such, it might carry more significant meaning for some. There is little doubt that in such encounters, opinions can be formed and prejudices can either be confirmed or eroded in ways that can strongly influence attitudes and behaviours elsewhere in life. They matter more than we have given them credit.

The nature of modern retailing

An overview of the complex and sophisticated nature of modern retailing reminds us that shopping is no longer (if it ever was) con-cerned exclusively with the simple exchange of goods for currency. We still must fulfil our basic requirements for food, clothing, shelter and fuel, but this takes up a diminishing proportion of both our time and disposable income. Taking Maslow's (1943) notion of the 'hierarchy of needs', consumers are increasingly concerned with non-essential goods and services, many of which may have little or no intrinsic substance. They are desirable through the symbolic value the providers and consumers invest in them. Value is now less based on raw materials or manufacturing costs and more on symbolic and aesthetic judgements. The social and cultural have grown alongside the economic. In effect value and values have become intertwined.

Factors beyond the calculation of price and worth come into play, changing the nature of the *relationship* between the retailer, the brand and the customer. Any high street shows that people often identify themselves (both as individuals and members of a group) through their choices and purchases as consumers (or their conspicuous non-consumption). The retailer needs to understand and empathize with that identity. It is as important as knowing how much a customer can afford to spend.

Shopping as social linking

The extent to which retailers balance the valuation of the relationship against the financial transaction has been synthesized into a four-part typology. This shows the extent to which retailers offer the prospect of social linking (Remy and Kopel, 2002). Shops, or commercial chains, may fall into one of the following categories:

- *Utilitarian valorization* – such companies are concerned with the transaction and little else. They include the extreme discounters and, to a lesser extent, some supermarkets.
- *Functional valorization* – relationships matter to companies such as banks who are increasingly trying to limit the 'fruitless' contacts with their customer by installing automats, while simultaneously encouraging small head-to-head spaces for more intimate contact that could prove valuable to them.
- *Hedonistic valorization* – shopping becomes a leisure activity in itself with sales outlets planned to appeal to all five senses to excite or divert the attention of the customer, such as FNAC, Sephora or Niketown.
- *Communitarian valorization* – shops are cult or tribal places in which being together with likeminded people associated with the same brand values appears more important than the sale itself, such as the specialist book or music shop, with a coffee machine.

Type of linking services	Transactional linking services	Relational linking services	Socializing linking service	'Tribal' linking services
Nature of the participation of the client	Economic – physical	Economic – contractual (physical and intellectual)	Social – hedonistic	Social – affective
Types of valorization in the Physical Support	Utilitarian valorization	Functional valorization	Hedonistic valorization	Community valorization
Role of contact staff	Strongly uniformized	Enhanced by proximity, the relationship with the customer	To share the firm's and the market community's values	Integrating the values of the community (the tribe)
Marketing techniques	Promotional offers sent to a whole segment, loyalty cards based on points	One to one techniques. Database, mailing lists, loyalty cards with associated services, newsletters	Charters, social and ethical commitments. Organization of non-commercial events	Local sponsoring, participation or organization of events in the community

Figure 5.4 Four typical linking services

Source: Remy and Kopel, 2002

The primary social link the retailer is interested in remains with the consumer but the lower down the list we go, the role of the retail environment as a more general social meeting place increases. Remy and Kopel (2002) have further developed this into a schematic for explaining the different relationships that would be expected to emerge in each place, as shown in Figure 5.4.

Although this typology was not devised with any intention of explaining intercultural exchange, it provides a useful framework within which to think about the possibilities of the retail environment. Clearly, where the economic transaction is valued above all else to the exclusion of social ones, we would expect fewer opportunities for people to overcome ethnic boundaries. Alternatively, you expect both the quantity and quality of social interaction to increase as one moves towards the right of the table. Yet it does not necessarily follow that this interaction will be more interethnic. Taking an idea from Robert Putnam (1993, 2000), groups with 'tribal' characteristics are based upon very strong 'bonding social capital', which means they draw their strength from the similarity and likemindedness of their membership, as well as their distinctiveness from non-members. What they often lack, however, is 'bridging social capital', which means they are less able to either admit outsiders or form relationships with other tribes. This is not to discount the possibility that some 'retail tribes' could comprise people of varying ethnicities, but this seems less likely.[13] The retail environments most likely to encourage interethnic engagement are likely in fact to be those described by the two central columns, where a reasonable priority is given to relational and social functions.

The relational nature of a company and retail environment is set by the proprietor and customer. Retailers will modulate their offer based upon their assessment of what their core customer base expects of them. If a retail survey concludes that people use their shop to grab a sandwich or newspaper before catching a train or going to work, they are more interested in the retailer's speed of service than what shopping there says about them as people. It is no good providing a warm, friendly, visually stimulating environment if customers are not looking for it. It might have a negative impact if customers think the retailer's expenditure on a pleasant environment is being passed on to them through higher prices.

Ethnicity and shopping behaviour

What happens if you attempt to assess customer expectations according to ethnicity? The evidence is limited but not negligible. A study of the differential use of shopping malls by English- and French-speaking Canadians did find small variations in the degree to which people shopped for purely utilitarian or more hedonistic reasons (Michon and Chebat, 2004). A study comparing black, Latino and white teenage shoppers was more definitive, though (Eun Young Kim and Youn-Kyung Kim, 2005). It found, first, that for teenagers in general the shopping mall was regarded as a 'third space' in which identities could be played out free of the restrictions of home or school and that they were 40 per cent more likely to visit malls than adults. However, black and Latino visitors were likely to be seeking out different experiences than their white peers in both scale and type. While white teenagers said they were there to purchase a specific item or to have a meal, non-whites were more likely to be there to see and be seen. Awareness of these tendencies has led some retailers to design their environments and product ranges with the aim of ethnically niching themselves, such as the Greenbriar Mall in Atlanta that has a decidedly African-American ethos.[14]

Most retailers segment and specialize, but some are becoming more aware that their potential market is ethnically diversifying and are looking for ways of dealing with this. At the same time there is increasing standardization, especially by mass chains who seek to acculturate their diverse customers to a common standard and uniform level of product and form of service encounter (Hopkins et al, 2005). In effect this is a globalized 'McDonalds' model of provision that offers an easy level of access but nevertheless requires concessions on the part of the customer. An Australian study found that in some such outlets, there was a lack of tolerance for customers who did not meet the image required of them in terms of, say, their accents (Braker and Haertel, 2004). The reaction of the retail staff is subtle (in the form of tone of voice or body language) but nevertheless expresses distaste.

The intercultural service encounter

A customer shunned or misunderstood may not only be business lost but business driven into the arms of a rival. The increasingly competitive environment is paradoxically moving retailers in the direction of greater sensitivity to cultural diversity. This is the conclusion of one study that considered how foreign visitors were dealt with in US hotels (Sizoo et al, 2005). It employed the Cross-Cultural Adaptability Inventory (Kelley and Meyers, 1989) to measure the sensitivity of restaurant staff. The results showed a very strong correlation between the hotels with the highest diamond rating and staff with greater cross-cultural adaptability. It argues for employers to invest more in training and recruitment to ensure their staff are more comfortable and competent with people of diverse backgrounds:

> *these employees will be more attentive to the needs of customers from other cultures. They will make greater use of suggestive selling, thereby creating opportunities to generate more revenue per foreign customer. Their interpersonal skills in a multicultural workplace will be more appropriate, and they will get more satisfaction from interacting with foreign customers ... service managers who hire and develop more interculturally sensitive employees will be providing their foreign customers with a better service environment and their organization with better results.* (Sizoo et al, 2005)

The limitation of this study is that it concerns the interactions of two relatively untypical groups: foreign tourists and employees of relatively sophisticated organizations with a clear financial incentive to acknowledge diversity. The day-to-day encounters that mostly characterize our diverse cities are people of different cultures who are both local but neither of whom have been given – or are expected to possess – any degree of intercultural sophistication. It is in these encounters where prejudices will most usually be played out. Take, for example, the inquiry made into the riots that tore through south-central Los Angeles in 1992 (Pyong, 1996). The disturbances were sparked by the racist beating of African-American Rodney King by white police officers. However, much of the subsequent anger, personal attacks and destruction of property were not inflicted upon the police or white people but upon the Korean owners of shops and other businesses in and around Compton.

Subsequent explanations for this apparent resentment focused largely on economic exclusion or jealousies. Yet one line of analysis looked at the black/Korean relationship as a zone of intercultural exchange. Bailey (2000) argued that the main reason for the tension and ultimate conflict between the two communities could be attributed to different communication styles in service encounters. Korean owners of convenience stores were observed to be taciturn and inexpressive in comparison to most of their African-American customers. This limited their interaction with customers to a minimum to complete the transaction. Black customers on the other hand were looking for socially expressive service encounters involving eye contact, small talk and laughter. Many blacks took the shopkeepers' failure to respond to their conversational cues as representing a lack of respect. The focus on these differences in communication styles then encouraged communities to highlight other aspects of difference and to minimize the common factors that they may share. The steady accretion of this over many years – combined with perceptions of economic or judicial inequality – led to the situation for which the King beating was the trigger.

Other studies have sought to demonstrate that African-American/Korean interactions are far from universally negative (Hye-Kyung Ryoo, 2005), and in doing so have emphasized even more the power (for good or ill) of interpersonal communication and the significance of the shopping experience at the front line of intercultural relations. It all comes down to two individuals putting ethnic stereotypes aside, taking the trouble to think about the expectations of the other and putting in a little effort to meet them.

In the UK too there has been more recent evidence that the local shop can be a place of great resonance in multiethnic neighbourhoods. In October 2005, the Handsworth district of Birmingham experienced – not for the first time – violent street disturbances. The difference between this and previous riots was that the violence was not targeted at the police or 'the state' but flared between two different ethnic communities, the African-Caribbean and the Pakistani Muslim. It was triggered by an unfounded rumour that a black girl had been caught shoplifting a wig and then raped by several Asian shopkeepers. Echoing south-central Los Angeles, this was fuelled by years of resentment both about the shifting economic balance of power and the build-up of innumerable unsatisfactory interactions (including service encounters) between the two communities (Cohn, 2005). What most shocked the British public was the unfamiliar sight of two minorities 'breaking ranks' to challenge each other. What we should highlight is the potential of the retail environment as an interface between groups where tensions can either be played out or assuaged.

The market as meeting place

The 'corner shop' is a microcosm of interethnic relations, but the classic location of social and economic exchange is the urban market. A recent study (Watson with Studdert, 2006) looked in detail at eight markets in the UK. It found that markets had faced considerable competition from other forms of retail and only catered significantly for certain social groups, namely older people, the disabled and young mothers. Watson with Studdert (2006) asked how markets performed as sites of social mixing and concluded:

> *Conflicts and tensions in markets were reported to be rare. However, there was some evidence of interracial tension at one of the sites, and some reports of shoplifting and drug use elsewhere... Overall, the markets tended to reflect the sociodemographics of the local community and where this was very mixed, such as in Ridley Road, the market appeared to act as a site of mixing and connection in very positive ways. The markets as a whole ... also appeared to provide opportunities for some mixing across different age groups, particularly in café sites.*

A fascinating study of public spaces in the East End of London by Dines et al (2006) looked in particular at an old but popular

BEING INTERCULTURAL

BOX 5.6 BUNNENGASSE MARKET, VIENNA

In the Otakring neighbourhood on the outskirts of Vienna, there are more than 50 nationalities including many Pakistanis, Turks, Maghrebians and Egyptians. It also features the largest permanent market for exotic products, which occupies a long street, the 'Brunnengasse'. The atmosphere is relaxed and cordial, and there are a large number of foreign restaurants. What is the secret of this successful coexistence? On the one hand, the Vienna Chamber of Commerce and City Council decided to allocate all empty shops to artists rent-free. Dozens of artists blend into the life of the neighbourhood and run numerous projects in association with the locals, ranging from providing services (sign painting and such like) to innovative and unusual projects. On the other hand, the annual 'Soho' festival in Otakring mobilizes a hundred or so artists and completely transforms the dilapidated image of the neighbourhood, while managing to avoid the phenomenon of 'gentrification'.[15]

---

market that was facing the prospect of substantial redevelopment against which there was much opposition. Queens Market in West Ham bears the evidence of successive waves of immigration to this part of London over the last century. It is widely acknowledged as a place for positive intercultural encounter. According to one member of the group campaigning to retain the market in its current form, the market represented the multicultural heart of the area, not only because of its wide range of international products for sale, but because it encouraged casual encounters between different groups. One trader is quoted in Dines et al (2006) as follows:

> *Next to the Bengalis selling biscuits is a Jewish guy selling curtains. They would never have met a Jewish bloke... It's most unlikely that they'd find themselves in a colleague situation where they can ask questions, they can joke with*

> *him... And he could ask them about their religion. I can't*
> *see another space where that could possibly happen. You*
> *could set up a society to bring Jews and Muslims together:*
> *he wouldn't turn up and they wouldn't turn up, because*
> *these sorts of outfits attract special people.*

Dines et al (2006) argue that the market, for all that it may show the ravages of time, plays a special role in the neighbourhood:

> *most people's memories of Queens Market were of a place*
> *that had evolved to reflect the new populations arriving in*
> *the borough. The market's accommodation of difference over*
> *time was considered integral to its identity by respondents.*
> *There was a general sense that having these spaces of regular*
> *contact, rather than more formally organised occasions for*
> *engagement (such as multicultural events in parks) – which*
> *do not attract everyone – were more important settings for*
> *developing tolerance and 'interethnic understanding'.*

The language of food

One aspect of the market associated with opportunities for cross-cultural discovery merits special consideration – food. The most visible sign of the increasing diversity of society is perhaps the presence of ethnic restaurants, not just in the high streets of major cities but deep into the suburbs and market towns of Europe, North America, Australasia and elsewhere. This diversity spreads to the shelves of mainstream groceries and supermarkets and to domestic refrigerators and kitchen cupboards too. While some people may still hold fast to their own ethnic food culture – be that wurst and sauerkraut, roast beef and Yorkshire pudding or dhal puri – the majority of us are becoming omnivorous, prepared to try anything. While many people may never have visited the home of a person of another race nor ever engaged in a meaningful conversation with them, they will have experienced the other in a restaurant or through a recipe.

This is true but is it merely trivial? Does the fact that nine out of the top ten favourite dishes in the UK originate from overseas

BEING INTERCULTURAL

BOX 5.7 BRING A DISH, SUSSEX

The Bring a Dish event is an intercultural networking celebration that unites a range of education, advocacy and supportive services, organized by the Celebrating Cultural Diversity Network (CCDN) in Hastings/St Leonard's-on-Sea. It promotes intercultural dialogue and builds a sense of belonging to the community. CCDN is a dynamic community-based organization that currently has a membership of over 2500 individuals, family groups and organizations from over 97 different ethnic groups living in East Sussex. The Bring a Dish event provides an opportunity for members of these communities to showcase their culture and increase their understanding of their neighbours' cultures by bringing a sample of food to a community event (Commission on Integration and Cohesion, 2007b).

---

suggest that the British are becoming more intercultural, or merely that they are addicted to novelty and that they have little indigenous food culture worth defending? Does exposure to new food open a door to other more profound cultural explorations or can it be discarded as carelessly as last night's polystyrene carton? Can we find some common ground across the tablecloth?

There is a lot of scepticism. One extensive study of restaurant habits in three English cities (Warde et al, 1999) found that while the users of ethnic restaurants were certainly a growing group, and one that largely identified itself with tolerant values and cultural curiosity, they were not necessarily typical of society as a whole:

> *The pursuit of variety in the field of food, and even more the affection for ethnic cuisine, may mask a straightforward class-based system of symbolic classification. Indeed, we maintain that distinction is claimed through extensive experience of specialized cuisine ... a broad repertoire of culinary experience ... is a practical tool of intra-class*

communication and a type of symbolic claim among fractions of the middle class with high levels of cultural capital… In England, experience of foreign cuisines is a mark of refinement, the possession of which is class-related.

These authors suggest in some sense that cosmopolitanism and cultural omnivorousness are becoming associated with a reconstitution of class distinction in UK society. So what ethnic restaurants and goods might give in terms of cross-cultural connection, they take away through class division.

Let us look at a place less obsessed with social class than the UK. Turgeon and Pastinelli (2002) celebrate the ethnic restaurants of Quebec City. They report upon a proliferation of ethnic cuisines in this Canadian city, which had until recently been quite conservative in it tastes. Turgeon and Pastinelli (2002) concur that users of these restaurants are people who are deliberately or subconsciously making a statement of their worldview:

Here the eating experience is expressed as a conversion, a ritual of transcendence, that enhances the diners' participation in contemporary cultural politics. Diners do not only take possession of people and places. They believe the conversion experience makes them better people and makes the world a better space.

This is something to ponder on the next time you stop off for a korma on the way home from the pub.

While the people of Quebec City are finding something of themselves through eating in diverse restaurants, are they finding each other? Are these restaurants places of worthwhile interethnic encounter? Turgeon and Pastinelli are less encouraging. They point out that hardly any of the restaurant owners they interviewed saw their role as providing a showcase of their culture, or as a social space for their co-ethnics, still less a place in which to cross cultural borders. Nor, indeed, had most of them been either professionally involved in or even interested in ethnic cuisine in their countries of birth. The motive was plain and simple – economic. There was little evidence of interaction between the owners and their clientele, or between diners of different ethnicity. If any interaction was taking place in ethnic restaurants it was being mediated through the waitering staff. Take the two Quebecois waitresses at Wong's Chinese Restaurant, both of whom have worked there over ten years and one of whom has married a Chinese man:

> *Even though they found their customers less curious than we were, they maintained that they were sometimes asked questions about Chinese culture and cuisine. Above and beyond serving as 'runners' between the worlds of the kitchen and dining room, these waitresses also play the role of intermediaries between their respective denizens, the immigrants and the local clients.* (Turgeon and Pastinelli, 2002)

By contrast, research from Bradford that took two largish samples of white and Pakistani people sought to identify whether shopping was providing a meeting place in this troubled city. It came to some rather positive conclusions (Jamal, 2003). Jamal found ethnic retailers in Bradford performed a range of functions both internally within their communities through 'institutionalizing' Pakistani culture in Bradford and providing social glue, but also in reaching out to and engaging with the white (mainstream) community. He also broadened his enquiry to include 'mainstream retailers' and came to the conclusion that the retail trade across the board was playing an important role in educating and informing Bradfordians about their multiethnic city. Figure 5.5 summarizes the findings according to consumers and retailers by ethnicity. They echo those of similar research among Mexican immigrants in the US (Penaloza, 1994) and represent a strong line of belief in the efficacy of the consumer society to regulate itself.

Retailers both reflect and shape society (Hollander, 2002). Policy-makers should be giving far more attention to the way people behave as consumers, the people and the professionals who mediate

	Ethnic consumers	Mainstream consumers

Ethnic retailers	Facilitate consumption of culture of origin by:
	
	• *Offering ethnic products at reasonable prices and convenient locations*
	• *Reinforcing cultural and religious identities of culture of origin by institutionalization through the establishment of cultural centres, use of festivals with emphasis on accompanying rituals*
	• *Providing support and help to newcomers*
	• *Encouraging frequent contacts with culture of origin and extensive use of ethnic media including newspapers, magazines, radio, TV and the Internet*
	• Educating and informing about new trends and products originating from culture of origin
	• Facilitate consumption of mainstream consumer culture by:
	  – Providing mainstream consumer brands at competitive prices
	  – Educating and informing about mainstream products
		Facilitate consumption of ethnic minority culture by:
		
		• *Offering ethnic products at competitive prices with convenient locations, and adopting current ethnic products to mainstream tastes; developing new ethnic products to suit mainstream consumer tastes*
		• *Educating and informing to facilitate transfer of meaning and personalized adaptations mainly through the use of in-store communications*
		• *Encouraging over-acculturation by inventing new products and associated terminologies*
		• Reinforce mainstream consumer culture by offering mainstream consumer products at competitive prices and convenient locations

Source: Jamal (2003)

Figure 5.5 Role of ethnic and mainstream retail enterprises in consumers' identity negotiations

	Ethnic consumers	Mainstream consumers
Mainstream retailers	Facilitate consumption and internalization of mainstream consumer culture by:	Reinforce consumption and internalization of mainstream consumer culture by:
	• *Offering mainstream consumer products and services*	• *Providing mainstream consumer products and services*
	• *Educating and informing about mainstream consumer culture and facilitating the creation of new consumer culture through the use of mainstream media as well as bilingual leaflets*	• Educating and informing about mainstream consumer culture through the use of all forms of mainstream media such as newspapers, magazines, radio, TV and Internet

	• Reinforce consumption of ethnic consumer culture by:
	  – Providing ethnic consumer products at competitive pricing
	  – Educating and informing about the use of ethnic products
	  – Using ethnic media to reach ethnic consumers (to a limited extent)
		• Facilitate consumption of ethnic consumer culture by:
		  – Providing ethnic consumer products at competitive pricing
		  – Educating and informing about the use of ethnic products

NB Items in italics considered to be of particular significance

that involvement and the potential of the consumer environment – the market place – to influence attitudes and action. Policy-makers understand all too readily how to intervene in certain fields like housing or social care. They are reluctant, perhaps with good cause, to stray into others. Yet there could be strong social and commercial reasons to explore initiatives to generate a much greater appreciation of skills in intercultural communication in the retail environment.

Friends and relations

Much discussion of interethnic and intercultural engagement has been dominated by concentrating on segregation and spatial separation, such as where one ethnic group lives in relation to another through various indices of isolation and separation. This has become the benchmark by which we assess the degree to which people live together or apart – and by a rather dubious leap of logic – as to how 'healthy' a society may be. In a word, proximity has become the overriding factor and hence the constant focus of policy-makers on patterns of residence and schooling as the most telling and influential indicators.

We do not deny its importance, but argue that proximity of itself may not be the defining factor – only one of several. We all know many anecdotal examples of neighbours living in the same street or corridor (perhaps for many years), whether from the same or different ethnicity, and who know nothing of each other nor have even exchanged a glance, still less a word. In a lift or at a bus queue one has only to observe the desperate attempts of the average crowd of people to avoid making eye contact or invading personal space. Being close to another is no guarantee of any form of meaningful interaction, still less that a productive relationship may be formed.

What is a meaningful interaction or productive relationship? A reliable sign that two people of different ethnicity have engaged in a way from which they and society might benefit is if they forge a liaison with some emotional content. This might be a friendship, a romantic partnership, a marriage or joint parenthood. After all, our very definition of a non-intercultural society, such as Apartheid South Africa or the 'Jim Crow' southern states, is one where non-routine cross-racial liaisons would be discouraged and sexual relations or marriage explicitly outlawed.

Intimate interactions

What is known about the more intimate aspects of life between races and what might this tell us of the prospects for an intercultural city?

First the statistics. A survey by the UK organization YouGov in 2004 found that 94 per cent of white Britons stated that most or all of their close friends were also white.[16] By contrast, only 53 per cent of non-white Britons said that most or all of their friends were mainly from ethnic minorities. On the face of it this might suggest that whites are far less cross-racially sociable or even segregated in their private lives, than non-whites. This does not necessarily chime with the predominant wisdom that it is minorities who are most likely to self-segregate. Since 87 per cent of the population of England give their ethnicity as white British (ONS, 2001), they are statistically far more likely to only ever come into contact with people of their own ethnicity than are non-white people who still represent a substantial minority. Echoing Allport's 'inter-group contact theory' (Allport, 1954), it is opportunity or lack of it that provides the primary influencing factor. We will return to this in a moment.

Meanwhile, statistics from the US suggest that just under 7 million Americans are in cross-racial relationships as married partners or cohabitees, which represents only 5.7 per cent of the total.[18] Furthermore, it appears that certain groups are more inclined towards 'marrying out' than others. Whites and African-Americans are the least likely to marry or cohabit with someone of another race (Gaines and Leaver, 2002). An even smaller 2 per cent of people in England and Wales are in an interethnic marriage.

Another way of looking at the issue is observing the growth in numbers of people of mixed race. Both the UK and US record 1.4 per cent of the population in this category and Canada records 1.2 per cent. Interestingly, 14.4 per cent of non-white English (as distinct from the UK as a whole) residents are mixed race and this group is predicted to rise significantly in both absolute and relative terms.

Racial mixing, as noted, has in the past been subject to official condemnation in many states and even today many societies strongly discourage it. Even where there is official sanction and explicit approval of mixed race relationships, it may take several generations yet before the social stigma is entirely eradicated. The recognition of 'mixed race' as an official ethnicity in the census of many advanced nations has at last created a 'place to go' for people who were often

Box 5.8 Mixen aan de Maas, Rotterdam

Mahmood is aged 30 and arrived in the city of Rotterdam only a few months ago after leaving Sudan in a hurry. Like Maria (35) from Cape Verde and Yusuf (36) from Syria, he was directed pretty quickly to an intensive Dutch language course at one of the district colleges. What he saw of Rotterdam he liked but spending all his time with other 'new Rotterdammers' he didn't really feel like he was really getting to know the place. Though he wanted to stay, he couldn't properly settle.

That was before he joined Mixen aan de Maas (Welcome to Rotterdam – Mixing by the River Maas). He turned up at an office in the city centre and was offered a vacant seat at a long table with what were obviously five other foreigners. Ranged along the other side of the table were six 'old Rotterdammers' and before he barely had time to feel nervous he was asked to start chatting to the person directly opposite him. His name was Han and he'd lived in the city all his life. He was friendly and knew a lot of interesting things. After four minutes the organizer clapped his hand and another person moved into Han's seat and asked Mahmood if he was interested in football and had he ever seen Feyenoord play. It carried on like this until Mahmood, Yusuf, Maria and the others had met everyone else in the room.

Their heads were spinning but their curiosity was aroused. Then the organizers took them on one side and asked them whether there was anyone they had met who they would like to spend a little more time with – in fact would they be willing to meet up with the person on five separate occasions over the coming weeks? Mahmood had really got on well with Wim, the Feyenoord fan. They decided to meet up every Thursday to watch a reserve team match, finishing off with a first team match against rivals Ajax. He was grateful for the €12.50 spending money the project offered him for this.

Maria and Yusuf had enjoyed the 'speed-matching' session too. She signed up for five weekly visits to Rotterdam's bustling market with Saskia, and Yusuf spent happy days sharing his love of motorbikes with Dirk. Saskia had been pretty apprehensive about the whole thing – she came from an outer suburb of Rotterdam and had never really spoken to a foreigner before, but her company had recommended she go on the course as part of its employee volunteering scheme. She enjoyed it so much though that she and Maria continued to meet up after the five sessions were up, eventually arranging meals for each other's families.

Back at the office Saskia was so enthusiastic about Mixen aan de Maas that her workmate Joanneke signed up for the next round. She met Reyhan, a Kurdish woman from Iran, and they agreed to visit the cinema together. Two weeks running Reyhan was late and on the third week she didn't turn up at all. Joanneke was pretty peeved by this, wondering if it was something she had said or whether the Kurdish woman was just being rude. She mentioned it to the people at the office and they went to visit Reyhan. It turned out that she had been fitting the meetings in between her two separate office cleaning jobs and on the week she hadn't shown up two of her four children had been too ill to go to school. She had meant to contact Joanneke but shyness overcame her and thought it would be best to just forget about the whole relationship. When Karolien and Minka from the office explained this to Joanneke she felt pretty bad at first but with their encouragement she and Reyhan met up again, this time with a much better understanding of each other. Things went fine from there on.

These fictional cases are typical of the 350 matches the project arranges each year and over 2000 people have passed through it in its first three years. For people who find the speed-matching rather daunting, the project also arranges group encounters, and everyone is encouraged to continue visiting the Welkom in Rotterdam café for social events.

The idea of Mixen aan de Maas seems almost too simple and obvious, but if it were then more cities would surely be doing it. It works because of the experience and wide combination of skills of the staff and the commitment that many leisure providers and employers in the city have shown to making Rotterdam an open and convivial place. It is also founded upon the extensive Dutch infrastructure of language education that aims to ensure no one falls through the net and becomes isolated from the mainstream of Dutch society.[17]

not previously acknowledged as belonging with anyone. This in itself is bound to encourage the enlargement and legitimization of a 'third space' for many forms of intercultural engagement, whether or not they lead to romantic attachment and procreation.

Preconditions of contact

Returning to contact theory, there has been recent work to establish what might be the conditions under which interethnic contact might best take place. Allport's (1954) original suggestion was that such engagement must be on the basis of equality between the parties, the sharing of common goals, the establishment of some form of intergroup cooperation and a supportive legal framework making contact acceptable. Pettigrew (1998) further expands Allport's theory by pointing to four causal mechanisms for intergroup contact:

- *Learning about the outgroup.*
- *Changing behaviour* – as a precursor to changing attitudes, in response to new norms encountered in the contact situation.

BEING INTERCULTURAL

Box 5.9 A weekend with another family, Villefranche-sur-Saône

Faced with a problem of violence between French and foreign communities, the community social centre in Villefranche-sur-Saône, France, launched an innovative project: 'a weekend with another family'. French families spend a weekend with an immigrant family and vice versa. On this occasion, people exchange food, converse with each other and talk about their recent past. It is an opportunity to get to know the culture of others better. Such an initiative can also be extended through correspondence to maintain the links between the people involved.[19]

This would include increased tolerance as a precursor to reduced prejudice.

- *Generating affective ties* – some level of emotional engagement.
- *Ingroup reappraisal* – questioning and perhaps rejecting aspects of the culture of one's own group as a result of exposure to other ways of thinking and acting.

All these mechanisms, Pettigrew (1998) argues, can occur in developing friendships and help explain why friendship may be a necessary part of the process of reducing prejudice in society. He connects these mechanisms to a process of generalization from interpersonal experience to intergroup attitudes, which is thought to be most effective at overcoming negative stereotypes.

Finally, Pettigrew suggests that the process of developing emotional ties, challenging stereotypes and changing how people think about other groups takes repeated encounters in the right conditions over time. It is not clear how much time is required because there are so many variable conditions. It seems people need to receive consistent messages over a variety of different situations to help them generalize their cross-cultural experiences.

Meeting places

So what situations might best create the conditions in which contact might take place and friendship emerge? We refer elsewhere to specific school-based conditions that help to foster relationship-building and a separate section for the workplace as a site of engagement between adults of different ethnicities. The other most obvious place to look is the neighbourhood – the boy or girl next door. Although it is dangerous to focus exclusively upon propinquity as the basis of contact, some lessons can be learnt.

While people encounter neighbours of different races and develop friendships with them, they do it to different degrees. Early studies of ethnic enclaves in the US found there was an inverse relationship between marital assimilation and segregation and that Italians, Jews and blacks were least likely to marry out (Peach, 1980). Sigelman et al (1996), looking at Detroit, found that the location of neighbourhoods influences the types and quality of encounters that whites and blacks have with each other, albeit differently. For example, while propinquity is the major determinant of the number of interactions whites have with blacks, the same is not true for blacks. They are more likely to be drawn to whites by other factors such as childhood experiences.

It has become too easy to take spatially based demographic statistics about who is living in the proximity of whom and to draw conclusions from this about who is or is not interacting with whom. Many relationships between people living at close quarters may turn out to be prejudiced, negative or non-existent. Proximity alone is a

BEING INTERCULTURAL

BOX 5.10 NATURALIZATION REVERSED, DELFT

Conscious that integration can sometimes seem to place all the onus to change on the shoulders of the newcomer, Delft City Council took a novel approach that it dubbed 'naturalization reversed'.

In partnership with the Mondriaan Onderwijsgroep education agency, native Dutch participants were introduced to the Turkish and Moroccan language and culture. A teacher of Mondriaan Onderwijsgroep and a Turkish or Moroccan volunteer ran the course that covered making contact, customs and traditions, food, history, politics, religion and included lessons in the Turkish and Moroccan languages. The course comprised six free weekly meetings.

Reasons for participation were diverse. Some people saw it as a way of strengthening their relationships with Moroccan or Turkish neighbours, while others worked with Turks and Moroccans and wished to know the language and customs of their colleagues. The individual Turkish and Moroccan naturalization courses started at the end of October 2004 and 40 places were quickly booked up, so they have been subsequently repeated.[20]

limited guide to quality. Furthermore, there is growing evidence that the neighbourhood itself is losing its influence as a defining factor in our social relations. An extensive French study (Bozon and Heran, 1989) analysed the locations in which married couples had first met over a period of 70 years. In 1914 over a fifth of spouses had met in their neighbourhood while by 1984 the figure had fallen to less than 5 per cent – and one can speculate that it will have fallen still further in the subsequent two decades. We must look elsewhere for the sites of intercultural encounter, which we do elsewhere, but what can we learn about the impact and value of cross-cultural friendship?

There is compelling evidence that the personal can influence the social. In other words, individuals who are involved in an interethnic relationship are also likely to change their feelings about ethnicity in general. In an authoritative meta-study of 39 pieces of research it was found that intergroup friendship was highly associated with decreased intergroup prejudice (Pettigrew and Tropp, 2000). Echoing Pettigew's (1998) fourth mechanism concerning ingroup reappraisal, many people rethink the negative perceptions and stereotypes they may have of another race. For example, African-Americans in a friendship with a white person were much less likely to believe in the predominance of white supremacist (Ku Klux Klan) attitudes throughout the white population (Sigelman and Welch, 1993). Recent evidence suggests that reappraisal alone is not effective without being seen to reappraise. In other words, minority group members may withhold commitment to a friendship until there are explicit signals from the majority group member that they value diversity (Tropp and Bianchi, 2006).

Finally, there is evidence of more extended and, one might say, *vicarious* influences. For example, whites who report knowing another white who has a friend of another ethnicity had less negative attitudes about non-whites than those who did not. It was also noted that an individual merely observing someone of the same ethnicity acting in a friendly manner to someone from an outgroup would themselves feel and behave differently in future (Wright et al, 1997).

The public domain

Public space

It is very easy to think of the city as its physical form – the familiar elements of its civic infrastructure such as the city hall and railway station, its shopping streets, office blocks, warehouses and residential apartments. This leaves out one vital but too easily overlooked zone – the space in between.

Public space has been accorded formal status within the city since the Greek agora and the Roman forum, and our modern city spaces are influenced particularly by the great piazzas of Italian renaissance cities such as the Campo in Siena. Another line of development has been the space of public leisure, exemplified best by the great parks of the 19th century. Public space, however, is not limited simply to the formal areas of democratic gathering, market trade or ceremonial pomp created by city leaders and their architects. People create public space, often in the places least expected or intended by their designers: a street corner, the semi-abandoned patch of grass between buildings where teenagers can avoid the prying eyes of adults, the beach or riverside, or even in motion on public transport.

Public space is not a static concept. If the teenagers' gathering point becomes too formalized, they may move on elsewhere or – if they are perceived to be a cause of concern – authority may move them. Currently, the erosion of public space by commercializing or privatizing areas formerly devoted to free passage, by shopping malls or gated streets, exercises us. How and where we behave in public is constantly under review and revision as behaviour and forms of regulation oscillate.

What might be the prospects for cross-cultural contact and inter-action in public space? We discount extreme cases such as Apartheid South Africa where ethnic segregation of space was state sponsored, or downtown Los Angeles where car-borne commuters may move from home to the office or shop without ever needing to enter a public space as a pedestrian. There are many spaces that people are obliged to share with citizens whom they might otherwise never encounter. Are these places of opportunity where a chance encounter with someone of another race could lead to something more substantial? Are they places of potential threat where a wrong step or a casual glance could lead to alarming consequences? Or are they simply zones of indifference in which we perform a well-choreographed 'mobility of avoidance' (Hajer and Reijndorp, 2002) – a necessary but tiresome chore that lies between more meaningful engagement?

One instinctively wants to agree with Richard Rogers and Anne Power (2000) in their enthusiastic assertion of public space at the heart of reviving our cities:

> *Combining physical attraction with the excitement of activity seems the recipe for success. This helps people to connect up in an informal, often random way. A sense of community, of shared interest, grows in functioning public spaces where streets, shops, cafes and public institutions help to weave together our private worlds. The public spaces of the city contrast with the tightly packed density of city buildings, the confinement of cars and buses, the scattered nature of private homes and suburbs... Rebuilding cities along their 'desire lines', their streets and public spaces, is the 'glue that holds cities together'.*

It should be thus, but Ash Amin (2002) speaks more for our current reality when he says:

> *My point is to caution against raised expectations from the uses of public space for inter-cultural dialogue and understanding, for even in the most carefully designed and inclusive spaces, the marginalised and the prejudiced stay away, while many of those who participate carry the deeper imprint of personal experience that can include negative racial attitudes... In the hands of urban planners and designers, the public domain is all too easily reduced to public spaces, with modest achievements in changing race and ethnic relations.*

We interrogate here a range of research conducted across four con-
tinents into the ways people of different cultural backgrounds use the
public domain and what this might contribute to – or detract from
– the intercultural city.

First, we ask whether the public domain is a genuine free-for-all.
Potential obstacles placed by architects, planners, retailers and the
forces of public order aside, some maintain that we ourselves present
the greatest threat to open space. The public domain is being carved
up by intangible lines of division between multifarious 'cultural
public spheres' (McGuigan, 2005). We are seeing the emergence of
many different publics, increasingly delineated by cultural factors
like gender, race, ethnicity, age, sexual preference and related lifestyle
choices. This is accentuated by the ability to access parallel media
outlets and information source. This means people exist increasingly
in cultural 'bubbles' with little intersection. When they do find
themselves in the same physical space, do they still share the language
and common reference points with which to enter into any form of
meaningful dialogue?

On the beach
The danger is that citizens may seek to translate their cultural public
sphere into physical territory necessitating the exclusion of those
who do not fit in. This has certainly been the explanation given
to one of the more surprising incidents of intercultural tension of
recent years. The popular imagination portrays Australia as one of
the more relaxed places on earth, at ease with itself and with its
increasing cultural diversity. As a nation in which 90 per cent of
human settlement lies within 30 miles of the coast, and in which
sport and physical expression are highly regarded, it is not surprising
that one of the most important public spaces in Australian culture
is the beach (Fiske, 1983). There was therefore a tremor of shock
when news emerged of racially aggravated violence between several
hundred Anglo/Celtic-Australian and Lebanese-origin youth over
several days in December 2005 in Sydney (Marks, 2005). Whatever
the specific reason for the outbreak of hostilities, they seemed to
be fuelled by a latent resentment on the part of white youths that

the Lebanese men were breaking established conventions of beach behaviour, particularly in the use of space and the treatment of women. Once a flashpoint occurred, the situation was exacerbated by the inflammatory language of various local radio station 'shock jock' DJs, enhancing the cultural public space into a media space, drawing large crowds to the area.

It is suggested by Hartley and Green (2006) that:

> *this conflict had little to do with the traditional cause of interracial strife, namely economic competition among 'have-nots' for resources such as land or jobs... What was at stake in the confrontation was culture – the use of the beach and the right way to 'be' Australian.*

Whether this is the case or not, Australians were certainly spurred into a response. The surf lifesaving clubs have recognized the need to develop a multicultural approach to their membership and 'Call the Same Wave' training programmes. This has led to an intake and training of a greater number of culturally diverse lifesavers. In addition Surf Life Saving Australia has developed a new uniform for Muslim women members. The head-to-ankle swimming costume, known as the 'burquini' has been enthusiastically embraced by young women from Muslim communities wishing to be part of the Australian beach culture.

While the average Northern European reader may find it difficult to conceive of the beach as an urban public space, there are many parts of the world where it most emphatically is, and not only Australia (as we saw earlier in the study from South Africa).

Out of town
This beach example reminds us that the intercultural *city* notion is becoming an increasingly significant factor in suburban, rural and coastal areas. The city, by its very nature, is a place of attraction to which people of all types have always come whether to work or play, to be noticed or to disappear, or simply to escape from somewhere else. In the past it has been a place to escape from the limitations

of rural life, tending to emphasize the homogeneity of those who remain in market towns and rural villages. Today it is not so simple – things are changing out of town.

There are three principal aspects to consider: BME groups in the countryside; gypsies and travelling people; and most recently the growth in migrant workers. In 50 years of migration of black minorities into UK cities, for example, there has been very little penetration beyond the suburbs of conurbations. Only 1.4 per cent (or about 136,000 people) of the population of rural England is non-white (CRC, 2005). This means that to minorities the countryside appears very white – indeed forbiddingly so – and outsiders stand out (Neal and Agyeman, 2006). There is also some evidence to suggest that black minorities receive a greater degree of racial discrimination than in cities and, particularly worrying, that their attempts to integrate through joining local organizations are sometimes prohibited (Tyler, 2006). It has also been suggested that rural public service providers are less culturally literate in recognizing the needs of minority communities (Pugh, 2004).

In the UK, the Commission for Racial Equality has argued that the group most excluded from and vilified by rural society are the 120,000 gypsies and travellers (Niner, 2002). They experience some of the worst living, health and educational conditions of anyone in the UK, as well as across Europe. They are also the least likely to participate in local civic activity and decision-making (Commission for Racial Equality, 2006). Because they have been communities routinely excluded and vilified for centuries, perhaps, the nature of the treatment of gypsy or Roma people stands today as the acid test of any nation's claim to be a tolerant, democratic and interactive society.

The arrival in the UK's rural areas of migrant workers (mainly from the EU) in large numbers has grown to a phenomenon – from virtually nothing over the last decade to 120,000 between 2004 and 2006.[21] This has been concentrated in particular areas such as Herefordshire, Lincolnshire and the Wash and the West Country, where foreigners are now a visible and audible part of rural life for the first time. In terms of building integration and interaction, a number of barriers exist: first, the perception that migrants are largely transient; second, isolation within communities often being housed away from local communities; and, third, the language barrier. The latter issue has been recently highlighted as a growing problem and barrier to rural integration (Buonfino, with Geissendorfer, 2007). Language teaching has failed to keep pace with the rapid growth of this new rural community.

The UK and Europe still have much to learn and do before it is possible to contemplate the integration and active interaction of ethnic minorities in rural areas and market towns. It would be worth looking to Canada, where there is a concerted campaign to encourage migrants to settle and integrate in small towns and the countryside (Canadian National Settlement Conference, 2003), summarized thus:

* Building a welcoming community:
  - ensuring the facts about migration are better publicized in the region than the misconceptions;
  - discouraging the locating of migrants in areas of high indigenous population disadvantage;
  - educating local employers and community groups in how they can sponsor migrants.
* Reception and early settlement of immigrants:
  - personalized support package for migrants;
  - easy availability of appropriate and quality accommodation, not just surplus stock;
  - access to language and translation services;
  - ensuring an adequate supply of trained ESOL (English for speakers of other languages) tutors for spouses and children;
  - early assessment of health, education and social care issues for spouses and families;
  - assistance gaining access to banking and other financial services and establishing creditworthiness (this can be one of the most frustrating experiences highly skilled migrants face);

   – assistance accessing religious and cultural needs.
- Sustaining settlement and building integration;
  – produce a 'tool kit' for small communities on how to integrate new neighbours.

There are a few positive examples from the UK. Wilder and more natural areas have often been perceived by minorities as unwelcoming or defined culturally as solely 'white'. There has been an attempt to address this through special projects to introduce minority ethnic urban dwellers to the countryside. The Mosaic Project[22] sets out to promote national parks to minorities as part of a shared cultural heritage, as well as places offering opportunities for physical recreation and spiritual renewal. An example of interracial contact emerging from this is Bradford woman Hawarun Hussain who described her experience to *The Guardian*:[23]

> *Someone just phoned me up and said, 'do you want a free trip to the Dales?' and I wasn't about to turn down anything free so I said yes. It was really incredible: I'd lived in Bradford all my life, but I'd never gone to the Dales because I'm used to an urban environment. You don't miss something if you don't know it exists. I mean, my parents are from Bangladesh; I'd been to the countryside there, but somehow I didn't connect that with England.*
>
> *Afterwards I took my sons to the Dales and they just went into a trance; all the way back they were saying: 'It's amazing, it's just like Bangladesh.' But this wasn't 10,000 miles away, it was 20 minutes from where we live.*
>
> *Through Mosaic, I met some of the Green Party councillors in Bradford. Politics had never really entered my life before, but I was surprised how much I liked these people.*

Hawaran is now a Green Party councillor in Bradford.

In the park
Urban parks have a different history and place in the popular imagination. They were created in the great European and US industrial

Amazing things happen when the Children's Museum of Pittsburgh

A precondition for an intercultural city is being curious about others. It should start at a very young age and cultural institutions and education play a significant role. The Children's Museum in Pittsburgh is an excellent example of fostering understanding across cultures.

Learning from history matters. Leading separate lives is not in itself a sin, but it can provide a fertile breeding ground for prejudice. This monument to the Jewish Holocaust in Berlin, a field of 2700 concrete slabs by Peter Eisenmann, is a stark reminder of the results of racial or religious hatred.

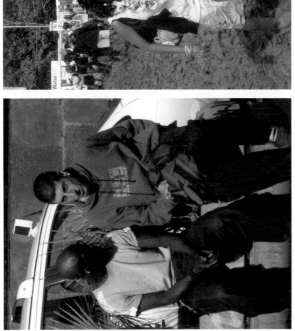

It is easiest to recognize intercultural communication when it is between black and white people, but in reality there are a mass of relationships between people of similar colour coming from vastly different backgrounds.

A Bosniac, a Croat and a Serb from the Abrasevican intercultural organization in Mostar. Its headquarters are located on the wartime front line from where it seeks to reunite communities.

The Bosphorus is an emblematic point linking Asia and Europe. Some scaremongers are trying to foster a clash of civilizations, yet the reality is different.

Mixing across cultures and doing things together has the greatest impact when it starts young and can have a lifelong impact.

Mixed marriages are eight times more prevalent in the American military than in the civilian population. The clue to this may be collective endeavour and interdependence combined with formal and quite rigid regulation and enforcement.

Marrying someone from a different background is the strongest commitment you can make to intercultural understanding. Mixed couples struggling through the mud at Womad.

Great cities like Istanbul are gateways where cultural influences collide. Here in Beyoglu a mosque stands in the heart of the wholesale mannequin district. The nakedness associated with the West and Islam are uncomfortable partners.

Different conceptions of openness and privacy. In the Dutch cultural context, as here in Amsterdam, the interior of people's homes is for all to see. Contrast this with how openness and privacy are seen within Islamic traditions as shown here in Marrakech.

Mixing kids from infancy is the best way of avoiding racial stereotyping and mixing people later on in life as in the Mixen aan de Maas project in Rotterdam can still be very effective.

Photo credit: Heather Magner

Identities today are in transition as are its symbols. What defines being British, German, Chinese, an Australian, an Arab or a Russian? A member of the Indian Gold family that own 11 tartan shops on the Royal Mile in Edinburgh, school kids expecting the Queen in Huddersfield, an Aussie cricket supporter in Perth.

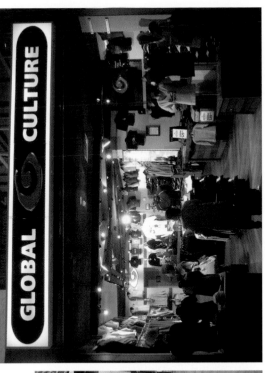

Shopping plays many tunes – at one moment it focuses on the truly authentic, then the pseudo authentic, at the next moment on being an emporium of hybrids. Desire has few boundaries and designers scour the world for ideas.

Food is the easiest way of sharing cultures. Increasingly there is an exploration of food fusion as in world music. Yet mostly we encounter food shops catering for the different tastes of the diaspora.

Street life in Paris: Café culture fosters casual encounters that may lead to more.

Street life in New York: The human throng and diversity of life, yet does it lead to a meaningful meeting of minds?

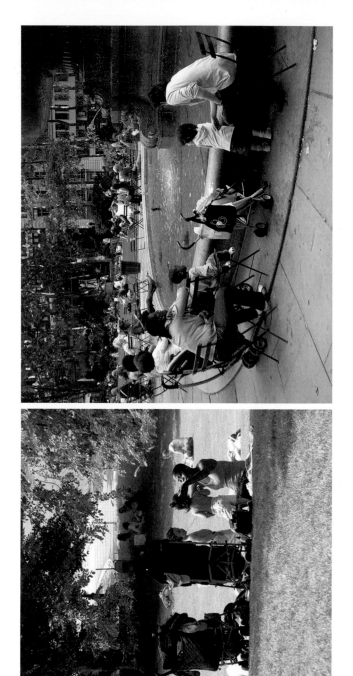

Cities need neutral territories where the communities of a city can come together and share mutual respect. This is why parks and public open space are crucial as here in Bryant Park, New York.

The jury is out as to whether tourism fosters intercultural understanding. Too often we simply gaze at another culture and do not mix with locals in a meaningful way. Looking at Paris and Edinburgh from above.

Sport can be a healer. Hosting the football World Cup was strongly symbolic for Germany. It offered Germans the opportunity to extend the hand of friendship to each other, visitors and the rest of the world. Two graffitis in Berlin. The first advertising an anti-racist fringe football tournament, the other a game between the former parliamentarians of East and West.

Photo credit: Phil Wood

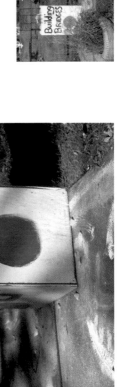

Words matter: The Heidelberg regeneration project in Detroit and the Hindi Diwali and Muslim Eid festivals being jointly promoted in Toronto.

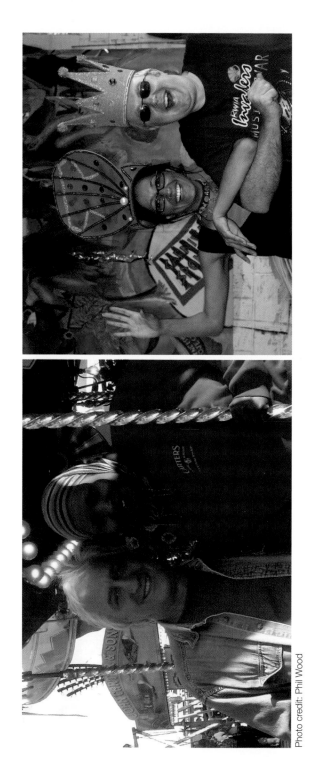

Festivals bring people together. Charles on the left at Womad and Phil at Preston Carnival.

cities as a physical and therapeutic outlet for people crowded into teaming urban neighbourhoods. However, they were never particularly established with the express intention of encouraging social interaction between different groups in society. Had participant observation existed in the 19th century, it would have confirmed that while there was great ethnic homogeneity, the various social classes and professional groupings used different parts of their local parks in different ways, at different times. Unsurprisingly, now that society is increasingly culturally heterogeneous, there are many varying perceptions of what and who the park is for:

> *Public spaces are not equally available at all times to all people. Certain groups may be effectively excluded or their access can be dependent upon time of day ... young people's use of parks is often not recognised by park managers because their use is often evening use ... the majority of daytime users thought it unlikely they would consider walking in the park in the evenings or after dark ... women hardly used parks early in the morning or last thing at night before closing, but were heavily represented during in the day. Dog-walkers are very fixed in their 'first thing in the morning, last thing at night' routine ... ethnic minority families would often come to the park only on Sunday afternoons, believing that numbers implied greater safety. The realisation of an increasingly complex and heterogeneous mix of urban population implies an even greater need for well managed public space.* (Comedia, 1995)

The irony is that as social complexity has increased over the last quarter century, the quantity and quality of management and maintenance of urban parks seems to have fallen in inverse proportion.

Parks have come to be seen not as places of freedom and opportunity but as territory to be defended with lines of demarcation, and no-go areas or frontlines (Gobster, 1998). A classic example was Alexandra Park in Oldham in the UK, which formed a disputed boundary between the Pakistani community of Glodwick and the predominantly white Fitton Hill estate. Once a fine example of Victorian civic pride, the park had fallen into disrepair and abandonment by the time the town was torn by race riots in 2001. Since then its extensive restoration has been seen as a symbol of Oldham's attempt to rebuild its self-respect and social cohesion. This has included the return to the park of the town's annual carnival and a description of it by the director of the National Parks Agency as 'the finest park in the land'. It has also contributed to Oldham Metropolitan Borough Council being short-listed for the Most Improved Council of the Year Award by the *Local Government Chronicle*.[24] Another example of culturally sensitive park restoration has been Handsworth Park in Birmingham, where the appointment of four new wardens who reflected the ethnic diversity of the neighbourhood has led to greatly improved communications, trust and usage (CABE, 2006).

BEING INTERCULTURAL

Box 5.11 The intercultural garden movement, Germany

Imagine an expanse of land about half the size of a football field in a sleepy neighbourhood in northern Cologne, right next to the Rhine river. The open field is punctuated by little vegetable patches measuring about 20 square feet. Tufts of lettuce, furry heads of carrots, sassy green tobacco leaves sprout up from the lush brown soil in the patches. Compost bins line one edge of the field while a bright blue hut decorated with a huge bird stands at another corner and houses all sorts of garden utensils. A water pump rears its head in the field's centre.

A group of gardeners, each with their own little plot of land, can decide what they want to cultivate. Some of the garden club members don't even have a plot; they just help out the others with ploughing, weeding and watering. The classic mini-gardens rented by individuals in Germany – known as *Schrebergärten* – are renowned for being tiny plots of land, made even smaller by fences closing them in like fortresses, each gardener relatively cut off from his or her neighbour. But in this huge garden, each plot is open to the other, separated only by a strip of grass. There is just a chain-link fence that surrounds the entire field to keep out rabbits and dogs.

The idea behind intercultural gardens is not separation, but integration. The intercultural garden club in Cologne was created in 2005 and has about 30 members, eight of them very active. The gardeners are originally from Turkey, Iran, the Democratic Republic of Congo, Cambodia, Japan, Poland and Germany. Previous members have been from Iraq and the Ivory Coast.

'Gardening is my hobby because I feel a connection to the earth,' said Khosro Sarhang, who is from Iran, but has lived in Cologne for 27 years. 'I don't like all of the rules and regulations of a normal *Schrebergarten* association,' he said. 'I like the freedom of our garden – that things aren't so strict.'

Besides the agricultural work, what unites the gardeners is that they all speak German with one another. It is good practice for those who are new to the country and are learning the language. In the evenings or at the weekends, after the garden work is done, club members barbecue and make salad. Sitting down together to share some of the fruits of their labour is better than sitting at home alone many say.

The intercultural garden idea is based on the 'community gardens' found in big cities in the US. There, old abandoned areas in urban centres are turned into gardens where all sorts of people can work the land.

The idea has taken off, with nearly 100 intercultural gardens in cities across Germany. It is also a European phenomenon, with hundreds of such gardens in Austria, France, Holland and the UK, among others. Participating gardeners often visit each other in different countries to exchange ideas.

The project has caught on so well, a foundation called Stiftung Interkultur was created in 2003 to coordinate the network of intercultural gardeners in Germany. Furthermore, Stiftung Interkultur coordinates on an international basis, with groups like the Black Environment Network and the Women's Environmental Network in the UK, the Community Gardens movement in the US, and the Council on the Environment of New York City. (Schaefer, 2006)

Pearson Park in Hull had also become a battleground, this time between local white youth and recently-arrived Kurdish refugees. In its midst was a bowling green and pavilion, jealously guarded by elderly men preserving their right to open it for just one session a week. The council appointed two new park rangers, including a Kurd, Dilzar Ali, who negotiated peace between the gangs and opened usage of the pavilion for a variety of intercultural leisure activities, Kurdish and English language lessons, a job club and a Hate Crime Report Centre. It now hosts large gatherings and barbecues where different ethnic groups can meet.

Finally, it seems, questions are being asked about what is the true (not just the financial) cost and value of good parks and of social contact, and politicians and professionals are being encouraged to respond in ever more creative ways:

> *The social interaction of diverse groups can be maintained and enhanced by providing safe, spatially adequate territories for everyone within the larger space of the overall site. Park managers tend not to think in these terms, concentrating on the needs of the resource, that is the material thing itself... What if on the other hand, management decided to encourage these uses?* (Low et al, 2005)

All this being said, we should still avoid raising expectations too high about the ability of parks to create interracial contact. A recent study (Dines et al, 2006) of public places in a highly diverse part of London compared people's feeling about markets, streets and parks:

> *Local parks were the settings for both routine and serendipitous encounters... However ... few people ... actually discussed parks as spaces of casual social interaction... It was when parks were used on a frequent basis, as cut through routes to somewhere else, or for mundane activities like walking a dog, that people were more likely to acknowledge their everyday encounters with others. A White British woman, who had started to jog around a nearby park, had*

been able to become acquainted with her fellow keep-fit
enthusiasts:

> *'Because you're doing the same thing and you've got a space*
> *in common. You might smile the first day you see them*
> *and you might the second day as well. And you might*
> *both collapse in a heap the third day and say hello and*
> *you do get to know people, not on a deep level, but if you*
> *saw them down the street you'd say hello. And that's the*
> *beginning of a community.'*

The woman saw these initial casual encounters as the
potential basis for closer relations. The salience of informal
exchanges in public space is a running theme ... it is worth
noting how the 'street' creeps back into her narrative as a
space for future encounters.

This seems to sum up the position well. A park – particularly a well-
managed and creatively animated one – can provide a place where
new social contacts can be sparked, to be consolidated elsewhere. But
in general they are places where people go to do things for themselves
(perhaps as an escape from social contact) or with people they already
know.

Third places
The contraction and enclosure of the public domain was first identified as a problem many years ago by Jane Jacobs (1961, 1969) but
the sense of impending crisis gathered pace in the 1980s. Typical
of the mood were the books of Ray Oldenburg (1989) in which he
extolled the virtues of the 'third places' that lie between work and
home, such as coffee shops, post offices, barber shops and bars. These
places serve community best to the extent that they are inclusive and
local:

> *The first and most important function of third places is*
> *that of uniting the neighbourhood... A third place is a*
> *'mixer'... Assimilation is a function to which third places*
> *are well suited. They serve as 'Ports of Entry' for visitors and*

*as places where newcomers may be introduced to many of
their predecessors... The neutral ground (space upon which
one is not burdened by the role of host or guest) of third
places offers the great ease of association so important to
community life. People may come and go just when they
please and are beholden to no one. Eventually one meets
or otherwise learns about everyone in the neighbourhood.
In this respect, third places also serve as 'sorting areas' ...
that is, people find that they very much like certain people
and dislike others. They find people with similar interests,
and they find people whose interests aren't similar but are
interesting nonetheless.* (Oldenburg, 1989)

Oldenburg's lament for the loss of such places of informal sociability
in the US city is heartfelt. He blames the phenomenon in particular
for the decline in male bonding in the US, the loss of cohesion within
ethnic minority communities and the general alienation of young
people. All true, but what does Oldenburg have to say about the
state of intercultural relations and the role of third places? Actually
nothing. Oldenburg's third places are essentially neighbourhood
spaces and one suspects that in the US of which Oldenburg speaks,
neighbourhoods in most cities are more strongly defined in racial
terms than in most other parts of the world. Third places were great
stores of what Putnam (1993) calls 'bonding capital' for people who
are alike, but seem to have much less of the 'bridging capital' that is
the basis of intercultural exchange.

In conclusion it is, perhaps, that such places are not necessarily
the ones that might seem the most obvious. Just because people
may share the same physical space, there remains a potential gulf
between that and their sharing the same life. Amin (2002, 2006)
is right to advise caution against our naïvely believing that we can
shape people's lives by shaping their public spaces. This is not to deny
a role, and a useful one, for the 'place-making professions'. Perhaps
a badly conceived and managed space can negatively detract from
intercultural behaviour more than a well conceived and managed
space can positively contribute to it.

Public institutions

There are serious questions to be asked about places of culture. For example does a positive encounter with a culture different from one's own in the rarefied atmosphere of a museum, library or concert hall make one more likely to feel positive towards a person from that culture? Would it make one more inclined to live next to them or befriend them? Or alternatively, might it simply be a process in exoticizing a culture, disembodying it from the day-to-day realities of living together and getting on?

Museums
Museums are often seen as having an ambiguous relationship with interculturalism. In the past they have been used expressly to reflect one culture back to itself, or to express it outwardly often to the exclusion or even in suppression of other cultures. Alternatively, some museums seem to have attempted to become collecting houses for the entirety of world culture.

Dutch museums have taken a lead in representing history through an intercultural lens. In 2000, the Rotterdam Museum of Modern Art staged an exhibition entitled 'Unpacking Europe', exploring the multifarious roots from which European culture has grown. One of the participants, artist Fred Wilson (cited in Stam, 2005) commented:

> *Basic things like paper, ink, glass, trousers, and the notion of zero are all imports, though now seem to have sprung from Europe, fully formed. The list seems endless. While Europe slept, medicine was developed in Egypt, footwear in Mesopotamia, the smelting of carbon steel in Tanzania. The Indians invented numbers, and the Chinese the compass. If most Europeans have known that Europe has been such a cultural melting pot, how could there be a notion of the 'exotic' (at best), or of ethnic hatred (at worst)? There are no 'them' and 'us', if 'we' are 'them'.*

Even so, there are very few places that self-consciously try to bridge cultures. One of the best is New Zealand's national museum, Te Papa, which communicates iconically. The name itself that translates as 'Our Place' resonates with symbolic meaning behind which lies a powerful expression of the bicultural nature of the country, recognizing the *mana* (authority) and significance of each of the two mainstreams of traditions and cultural heritage – Maoris and Pakehas – so providing the means for each to contribute to the nation's identity... A place where truth is no longer taken for granted, but is understood to be the sum of many histories, many versions, many voices. This sensibility is built, in part, into the physical fabric. A long, noble, reflection-inducing staircase proceeds past outward-looking bays towards the top, where a dramatic promontory projects us out towards the drama of sea and sky, before we reach the *marae atea* (the traditional Maori meeting place) that is a symbolic home for all New Zealanders. This requires little explanation and is instinctively understood (Beckman, 2006).

Meanwhile, in the US, the Brooklyn Museum has attempted to draw its local community into an intercultural engagement through its First Saturdays programme. Through creating a diverse programme that reflects and showcases local cultures, and waiving admission fees (always helpful), the museum has substantially increased the numbers and variety of people through the door. The programme, which started in 1997, included world music, film/performance, gallery talks and a dance party. *Time Out New York* applauded the 'impressively diverse crowds' who attend these events (Spitz and Thom, 2003).

Neil McGregor, Director of the British Museum, takes another tack. He describes museums in the UK as 'places where you can disagree without fighting over what it means to be British'.[25] He is making an important case for the museum not only as a place where the public may educate itself about its own and other cultures. He goes beyond this to suggest the museum is a place for discussion, argument and negotiation over what it means to live in a diverse society. This is a bold claim – and probably sets a bar below which many lesser museums might still fall. It is significant for one of the global leaders in the field to be expressing the point so confidently.

Recent work in Australia has attempted to move beyond educational and representational methods to place museums at the heart of creating a new space for intercultural dialogue. For example, the Migration Museum in Adelaide works toward the preservation, understanding and enjoyment of South Australia's diverse cultures through telling the stories of individuals and communities. The museum is active in developing changing exhibitions and working across the community to highlight relevant social issues that have a migration perspective.

Taking advantage of recent technological advances, it is possible to employ virtual reality to immerse the visitors in an environment that requires them not only to think themselves into the mind of someone of another culture but also to feel and embody it too. The Video Wall at the Museum of Sydney depicts Sydney from first human contact through to settlement and invites the visitor to step across the invisible line of separation that normally characterizes a museum exhibit:

> *Rather than the exhibition being centred on 'mechanical modes of interaction' the visitor is required to move in and around the space, taking in the visual experience. Further still is the use of Australian Indigenous cultural heritage in the exhibition to communicate the notion of cultural presence. The exhibition ... uses the juxtaposition of images ... to communicate the ways in which different cultures have approached the space of Sydney, including Indigenous and non-Indigenous Australians. [It has been described as] 'mov[ing] from past to present, making it clear that there is a continuity of Aboriginal presence in the Sydney area'. The approach to interactivity and content then in the Video Wall generates a dialogue between real and virtual, museum and visitor, space and body.* (Thornton, 2005)

This is an exciting new direction because it allows us to conceive of museums not only as places where one might be challenged to rethink interculturally (in a slightly detached sense), but where one physically has to engage in behaving differently too.

Libraries

There has been a strong case made for the role of public libraries as 'one of the few remaining cross-cultural meeting places' (Audunson, 2005). At their best they can be cosmopolitan treasure houses of many different cultures in which an encounter – by chance or via the guiding hand of a librarian – with an unfamiliar text or piece of music can open up a new world (Larsen et al, 2004). They can also be seen as safe and neutral places in which potentially suspicious strangers might make a first encounter without too much being asked of them, as well as launch pads for subsequent collective action (Matarasso, 1998). However, too often, of course, resources cannot match the ideals of the librarian. Libraries are often hobbled by being housed in inadequate or even off-putting premises harking back to more hierarchical and monocultural times, or are unable to afford enough stock to reflect the cultural diversity of their neighbourhood.

One country in which the library service has been resourced and entrusted with taking a leading role in achieving integration and social cohesion is Denmark (Berger, 2002). Two different examples exemplify the Danish approach.

A national library collection for 'guest workers' was first established in 1984, but it has now been transformed into the Danish Library Centre for Integration.[26] Its role is, first, to act as a national resource of non-Danish language materials available to libraries throughout the country. Second, it acts as a centre of excellence for management and staff development in international and intercultural knowledge and skills.

The experience in Denmark has in turn enabled the creation of a large network of city and local branch libraries around the country with high levels of expertise in delivering to the needs of highly diverse urban populations and providing a space of cultural encounter. A good example of this is the Library and Community Centre in Gellerup, a suburb of Århus. The branch serves a population of 19,000 of which 45 per cent are ethnic minorities and

BEING INTERCULTURAL

BOX 5.12 FACT – MYTH = PEACE, HULL

The Humbermouth Festival is an annual literature festival that attracts major writers and artists to the city over a 16-day period. Hull City Arts Unit organizes the event and offers grants to local individuals and community organizations to produce work for the festival. The start of the festival coincided with Refugee Week's 'Gig in the Garden' and the two events were linked. The intention was to challenge myths about asylum seekers, refugees and the minority communities through language and text.

The Libraries Connect Project set up the 'Fact – Myth = Peace' exhibition, which consisted of a rainbow coloured footprint trail leading across Queens Gardens, linking two seated public areas. An exhibition of photos, texts and quotes were placed in these areas that which challenged the myths and misconceptions about asylum seekers and refugees.

This was also incorporated in a bookmark, 'Walk a Mile in my Shoes' that was available for people attending the event at the library display stand. Library staff and representatives from the refugee and minority communities held a craft session, inviting people to create their own bookmarks in different minority languages and texts. These include Arabic, Kurdish, Chinese, Urdu, Bengali, Punjabi, Hindi and Portuguese (Commission on Integration and Cohesion, 2007b).

---

about 70 different languages are spoken in the area. Around half the population are in receipt of benefits and most are council house tenants. Gellerup's strategy has been to make the library the hub of a series of essential services required both by minorities and ethnic Danes, and to focus in particular on the needs of women. In explanation of the latter, Gellerup has adopted an African proverb as a point of reference: 'When you educate a man, you educate a man. When you educate a woman you educate an entire village' (cited in Spackova and Stefkova, 2006).

BEING INTERCULTURAL

Box 5.13   Mensenbieb: A people's library, The Netherlands

Many people borrow books from libraries in order to learn and increase knowledge. In this Dutch project, you are encouraged to borrow a person in order to learn something new and to test your prejudices. A group of volunteers with different cultural and ethnic backgrounds come together to be 'lent out' to interested members of the public. This can take place in diverse settings: in a mobile library, in a library, in a café, in a school, depending on the exact target group. Using sandwich boards and stickers, with prejudices ranging from 'blonds are dumb' and 'women can't drive' to 'foreigners don't want to integrate' and 'Muslims are extremists', the general public is encouraged to enter into dialogue about prejudices and to meet with different volunteers to test their ideas. The motto is: 'Don't lend somebody else's point of view: judge for yourself'.

The project is marketed in a creative and cost-efficient way. The concept of 'lending' people out for discussions is an attractive one for the media. A lot of effort is therefore applied in the communication and marketing sphere, and resulted in enormous media success and widespread dissemination of this idea.

There have been more than 1000 visitors to the 'library' during five festivals. Particularly notable has been the spontaneous contact between diverse groups of people who wouldn't normally come together, stimulating open dialogue on subjects that are sometimes difficult to broach. Millions of people in The Netherlands have heard about the project one way or another (via newspapers, national TV, radio, websites, etc.). Spontaneous debate and discussion have arisen throughout The Netherlands via internet and web logs on the topic of prejudices.[28]

As such the library is housed jointly with a health centre with a visiting nurse, midwife consultation, dental examinations and health education. The library also provides an IT training centre, employment information and houses several voluntary organizations, including the Daisy Association that connects ethnic Danish volunteer students with ethnic minority school children and adult learners to help them with school homework or such things as driving examinations.

The centre has been achieving marked successes in the neighbourhood with immigrant unemployment falling (in spite of a continuing increase in the immigrant population) and the number of people participating in spare time activities has risen from 57 per cent in 2003 to 80 per cent in 2005, which suggests there must be a high level of interaction between different ethnic groups. In 2004, Århus Library Service was the winner of the US$500,000 Bill & Melinda Gates Foundation 'Access to Learning Award'.[27]

Meanwhile in the UK, the library services seem bedevilled by regular pronouncements on their decline or even imminent demise.[29] Far from being the dynamic hub of a vibrant intercultural community, the libraries appear to be fighting merely to survive. There is however a new confidence emerging, perhaps best exemplified by the new breed of libraries being developed by the London Borough of Tower Hamlets for what is one of the most diverse local communities in the world, the Idea Stores. Designed by architect David Adjaye to look like no other libraries, Idea Stores will eventually replace every library in the borough. The objectives of the council are:

> *to bring the community together and to empower individuals to help themselves, whether it is learning to read, pursuing hobbies, expanding their knowledge or seeking a job... An Idea Store is an ideal place to browse and borrow books, read a newspaper or magazine, learn new skills, surf the net or to relax and meet friends over a coffee in a fun and stimulating environment.*[30]

The physical presence of an Idea Store is striking. It does not have a defined threshold between street and library so one is drawn inside without the feeling one is crossing any kind of boundary. This helps to create the sense of neutrality of the space that encourages users to interact. It seems significant that Adjaye was the architect chosen to bring this new concept to life. Born in Tanzania of Ghanaian parents, he grew up in several different parts of world, trained in London and now lives mainly in the Middle East and Africa. He describes his upbringing as placing him in a situation in which he had to:

> *negotiate different notions of publicness, different notions of privateness, different notions of civicness, by shifting through many places in probably the most formative time in my upbringing. That had a subliminal effect which later became triggered as a desire to work within this world. There is no doubt there is a link between the two.* (Allison, 2006)

Recent research suggests that the Idea Stores are managing to balance the maintenance of traditional library functions with their newer responsibilities for social inclusion and interaction (Hartley, 2005).

There is also an interesting paradox emerging. We hear reports of concern that the public realm is becoming increasingly constrained and regulated, not only through the growth of mall-based retail development but also through the spread of CCTV and the like. The growth of personal surveillance technologies such as mobile phone/camera/videos and the recent emergence of websites such as YouTube also add to the sense that when in the public sphere one is very much under observation. We might speculate on what the effect of this might be on people who are contemplating interethnic contact, if that contact might be considered in any way illicit or transgressive. Would a Pakistani girl risk being seen with a white boy in a public street, particularly if it could be captured, reproduced and used by those who would seek to discourage cross-ethnic contact? The paradox here is that the parties in such a liaison might be more likely to shun the street and prefer the once highly regulated but now reassuringly discrete surroundings of a library.

Sport

Sport, especially team sports, holds a strong promise for understanding within and across cultures. Research into sport as (literally) a field of ethnic engagement has produced clear conclusions. Brown et al (2003) looked at the attitudes of black and white sportspeople across a range of sports. They found that white athletes who were in teams with black athletes reported more tolerant racial attitudes than those who were not and attributed this to the positive impact of sharing in a common endeavour. However, they also noted that blacks and whites on different sides did not display the same levels and, indeed, competition might actually reinforce prejudices. In looking at individual as opposed to team sports, they noted that two of Allport's (1954) necessary conditions for intergroup contact were absent – interdependence and non-competitiveness – and concluded that without mediating circumstances, interethnic individual sports such as golf or tennis might lead to negative forms of interaction. Brown et al (2003) felt that in considering all the potential means by which policy-makers might encourage greater ethnic interaction, (well-managed) sport was one of the most promising because it was a popular and natural impulse of so many young people and thus was less likely to appear socially engineered.

The report *Sport and Multiculturalism*[31] is probably the most comprehensive piece of research into the role of sport in fostering cultural exchange. In reviewing policies and initiatives in the 25 EU states it compares how sport is being used in policy terms identifying four specific approaches:

- *multiculturalism* – encouraging the experiencing of diversity;
- *separatism* between communities;
- *assimilation of* ethnic groups into national sports culture;
- *interculturalism* – creating a sense of togetherness.

The authors characterize the UK sports policy approach as multicultural, focusing on the notion of cultural diversity and the cultural heterogeneity of ethnic minorities communities, but not necessarily on building bridges. Increased efforts are now being made to eradicate barriers in the various sports forms, from which a platform for intercultural sports exchange can be built, but in the face of continuing racism and exclusion, particularly in sports club structures, priority has been on getting ethnic groups to participate at all in co-ethnic contexts in the first place, as distinct from encouraging participation across cultures.

The Maimonides Foundation in London is a joint Jewish and Muslim interfaith organization. It has employed sport as one of the main strands of its activity. At its annual Interfaith Football Programme over 120 Jewish and Muslim students between the ages of 9 and 12 take part in a football tournament in mixed faith teams (Institute of Community Cohesion, 2006).

In sport-mad Australia, the majority of sporting codes have until recently been dominated by the white majority. Soccer was the exception where teams had developed along ethnic/nationalistic lines, leading at times to fierce interethnic rivalry. The recent restructuring of the game into a national A-League competition has resulted in intercultural teams on a city basis. This restructuring has changed the face of Australian soccer and brought about a profound shift in the nature of the game and its acceptance across the community.

Activities against racism are perhaps more strongly developed in football than rugby, cricket and the other sports. For instance, the European network Football Against Racism in Europe initiated the 'Fair Play. Different Colours. One Game' campaign in Austria and a programme in Vienna to interculturally sensitize referees. The Belgian federation and FIFA project 'Show Racism the Red Card' (now also in the UK), 'The United Colours of Football' and 'Go for Girls' initiatives are other examples. These worked on two themes curtailing racism among football fans and discrimination in the clubs. The King Boudewijn Foundation also funded the Coloured Sport Clubs initiative whereby 24 sports clubs were selected to receive financial support to implement a sports and participation policy for foreign youth. Similarly in the UK in 1993, the 'Let's Kick Out Racism in Football' initiative was launched and supported by the governing bodies, as well as at the club level with projects such as the 'Foxes Against Racism', founded by Leicester football club, and the 'Football Unites, Racism Divides' campaign by Sheffield United. In addition, stars such as Thierry Henry have highlighted the nature of racism experienced by refugees and asylum seekers.

The city of Leicester has been particularly concerned with sport as a means of integrating refugees and asylum seekers. The Voluntary Action Leicester: Asylum Seekers and Refugee Sports Development Project focuses on sport as its primary vehicle for working with refugees and asylum seekers, and uses sport as a means of drawing them into social networks. The group has focused predominantly on football but has also used netball as a vehicle for reaching female refugees. The group has been particularly successful in competitive sport, winning or doing well in a number of local football competitions. It was recognized that if introducing refugees to a local club, it was best to identify clubs struggling for players so that new players were seen from the start as part of the solution to the club's problem, rather than being seen as a 'problem' of integration at the club (Henry et al, 2005).

Among the conclusions that were drawn by Henry et al (2005) from organizations providing sport for refugees and asylum seekers in Leicester were:

- Refugees and asylum seekers themselves demand access to sporting opportunities once primary preoccupations such as health, housing and security have been resolved.
- Sport can play a role in increasing the levels of interaction between refugees and local host communities, but competitive situations have to be managed appropriately.
- Team sports provide the greatest potential for increased interaction with host communities.
- While funding may be available from various sources, the bureaucracy associated with making an application discourages applications.
- The dominant sporting practices tend to be associated with male participation, thus care is required to ensure gender equity.
- Sports leadership training can be useful for enhancing other competences, for example language and communication skills, improving self-esteem and enhancing employability.

Finally, perhaps, one should not underestimate the potential for an iconic sporting event, team or individual to capture the imagination of the public and to create a new common space and understanding. In this respect, the emergence of the young boxer from Bolton, Amir Khan, has aroused interest far beyond the world of the ring in sport as an intercultural bridge:

> *He has provided a public space for all those British youth for whom Pakistan is both a foreign country, far removed from their own experience, and a strong emotional presence... And he offers us something no other sporting champion has ever offered: new insight into multiple identities and what it means to be simultaneously British, Muslim and Pakistani.* (Sardar, 2006)

Arts

By their very nature the arts are predisposed to being intercultural. Being interested in what lies beyond the horizon or across a boundary is often what inspires people to make a career in the arts. Being awkward, rule-questioning, transgressive even, are common characteristics that emerge from the biographies of artists, and this inevitably leads to the curiosity to want to explore cultures other than their own. It might be added that the seeking out of conflict, the fusing of opposites and resolving incompatibility are all techniques reported by some artists as triggers in their search for a creative breakthrough. Finally, artists as individuals and a group are often naturally impelled to seek to communicate a message and to reach out beyond their immediate community.

However, artists often walk a fine line between tradition and innovation – the challenge of being 'out there' and 'in here' at one and the same time. This has particularly been the case for artists of colour working within the UK for last three decades – a period in which arts policy has been closely associated with postcolonization to celebrate and reinforce cultural distinctiveness, the growth of cultural fusion and hybridism, and the current questioning of multiculturalism. Artists, particularly if they are associated with the culture of a minority community, may be expected by that community to reflect, uphold or even defend the integrity or purity of an art form. The 'cultural mainstream', meanwhile, may seek to portray these artists as exotic but of limited general appeal.

What, then, can be learnt through observing the arts through an intercultural lens? Evidence suggests that the key to integration lies in identifying that area that UNESCO called 'the shared space' in its major 1995 report, *Our Creative Diversity* (Perez de Cuellar, 1995). The playwright David Edgar (2005a) has studied and written about many ethnic conflict areas. He believes that:

> *Where hope resides uniquely it is in culture. The secret is to create third spaces, unfamiliar to both [sides], in which different groups can share a similar experience of discovery. Sometimes such spaces allow people to detach aspects of their own identity (cultural, vocational, sexual) from what they have hitherto regarded as its essential and dominating character. It is in such spaces – youth groups, drama workshops, sports teams – that some of the most imaginative and successful forms of community healing have taken place.*

Speaking specifically about Burnley, Edgar (2005b) has said:

> *The most successful interactions occur when people from different backgrounds share experiences which are new to both. This is why drama works so well. Indeed, for a group of seriously racist white teenagers... the only successful point of youth work contact was doing drama... It's hard not to be inspired by the work of the Burnley Youth Theatre, who used material drawn from arts workshops as evidence to persuade the inquiry into the 2001 riots of the deep-rooted extent and nature of white racism in the town. However, when the group decided to bring together young white and Asian men to make a play about the conflict, they decided to base it not on their experience of the riots nor their day to day lives but on their vision of the future, presenting three possibilities for Burnley a hundred years hence, all*

expressed in a rich, partially invented language. Here was
imaginative theatre enabling young men to confront their
deepest fears and hopes and create a work of art.

Someone who wrestles with these ideas almost daily is Keith Khan.
Brought up in the rich cultural mix of Trinidad, he came to the
UK to direct theatre and dance projects. He found the only way
multicultural Britain could deal with him was to put him in the box
marked 'Minority Arts':

> *If I'd stayed being 'Asian' . . . I could see a future of touring*
> *on a circuit of venues that are the 'Asian touring circuit',*
> *while I myself was trying to move the work into being*
> *more international. . . I can't imagine why I'd want to do*
> *that!* [32]

So when his international production of 'Aladdin' did go to major
theatres in the UK, it did not find an audience when compared
with its singular success in North America. Audiences were not
being encouraged, he felt, to go beyond race lines, and venues were
compartmentalized in their thinking.

Khan was until recently the artistic director of Rich Mix, a
pioneering GB£20 million-plus project in Spitalfields that sets out
to redefine what a cultural institution should be, not as a place to
consume artefacts or experiences but as an interchange for ideas,
people and cultures. He describes how it will engage with its
surroundings:

> *You've got the heart of the British fashion industry, in Brick*
> *Lane, as well as major leather manufacturers. It's also the*
> *heart of all the creative industries, web graphics, and a huge*
> *nightclub circuit. It also has the Bangladeshi community.*
> *But at present, there isn't much of an interchange between*
> *those audiences anyway. Rich Mix may become the place*
> *that people end up sharing a space in, although I'm not yet*
> *sure that just by sharing a building together you begin to*

make those connections or whether or not you have to force them.
There's no common culture. But that's not what we're trying to do. We're actually trying to reflect the complexity of what's around rather than trying to say there is a common culture.[33]

The London Borough of Tower Hamlets certainly hopes that this intercultural innovation will become the 'creative engine room' and bring with it diversity advantage in the form of new creative ind-ustries jobs and business and the attendant processes of regeneration. It hopes this can be done in a way that goes beyond the shallow 'con-sumerist multiculturalism' that portrays urban diversity as a mere exotic spectacle, and also that it can be challenging without upsetting too much the sensibilities of its neighbours, the City financial district and the local mosque-based communities. This truly is the archetype of an intercultural city project.

Other 'shared spaces' do not necessarily have to be located in buildings. Carnivals in the UK have become perhaps the most vis-ible intercultural events of all. For example, the introduction of sound systems and floats on big lorries are specific British Jamaican innovations on the Trinidadian tradition that originally formed the Caribbean carnival in the UK. To this is now added Brazilian and other Latin American themes, plus new forms of music such as garage and drum and bass, which are unique British hybrids. However, the intercultural character of UK carnival is not perceived or communicated as such. On the contrary, the marketing of it often emphasizes its 'ethnically exotic' character, thus freezing it in time and taking it back to its country of origin.

This ambiguity of whether festivals represent change or continu-ity remains potent. For example, the annual Bradford *mela* is the largest Asian-inspired festival in the UK and over many years has offered an important meeting ground of cultures in a segregated city. Troubling signs emerged in 2006, however, that there was a body of opinion that wished to narrow its focus and squeeze out intercult-ural elements. The Yorkshire-based Jamaican-origin jazz musician,

Dennis Rollins, was invited to perform on the main stage. Unfortunately, after only a few tunes his set was abruptly halted by a hail of abuse and projectiles from a section of the crowd, the message being that he did not belong in the *mela*.[34]

Alternatively, there are dangers inherent in an overzealous exercise of interculturalism. For example the town of Oldham has also had a reasonably large Asian *mela* over several years. Following the 2001 riots, a new grant-funding policy was introduced by the council and Local Strategic Partnership, according higher priority to activities that were seen to be cross-cultural above those that derived from one culture. Grant aid to the *mela* was subsequently cut and the event did not take place. The *mela* organizers felt their event provided a platform from which the town's Asian communities were able to reach out to each other and to other communities in the town. But they had been judged to be separatist. They felt they had been the victims of a knee-jerk reaction when a more subtle approach to community relations was required.[35]

There are nevertheless many good examples of how skilled management can foster new relationships and collaborations and open up a *mela* to other voices without alienating the traditional sectors. The Edinburgh *mela* has done this and as it has become more intercultural, it has seen a growth of visitors and participants every year. It has been notable for intercultural transfers between India, Pakistan and Scotland and for the development of hybrids, such as the *dhol* drummer and pipe band!

An even more explicit attempt to employ culture in the service of ethnic interaction was the Four Wards Intercultural Project in Leicester.[36] The project set out to organize five events with the intention of creating 'intercultural bridging' between four parts of the city with very different ethnic profiles. These were:

- an exhibition challenging stereotypes of Pakistani women's place in the workforce held in Belgrave;
- an evening of Asian music and dance at Aylestone Working Men's Club in Saffron;

- an intercultural football tournament in Braunstone with teams from each ward;
- a children's concert for schools from each ward;
- a Sikh play presented by a Muslim group to an audience from the four wards.

While not all community organizations invited were willing to co-operate, participation exceeded expectations. The organizers were particularly pleased because participants were local residents and activists who would become opinion-formers in their own communities. The organizers are now looking to further develop the project in two ways: extending the principle across all wards of the city; and focusing upon one ward in greater depth to address in particular the integration of newly arrived communities.

Aside from providing a physical zone of interaction, the arts create an experimental mental space in which new cross-cultural relationships can be rehearsed and imagined. Take, for example, the theatre company, Tara Arts, which over 20 years has spawned many uniquely British-Asian artists and art forms. Tara actors have gone on to success in mainstream theatre and especially on TV, such as Sanjeev Bhaskar who became a comic actor and co-author of the BBC hit comedy series *Goodness Gracious Me* and *The Kumars of Number 42*. One Tara actress, Sudha Bhuchar, wrote the BBC radio series *Girlies*, and went on to establish the Tamasha theatre company that has had a string of hits with its intercultural mix of contemporary eastern music and dance-based plays about young British Asians such as *East is East, Balti Kings* and *Fourteen Songs, Two Weddings and a Funeral*, which won the Barclays New Musical Award in 1998 and the BBC Asia Award for Achievement in the Arts in 1999. Tara protégé, Ayub Khan Din, wrote the play and subsequent film script, commissioned by Channel 4, of *East is East*.

Film too has been a place for experimenting with potentially controversial social trends, but has spawned a small industry of successful cultural business ventures. In the 1990s, British Asian commercial films took off and captured mainstream audiences by comically subverting stereotypes of race, class and 'the North' in *East is East* (1999), Gurinder Chadha's first feature, *Bhaji on the Beach* (1994) and Udayan Prasad's *Brothers In Trouble* (1996), which portrayed the troubled existence of illegal Pakistani immigrants in early 1960s mill towns. Romance across the cultural and racial divide was a common narrative theme in *Bhaji*, *Brothers in Trouble* and *Sammy and Rosie Get Laid*. As British Asian film has become fashionable, the musicians who wrote the film scores, like Nitin Sawhney and Talvin Singh, have become established in the British music charts.

While the controversial subject matter of much of this material may have persuaded a minority of people of the need to maintain and redouble cultural separation, there can be no doubt that for a majority of Britons of all races, it has provided a new and positive meeting ground and common reference point.

Cyberspace

Just over one billion people, some sixth of the world's population, were using the Internet in January 2007.[37] Since the turn of the century, Internet usage has grown by over 600 per cent in Africa and almost 500 per cent in the Middle East. While English is clearly the dominant language of the Internet, there are 20 other European languages with at least a million Internet users each and a further nine Asian languages.[38] Of the estimated 313 billion web pages in cyberspace, almost one third (31.6 per cent) are in languages other than English.[39]

For all these reasons there has understandably been much interest and speculation around the impact of computer mediated communication (CMC) upon international relations and intercultural contact and understanding (see Hart, 1998). In this section we explore the potential of cyberspace as a zone of intercultural contact.

Computer mediated communication

In discussions about cyberspace over the last two decades or so, specific references to its intercultural potential have tended to be divided. Some have argued that because it brings with it a *lingua franca* as well as common codes and protocols, it offers a level playing field for international discourse. Others counter that while this may be true, the price that has to be paid is too high – that of cultural imperialism. They argue that the Internet is simply a more pervasive example of the inexorable march of mass media, with an

---

BEING INTERCULTURAL

Box 5.14 Radio Salaam Shalom, Bristol

This is the UK's first Muslim and Jewish radio station, the result of a hugely successful process of Muslim–Jewish dialogue that began in 2005 involving the Bristol Muslim Cultural Society. The project was supported by faith community capacity building funds (from the Department of Communities and Local Government). The radio station is aimed at bridging the gap between Jewish and Muslim young people by promoting interaction and mutual understanding. This project is the first of its kind in the UK and its development is a good example of an innovative approach to community relations and proof of the tremendous contribution to the community cohesion agenda that faith communities can make.

Radio Salaam Shalom's key success is bringing Muslim and Jewish communities together to consider their shared local values and experiences as residents of Bristol. The project has been successful in bringing together a range of individuals from both communities, across all ages: the youngest volunteers are aged 11. The radio show has received support from the BBC.

The Muslim Jewish Forum emerged to strengthen relations between the two communities in response to foreign events that posed potential challenges. It aims were to provide a point of access for interaction between the communities and with other groups, and to develop projects with shared values and develop a strategic partnership. The success of the forum's model of interfaith working has led to it being adopted in national and international areas and it has become a key stakeholder in developing bilateral dialogue with central government departments (Commission on Integration and Cohesion, 2007b).

irresistible ability to penetrate the furthest corners of the world and swamp local cultures with the English language and a monoculture of US consumer capitalism. As if to confirm the worst fears of those holding such views, net gurus such as Douglas Rushkoff believe that 'The underlying force threatening the paranoid enemies of so-called American Imperialism is progress itself. If progress looks American, that's not America's fault' (cited in Herschlag, 1996).

It is notable, however, that when this statement was made it was estimated that over 90 per cent of the web was in English and, as we have seen above, in the subsequent decade the linguistic imbalance has been at least partially addressed.

In general there is now little support for a bald accusation of the web as a one-way street to global uniformity, not least because it has been demonstrated that the web provides multifarious opportunities for two-way communication and influence as well as diverse and unpredictable 'bottom-up' cultural phenomena. The web is not simply a medium of content delivery but also a mode of content production in which many can participate. But does this make it more or less helpful in achieving intercultural exchange and understanding?

In theory at least, the billion of us who are able to access the Internet could use it to communicate with and get to know each other. The irony, however, is that a medium with the potential for spreading global peace, love and understanding is equally capable of conveying prejudice and hatred and of being hijacked by the forces of international terror. Furthermore, the counter-terrorist response to this by government agencies threatens to take away more of our liberties than the Internet offers, as well as accentuating fear of the outsider (Weimann, 2004).

More positivistic readings of the intercultural potential of CMC fall into three broad strands, according to Robert O'Dowd (2001). First, it is argued that CMC, and particularly email, has a reduced social dimension in which aspects of a user's race, gender, social class and accent can be hidden, and which also precludes non-verbal cues such as frowns or hesitation that might otherwise cause cultural misunderstanding (Warschauer, 2000). There are great advantages for CMC in bringing about better cross-cultural relationships because:

Skin colours and other biases based on visual factors will be minimized. Individuals who by ethnicity or personality are less outspoken in face-to-face situations may contribute more abundantly to news groups and forums that provide off-line time to prepare a response, or where they enjoy anonymity or less exposure. (Simons, 1998)

This may be true but, as O'Dowd (2001) reminds us, one has to ask just how genuine a relationship really is if it is predicated upon the concealment or ignorance of cultural difference. While many proponents of web-based social networks celebrate their supra-ethnic or colour-blind qualities, others argue that this ignores the fact that in most cases they default to an assumption of white skin (Kang, 2000).

We might also consider that while international email traffic is clearly increasing year on year, one wonders just how much of that is simply taking place within established national, company or family networks dispersed around the world and how much is the genuine forging of new cross-cultural relationships?

Second, and perhaps more plausibly, as the web becomes more sophisticated through the use of multimedia and hyperlink connectivity, it considerably enriches the ways in which users may communicate and share information and feelings. While individualistic cultures (such as North America and Northern Europe) feel at home with the terse and direct approach of one-to-one email, other cultures (such as Southern Europe and East Asia) prefer to communicate through more collective, iterative and narrative means that are better served by more recent technological developments.

Third, some claim the potential of the web to create a global village in which all voices may receive an equal hearing. For example:

As we cast our communicative nets wider, searching for contacts to foreign cultures across the globe, the spectrum of voices from otherwise obscure individuals helps us learn tolerance for difference as well as similarities. (Lixl-Purcell, 1995)

While inspired by new technology, such idealism seems rooted in an age-old belief that if only we were all able to meet each other we would all get along. However, as we have seen elsewhere in this book in discussing the work of Gordon Allport (1954), while contact is vital in achieving greater intercultural understanding, it is only a step, and in the absence of other factors it is not enough. Furthermore, contact on its own may even lead to negative outcomes. Research designed to encourage students of different nationalities to communicate via email has often done little more than reinforce previously held stereotypes and prejudices about the other, for example in the case of Mexicans and Americans (Meagher and Castaños, 1996), and Germans and Americans (Fischer, 1998).

O'Dowd (2003), building on the work of Byram (1997), concludes that in order for truly intercultural CMC to occur, the participants require the following characteristics:

- *Attitudes of curiosity and openness, readiness to suspend disbelief about other cultures and belief about one's own;*
- *Knowledge of social groups and their products and practices in one's own and in one's interlocutor's country, and of the general process of societal and individual interaction;*
- *Skills of interpreting and relating: ability to interpret a document or event from another culture, to explain it and relate it to documents from one's own;*
- *Skills of discovery and interaction: ability to acquire new knowledge of a culture and cultural practices and the ability to operate knowledge, attitudes and skills under the constraints of real-time communication and interaction;*
- *Critical cultural awareness/political education: an ability to evaluate critically and on the basis of explicit criteria perspectives, practices and products in one's own and other cultures and countries.*

A tall order indeed! What this suggests is that while email and the Internet might represent a quantitative jump in the numbers that might interact and the potential distance between them, the effectiveness of the communication ultimately comes back to quality. Culture clash, prejudice and miscommunication are the same whether they are conducted face-to-face or down a wire and technology is no substitute for preparation, consideration and empathy.

Social software

Most research cited focuses on email and websites, but the technology and its social applications move on apace, with the arrival of peer-to-peer computer networks (such as Napster) and latterly even more sophisticated forms of social software. This social, or collaborative, technology began with Usenets for special interest groups, moving on to chat rooms and Internet forums in which social contact became the end in itself, and then on to blogs and wikis in which groups of people may compile online journals or encyclopaedias.

From this have developed more explicitly social network services. For example, some sites provide dating services where users will post their personal profiles, location, age, gender and so on, and are able to search for a partner. Other shared goals or interests include business networking (Ryze, Ecademy and LinkedIn), emotionally supportive phone counselling (Phone Buddies), social event forums (Meetup) and recreational hobbies. Some of these have captured the imagination of millions and become Internet phenomena, notably MySpace, rapidly arousing the commercial interest of major companies such as Rupert Murdoch's NewsCorp – proof, if any were needed, that the desire for social interaction remains a fundamental force of human nature.

However, when we focus specifically on the propensity for the web to engender interethnic relationships we are inevitably drawn to something rather more sleazy, the international online dating and marriage services. Many skirt the fringes of pornography and organized crime. They have been described as 'cruising sites of ethnosexual desire' (Nagel, 2003) and play heavily on neo-colonial stereotypes of feminine compliance and exoticism. Some such encounters undoubtedly do lead to positive and mutually fulfilling relationships across national and racial divides, but most evidence suggests rather more one-sided and indeed abusive relationships (Lee, 1998).

Of urban UbiComp and MMOGs

So far we have explored the potential of people of different cultures in different locations communicating with each other through the medium of the computer – but our scope has been limited. How can CMC be liberated from the confines of the desktop?

The answer may lie in the emergence of a new generation of 'ubiquitous computing' or 'ambient intelligence'. UbiComp integrates computation into the environment, rather than having computers that are distinct objects (Paulos et al, 2004). The continuing reduction in size and cost, but expansion in capacity, of microprocessors has enabled the potential for them to be embedded into all aspects of our lives, from dustbins that remind us when they are full to refrigerators that compile next week's shopping list. Add to this GPS technology giving us the possibility to create digital maps of our cities and neighbourhoods in unimaginable detail and complexity. When combined with the all-pervasive presence of personal technology such as Bluetooth-enabled mobile phones and the extension of wireless communication zones, there emerges the possibility for us to interact with our cities – and those we share them with – like never before.

The Lovegety, one of the earliest and most well known commercial gadgets for urban social networking, helped strangers in Japanese cities find potential love matches. Popular in the late 1990s, the portable matchmaking device easily attaches to a cell phone and the three-button oval device provides talk, karaoke and 'get2' functions. Once the user selects the mode, the Lovegety searches for other device holders of the opposite sex within five metres, beeping when it finds one.

More recently, services such as Dodgeball exploit local social networks to provide introductions. Through the dodgeball.com web site, a user can identify or add friends to their online profile. When out on the town and looking for company, a dodgeball.com user may text specifying his location, and the site will tell his friends of his whereabouts and vice versa, also alerting him if friends of friends are located within ten blocks. The operative word here is 'his', with the service being marketed primarily to young men seeking to meet young women. And so rather than the city being perceived to be peopled by ominous strangers, dodgeball.com portrays it as teeming with potential dating opportunities.

While they are not usually so extreme or blatant as Dodgeball, pervasive computing technologies are often presented as being capable of transforming people from strangers into friends who might be available for social interaction.

Swedes Rebecca Hansson and Tobias Skog (2001) are also concerned with the city's propensity to suppress our affective and sociable tendencies and the potential of UbiComp to come to our aid. They have prototyped the LoveBomb that, Hansson and Skog (2001) tell us, is:

> *a persuasive mobile device which fits within the palm of the hand. It has two buttons, one with a heart and one with a tear pictured on it. When a button is pressed, an anonymous message will be sent to people (LoveBomb owners) who are positioned within a certain radius from the initiator of the message. The LoveBomb uses tactile cues – the heart message makes the device vibrate in a manner that resembles pulsating heartbeats, while the message of sorrow is characterized by irregular vibrations. If a LoveBomb receives several messages of the same kind within a specified time limit the conveyed cue increases in strength.*

Hansson and Skog (2001) note the similarity with the earlier Japanese LoveGety device for lonely hearts but point out that:

> *An important distinction between the LoveGety and the LoveBomb is that the LoveGety is intended to help users*

in their search for a partner, whereas the LoveBomb is designed to encourage users to actively and anonymously express their feelings to strangers.

At a more sophisticated level, Eric Paulos and Elizabeth Goodman (2004) explore the notion that every day in our routine movements around our urban environment, we encounter figures who we recognize but with whom we have never exchanged a glance, still less a word – the 'familiar stranger'.[40] Neither unfamiliar nor friendly, familiar strangers contribute to urban dwellers' sense of place without penetrating their anonymity and, though strangers, they may also contribute to urbanites' sense of safety. Paulos and Goodman's device, Jabberwocky, detects the people its user encounters in travels throughout the city, lighting up when it detects someone the user has encountered before. It is also possible for people to digitally tag an urban place or object of significance to them by attaching a mote, a 23mm diameter low-power embedded processor with wireless connectivity to 30 metres. While not designed as a friend-finder, Jabberwocky nonetheless renders spaces intelligible in terms of occupancy and patterns of hidden and potential familiarity. Rather than simplistically evaluating the city in terms of friends, strangers and potential acquaintances, it highlights the connections and relationships between people and their shared space. As Paulos and Goodman (2004) explain:

> *As two people approach one another, each person's individually carried Jabberwocky transparently detects and records the other's unique identity. Over time each Jabberwocky accumulates a log of unique entries of people that have been previously encountered. Similarly, a person is able to 'digitally tag' a place (i.e. park, plaza, bus stop) or object (i.e. bench, bridge, parking meter) by attaching a fixed Jabberwocky to it. The combination of fixed and mobile Jabberwockies is the essence of the Familiar Stranger system.*

Clearly we are still at an early – and slightly eccentric – stage in the development of ubiquitous computing for urban conviviality but the direction these developments are taking should be apparent. What is also apparent from a study of the literature is how little, if any, of it concerns itself with engendering sociality across ethnic or racial boundaries. UbiComp is currently largely of interest to a small minority of people who have privileged access to the equipment, knowledge, time and, significantly, the discretion and confidence to move freely around the city. However:

> *Although researchers and knowledge workers might occupy this privileged position, we share urban spaces with people who, due to disability, economic status, immigration status, employment, race, caste, and other reasons, find themselves unable to move about easily or, conversely, have mobility forced upon them.* (Williams and Dourish, 2006)

There is another branch of advanced social software research that has concerned itself with intercultural issues, however. Computer video games have become an important part of the lives of many millions of people around the world and created an industry that is now outperforming Hollywood. The reason seems to be that games are more engaging than movies and their interactivity captures the attention across cultural boundaries. The current generation of games are highly sophisticated, demanding enormous resources of computing power as well as time commitment from large numbers of people – often in dispersed locations. Hence their rather portentous but proper title of massively multiplayer online games (MMOGs).

The power of these games is their ability to simulate alternative worlds. While most of these worlds are merely the backdrop for 'shoot 'em up' adventures, some games make the very creation of a new virtual world (and society) their core purpose. Starting with SimCity in 1989, these simulation city-building games have built in popularity. 2006's City Life enables the user to construct a virtual urban community complete with economy, social structure and class system. While most MMOGs are designed for entertainment, they are built upon powerful theoretical principles including experiential constructivist learning, which is the idea that learners construct knowledge for themselves. A properly focused MMOG can stimulate learning while increasing student interest and engagement and this is why they are attracting the attention of people far beyond the entertainment industries.

MMOGs have for several years now been the subject of research into their potential to convey intercultural knowledge and understanding to young people (see Sisk, 1995). According to Raybourn (1997):

> *There are several benefits to using simulation games to facilitate intercultural learning. First, players learn critical thinking skills that better prepare them to rationally plan future strategies as well as spontaneously intuit the consequences of their decisions. Second, players also learn to apply the theories and models explored in the simulated situation to real-world situations. The simulation gaming process also provides players an opportunity to practice real-world behaviors associated with competition, empathy, and communication in a simulated reality. Third, perhaps one of the most valuable benefits for social scientists and interculturalists is that a simulated reality is a safer arena for many people to confront cultural differences. Particularly when addressing some cross-cultural issues of potential controversy, simulation games provide a safe place to explore dangerous questions.*

This potential has become even more apparent with the appearance of a new phenomenon in the genre. During 2006 the media began to pick up on the rapid adoption of a new product created by Linden Lab in the US – Second Life. Hardly a game, as it involves no winners or loser, points system, levels or other familiar features, Second Life invites users to become 'residents', and visit its virtual world almost as if it were a real place. They explore, meet other residents, socialize, participate in individual and group activities, and buy items (virtual property) and services from one another. As they spend more time in the world, they learn new skills and mature socially, learning the culture and manners of a virtual environment. By December 2006, Second Life had achieved 2 million registered accounts and a concurrent usership of 20,000 – having doubled in size in only eight weeks![41]

Because of its all-pervasive nature, its penetration and its ability to create sophisticated human and social characteristics, it is arousing much excited interest among people with an interest in intercultural communication. One educator, Pacino (2007) believes that under expert guidance, American children can use Second Life to begin to discuss and think about issues of cultural difference that they might otherwise find too difficult to address:

> *Any class lesson that tries to deal with the current clashes between cultures must come to terms with the strong emotions, biases, and beliefs that we carry with us. In order to observe and analyze many of these volatile behaviors we need a setting where they can be expressed forcefully yet in a safe environment. We need a presentation mode that will give us the opportunity to experience these behaviors, and then be followed with enough distance to be able to discuss and reflect on them dispassionately.*
>
> *Second Life is a 3D virtual environment that is easily accessible with a computer and an internet connection... Second Life provides anyone the opportunity to engage directly with people of other cultures.*

In conclusion, we are seeing a growing concern with the communication and conviviality deficit that exists in the modern world, be it at street, neighbourhood, city or international levels. Past technological innovations such as the motorcar may have contributed to this, but many now believe that today's technology can make a major contribution to winning back that which has been lost. Of course, as noted in considering IBNIS, the neighbourhood information system, social software can be a double-edged sword enabling birds of a feather to flock even more closely together than they have before. Yet the potential for strangers, separated by cultural and physical distance, to form an interaction that might otherwise have been inconceivable, cannot be denied, and opens up the possibility for exciting explorations of how the future intercultural city could be realized.

SUMMARY

This has been an extensive tour of territory that might superficially appear to be familiar. Actually it turns out to be largely overlooked, unknown, taken for granted or forgotten about. In general, we know less than we assume about the way people are living together and far less than we really should. From the evidence that is available, however, a number of messages start to emerge.

First, irrespective of ethnic diversity, sociability is under serious threat in modern urbanized societies. Some say this is because we are turning inwards as technology and our search for self-realization diminish our reliance upon other people. Others say the public realm is becoming so penetrated and co-opted by commercial interests that the public no longer behave as citizens of a common entity but as atomized consumers. We add that the risks – perceived or real – associated with modern life have made people fearful of the unknown and of each other, when the real risk is of abandoning the public domain to be contested by the forces of security and surveillance and those of crime and disorder (Landry, 2004). We should be not asking ourselves, 'How can we help the different races to get along?', but 'How can we reverse the erosion of our public sphere and regenerate the spaces and institutions that bring us all together across the many factors that might possibly divide us – age, gender, class as well as ethnicity?'

Second, some empirical evidence on social behaviour suggests that different ethnic groups prefer avoidance to interaction, but we should remember that what little research has been conducted has largely been conducted in countries with far higher levels of segregation than Europe. What this teaches us is not to take for granted that interaction will happen by chance. If we want it we must create the conditions for it to happen. At the same time though, we need programming with a light touch, building on shared interests and common curiosities and spaces to help people bridge the gap without forcing outcomes. Top-down interculturalism alone will not work.

Third, we have sought evidence of situations in which strategic intent, careful planning and skilled intervention have been able to transform avoidance and indifference into engagement and cooperation. There are domains that are more conducive to ethnic interaction and there are methodologies, competencies and attitudes that can make it into a manageable and realizable process. Ash Amin (2002, 2006) anticipated this in arguing that it is the places in which we are obliged to be, combined with the opportunity or incentive for 'banal transgressions', which displace us from one cultural space into another, where a new intercultural sociability is being formed. The story we quote of the US armed forces, where blacks and whites are eight times more likely to form interracial marriages than their civilian counterparts, bears repeating, but this is perhaps taking things to the extreme. The point is that we need to create conditions in which people's sense of need to know each other and of an overriding common purpose trump their ignorance, fears and prejudice.

Fourth, we should be looking at actions and ideas that displace people from their cultural moorings, just enough for them to begin to see the world through the eyes of another, without forcing them on to the defensive. This is work for skilled practitioners and is risky too, because it takes people on a route from avoidance towards engagement but through areas of potential conflict. Nevertheless, the policy of brushing potential conflicts under the carpet has surely now been discredited and the time has come to recognize that only through active debate, disagreement, mediation and resolution can we truly become active citizens in a democratic public space.

Fifth, there is ample evidence of intercultural spaces in both the public and the commercial spheres where the right combination of strategic focus and will, alongside skill and attitude, can produce situations that are not only harmonious but also creative and developmental. In such situations, opportunity and growth interactions can be maximized without compromising or undermining the ongoing need for grounding interactions. From Burnley Youth Theatre to Oldham's Unity in the Community sports programme; from Danish libraries to Vancouver's community houses; from the large corporate company that has given all its frontline staff intercultural awareness training to the Gujerati postmistress who knows all her customers and introduces them to each other: there are many possibilities and reasons for optimism.

Sixth, we should take a step back and reflect upon what this suggests for the understanding and realization of diversity advantage.

Finally, the common factor is the need for a firm resolve that the creep towards monocultural isolation is neither inevitable nor inexorable, and a belief that interculturalism in our public life is not only a better alternative but something that is desirable, attainable, sustainable and will actually add value to our urban communities and economies.

NOTES

1 This largely American notion is contested and controversial in the UK context with some academics such as Ludi Simpson (2007) claiming it has little relevance, while leading policy-makers such as Trevor Phillips and Sir Herman Ouseley argue that it has.

2 UK Government Response to the Report of the Select Committee on Environment, Transport and Regional Affairs on the White Paper *Our Towns and Cities: The Future – Delivering an Urban Renaissance, 2000.* Accessed at www.communities.gov.uk/index.asp?id=1127184 paragraph 15 on 28 December 2006.

3 For further information, see www.citysafari.nl/.

4 www.bradfordhomehunter.co.uk/.

5 Deborah Jones (2007) *The Globe and Mail,* Canada, Monday, 18 June.

6 URBACT. More information: www.brugfolkeskolen.dk/sw11393.asp.

7 Devised by the Southern Poverty Law Centre, the campaign's website is at www.tolerance.org/teens/index.jsp.

8   www.bradfordschools.net/slp/.

9   Interview by the author (PW) with Saied Laher, Community Partner-
    ships Manager, Kirklees Metropolitan Council, March 2007.

10 From interviews by the author (PW) with Ayub Bismillah, headteacher
    of Warwick Road Infants and Nursery School, Batley; Bibi Laher,
    headteacher of Spring Grove Junior, Infants and Nursery School,
    Huddersfield; and Elodia Eccles, headteacher of Southdale Church of
    England Primary School, Ossett.

11 For example *Brown et al.* v. *Board of Education of Topeka et al*, Supreme
    Court of the US, 17 May 1954.

12 It is interesting that in *Bowling Alone: The Collapse and Revival of
    American Community* (2000), Robert Putnam is ambivalent about the
    value of the workplace in building social capital, arguing that short-
    term contracts, surveillance and job insecurity undermine sociability.

13 Drawing upon the work of Michel Maffesoli (1996) and the market-
    ing guru Bernard Cova (Cova and Cova, 2002), this is claimed as a
    distinctly 'latin' response to the individualism of 'northern' approaches,
    proposing to replace the whole concept of marketing with 'societing'.

14 www.shopgreenbriar.com.

15 http://urbact.eu/projects/udiex-udiex-alep/synthesis-and-prospect/
    case-studies/workshop-6-the-role-of-culture-for-social-inclusion/
    workshop-6-culture-vienna-villefranche-sur-saone-bucharest-setubal.
    html accessed 11 June 2007.

16 www.cre.gov.uk/media/YouGov_researchfindings.html.

17 Interview with author (PW) in June 2007. All the names used in
    this example have been changed. Further information at: www.
    welkominrotterdam.nl.

18 US Census Bureau (2000) at www.census.gov/main/www/cen2000.
    html.

19 http://urbact.eu/projects/udiex-udiex-alep/synthesis-and-prospect/
    case-studies/workshop-6-the-role-of-culture-for-social-inclusion/
    workshop-6-culture-vienna-villefranche-sur-saone-bucharest-setubal.
    html accessed 11 June 2007.

20 European Urban Knowledge Network at www.eukn.org/eukn/.

21 Based on registration to the Workers Registration Scheme.

22 See www.mosaicpartnership.org

23 *The Guardian* (2006) 'Good lives: The people making the difference',
    9 May.

24   www.lgcawards.com/images/contentpage/most%20improved%20cou
ncil.pdf.

25   Taken from a speech at the Commission for Racial Equality *Race Convention*, 27 November 2006.

26   www.indvandrerbiblioteket.dk/engelsk.

27   See www.gatesfoundation.org/GlobalDevelopment/GlobalLibraries/
Announcements/Announce-040824.htm.

28   European Urban Knowledge Network at www.eukn.org/eukn/.
Further information at www.mensenbieb.nl.

29   For example, Ezard, J. (2004) 'British libraries could shut by 2020',
The Guardian, 28 April.

30   www.ideastore.co.uk/.

31   *Sport and Multiculturalism* (2004) produced by PMP in partnership
with the Institute of Sport and Leisure Policy Loughborough University
as part of the European Commission's Studies on Education and
Sport.

32   Keith Khan interview with Munira Mirza at www.uel.ac.uk/risingeast/
archive02/interviews/index.htm.

33   Keith Khan interview with Munira Mirza at www.uel.ac.uk/risingeast/
archive02/interviews/index.htm.

34   Interview between Dennis Rollins and the author (PW), August
2006.

35   Interview between the author (PW) and organizers of Oldham Mela,
April 2005.

36   Organized by the Society for Intercultural Understanding Leicester
(SICUL) and Leicester Cultural Partnership, an evaluation report is
available at www.emen.org.uk.

37   Internet World Stats at www.internetworldstats.com/stats.htm.

38   Global Reach at www.glreach.com/globstats/index.php3.

39   Global Reach at http://global-reach.biz/globstats/refs.php3#27.

40   As first identified in Milgram (1977).

41   Offical Linden Blog at http://blog.secondlife.com/2006/12/29/a-
concurrency-of-20000/.

6

Diversity Advantage: The Benefits of Cross-cultural Interaction

We have taken a long and comprehensive tour around the reasons why people choose to avoid each other and the many ways in which they might be encouraged to live together and cooperate. We have argued our belief that getting on and being intercultural is in every way preferable to moving apart, even while there are optimal levels of diversity and there are some – albeit transient – advantages to separation.

Some people, however, are never satisfied with the entreaty simply to 'do the right thing'. They need a reason and we should try to give them one – the *diversity advantage*. Now money isn't everything but it means a lot to many and so, unless intercultural diversity can't add to the bottom line of companies, cities and nations, an awful lot of people aren't going to give it much credence. We have already noted that economists have been able to determine in fairly general terms that migrants are more likely to have a positive than a negative economic effect.

HYBRIDITY AS A DRIVER OF INNOVATION

Let us now dig a little deeper to understand how this process of realising the diversity advantage actually works. Although new ideas and innovations have always been significant throughout history and, as we have seen, cross-cultural interactions have been a major source of these, it is now claimed that the times we are in are different in both scale and degree. As analysts of the new economy such as John Kao, Richard Florida, Daniel Pink and John Howkins argue, businesses, whole industries, public sector agencies and cities must now reinvent themselves simply to keep ahead of the pace of technological change and the demands placed upon them by the expectations of us, their consumers and constituents. It is no longer feasible to rely upon a few specialized and privileged individuals in research labs to have all our best ideas for us. Innovation is – and must be – a more collective process. Richard Dawkins (1976) expressed it well when he first posited the concept of memes as the building blocks of our civilizations:

> *Examples of memes are tunes, ideas, catch-phrases, clothes fashions, ways of making pots or of building arches. Just as genes propagate themselves in the gene pool by leaping from body to body via sperm and eggs, so do memes propagate themselves in the meme pool by leaping from brain to brain via a process which, in the broad sense, can be called imitation.*

Frans Johansson (2004) has gone on to distinguish between two different ways of generating ideas. Many of the things we call innovations are refinements of an established product or process, squeezing out (often with great expertise and ingenuity) extra efficiency or value through analysis of usage and demand. These can be termed *directional* because they are pushing forward on a largely predetermined path. Separate and more significant, however, are the *intersectional* innovations that according to Johansson (2004):

> *change the world in leaps along new directions. They usually pave the way for a new field [but] do not require as much expertise as directional innovation and can therefore be executed by the people you least expect. Although [they] are radical, they can work in both large and small ways . . . the*

design of a large department store or the topic of a novella
... a special effect technique or the product development for
a multinational corporation.

Johannson (2004) goes on to speculate on the conditions in which intersectional innovations can best be encouraged and concludes that:

[Diverse teams] have a greater chance of coming up
with unique ideas [as they] allow different viewpoints,
approaches, and frames of mind to emerge... People who
have experienced the innovative power of diverse teams
tend to do everything they can to encourage them.

Such a person is Steve Miller, former CEO and chairman of Royal Dutch/Shell, the world's fourth largest company who says (cited in Johansson, 2004):

You begin to find that you get some really neat ideas
generated from creating a culture where people of different
ethnicities, cultures, backgrounds, [and] countries ... come
together. Invariably you find that the best ideas come from
this mosaic of players working together in a team on a
project. They will come up with an answer that is different
from what any one of them would have come up with
individually.

HYBRID INNOVATORS STATESIDE

When the Italian Stefan Marzano took over product design for the Dutch electronics giant Phillips in the 1990s he found a competent but rather staid organization. He deliberately introduced diversity and cultural hybridity into his department of 500 staff, eventually ending up with 33 nationalities on his team. Phillips' Hong Kong design office, for example, eventually comprised only three Chinese alongside others from Germany, Ethiopia, Singapore, Belgium and the UK. Marzano argues that it was this radical reconstituting of the staffing mix that put Phillips' products back at the cutting edge by the end of the decade. One of his staff, Grant Davidson (cited in Zachary, 2003), says of the diverse teams:

> *You get a richer environment, you have more insights, because people reason from their own background. The result will be richer than if you don't have a multicultural environment. I'm sure of this because we've reaped the rewards. We have an absolute advantage from having many cultures.*

In the mid-1990s Annalee Saxenian (1999) was one of the first people to notice that there was more to the Silicon Valley phenomenon than met the eye. Not only was it bringing about a revolution in the way ideas were transformed into new products and innovations, it was doing it through bringing together a diverse mixture of overseas talent, particularly from China and India. Recently she has returned to this theme (Wadhwa et al, 2007) and in research across the whole of the US she found the trend to be even more pronounced. She found that foreign nationals residing in the US were named as inventors or co-inventors in 24.2 per cent of international patent applications filed from the US in 2006 and this count does not include the immigrants who became citizens before filing a patent. This figure had increased from 7.3 per cent in 1998 and the largest group of these immigrant non-citizen inventors were Chinese (mainland and Taiwan-born). Indians were second, followed by the Canadians and British.

Saxenian's team also returned to Silicon Valley and another high tech growth cluster, Research Triangle Park, North Carolina. Wadhwa et al (2007) found that:

- over half (52.4 per cent) of Silicon Valley startups had one or more immigrants as a key founder;
- compared with the 1999 findings, the percentage of firms with Indian or Chinese founders had increased from 24 to 28 per cent. Indian immigrants outpaced their Chinese counterparts as

founders of engineering and technology companies in Silicon Valley. From 1995 to 2005, Indians were key founders of 15.5 per cent of all Silicon Valley startups, and immigrants from China and Taiwan were key founders in 12.8 per cent;

* in Research Triangle Park, 18.7 per cent of startups had an immigrant as a key founder. Indians constitute the largest immigrant founding group, with 25 per cent of startups, followed by immigrants from Germany and the UK, each with 15 per cent.

Clearly immigrants (often in collaboration with Americans or with immigrants of other backgrounds) have become a significant driving force in the creation of new businesses and intellectual property in the US – and their contributions have increased over the past decade.

While, as we have seen earlier, the US exhibits some of the highest toleration for segregation and polarization, it also creates some of the greatest opportunities for diversity advantage, as many have found.

Andrew Grove, one of the founders of Intel and still its chairman, was born András István Gróf in Hungary in 1936, the only child of Jewish parents who were in the dairy business. According to his autobiography (2001), Grove found his way to the US through the combined efforts of numerous relief and charitable organizations. Relatives in New York City helped him adapt to his new life and he entered City College of New York and graduated in 1960 with an undergraduate degree in chemical engineering followed in 1963 by a PhD from the University of California at Berkeley. The rest is history. In 2000 Grove spoke about his life as an immigrant and gave the warning that in an era when many would have the US close its borders and eject every foreigner, his presence and success is a reminder that the US has been the place for those seeking a better life for almost 400 years:

> *It is a very important truism that immigrants and immigration are what made America what it is... We must be vigilant as a nation to have a tolerance for differences, a tolerance for new people.'* (Sager, 2000)

Box 6.1 Diversity rescued the company, Atlanta[1]

Vic was an architect, Joyce a construction manager. They were early and eager adopters. They knew CAD (computer-aided design) like Ford knew cars. Their clients were the big-name architects who created front elevations and plastic scale models for new buildings – then hired their company to grind out the thousands of drawings necessary to actually build them.

Joyce and Vic were so committed to quality they resolved to employ nothing but top graduates of the best architecture schools. Work poured into ASSI from an up-and-coming retailer called Home Depot. Before long, Joyce, Vic and their dozen young employees appeared on the cover of Fortune as a company of tomorrow. The cover kids of ASSI.

Deep down, though, Joyce and Vic sensed problems. When the company moved to bigger offices, everyone wanted a cubicle with a view. Joyce and Vic accommodated the staff to the point of seating everyone next to a window – no small feat in a modern office building – only to hear the staff complain about glare. When Joyce or Vic tried to have a private lunch with a staffer, the entire staff assumed that something was amiss. 'We couldn't do anything right', Joyce told me, 'It was like a spontaneous unionization drive'.

Then, within barely a year, the cover-kids staff walked out. En masse. Only in retrospect did Joyce and Vic realize their error. Their rigorous hiring profile – only the best grads from the best schools – effectively guaranteed a monocultural workforce, one that was young, single, childless, white, from well-to-do families and from the northeast. That's a lot for any dozen workers to have in common. They thought like a bloc. Acted like a bloc. Walked out like a bloc.

The exodus left Joyce and Vic with bills piling up and clients awaiting drawings. ASSI needed staff instantly, but this time such selectivity was not an option. If you qualified for the work, it was yours. That architect from Vietnam? Hired. A woman re-entering the workforce? Hired. People who had attended lesser schools in the south. People who didn't grow up as rich kids. People with spouses (and not). People with children (and not). People with mortgages (and not). Part-timers as well as full-timers. Ultimately temps, contractors, even employees shared with other firms.

This crazy-quilt crew was never going to win ASSI a return trip to the cover of Fortune, but it was a crew that worked together brilliantly. When problems came up – business problems, personality problems, whatever – the diversity of views tended to dampen them. Beyond that, the greater number of sensibilities created a greater number of potential solutions to any problem. However unplanned, diversity had rescued the company.

Many others have repaid the US for its openness through inventiveness, innovation and through the financial rewards and economic advantage this has accrued (Peters, 1996). Take Fred Kavli who is Chairman of the Board and CEO of the Kavlico Corporation in Moore Park, California. Kavli emigrated from Norway in 1956 with a physics degree in hand, and founded the company on a shoestring two years later. 'This was the land of opportunity – especially then. There was no other country I could go to do that' (Peters, 1996). Kavlico makes sensors, primarily for aeronautical controls and automotive pollution controls. One hundred Kavlico sensors operate on the space shuttle.

Kyong Park is Kavlico's Vice President for Research and Development. A physicist, he came to the US from Korea in 1969 to pursue his education. Park joined Kavlico in 1977 and holds 24 patents. With Kavli's assistance, Park was able to stay in the US to pursue his career. He preferred to stay because Korea was under a 'corrupt' military government in the 1970s, where bribery was rife and 'only people with connections had opportunity. Here, if you work hard you have opportunity. People from outside really appreciate this society and this culture' (Peters, 1996). According to Kavli, Kyong Park was instrumental in the pressure sensor development that brought Kavlico into the automotive pollution control market. This has helped to propel Kavlico's growth from US$4 million in sales and 120 employees in 1977 to US$156 million in sales and

1500 employees in 2003, shortly before its acquisition by Schneider Electric.

Ram Labhaya Malik of San José, California, emigrated from India in 1971. An engineer, he is co-inventor of an air purification system now in use in the US Army's Bradley Fighting Vehicle, a front-line troop carrier. The system protects personnel inside from nuclear, chemical and biological contamination. One of his co-inventors emigrated from The Netherlands, the other is US-born.

Michael Pryor of Woodbridge came to the US from England with a doctorate in metallurgy. He holds 130 US patents, and became Vice President for Metals Research at the Olin Corporation in 1973. At Olin he calculated that the research department he directed produced a three-to-one monetary return on investment. Its innovations include alloys, manufacturing processes and the process used to produce the metal composites needed to mint quarters and dimes ever since the 90 per cent silver to 10 per cent copper blend was discontinued. Pryor recruited both US-born and immigrant scientists for his labs, and expressed particular admiration for Indian and Asian metallurgists (Peters, 1996).

Aleksander Owczarz is a mechanical engineer at Semitool Inc., a Montana company that makes capital equipment for the semiconductor industry. Dissatisfied with the system in Poland, he emigrated in 1978 to seek new opportunities in the US. He stopped counting his patents when his 25th was issued. One patent is for a precision cleaning machine for wafer boxes and wafer carriers and over 20 Semitool employees work full-time manufacturing it. It is sold in the US, Europe and Asia; sales were projected to grow to US$15 million per annum. 'It's not just bright people' that lead to technological innovation', he said. 'The combination of bright individuals and the right environment is what makes people productive here' (Peters, 1996).

It is no great surprise that the US has been the haven for footloose international talent, or that it has enabled many of these immigrants to fulfil their potential and enrich both the US and themselves in the process. But how are other places, specifically the UK, coming to terms with this?

BOX 6.2 KARIM RASHID, DESIGNER

Born in Cairo of an Egyptian father and English mother, Rashid has applied his taste to shopping bags, plastic chairs, even 'very trippy' manhole covers. His Garbo wastebasket is considered a hit. More than one million of these curvy, translucent pails – in lilac, lime and ice blue – sold in North America in the late 1990s. The pail, priced at US$10, caught the attention of art critics. A 'Garbo' even ended up in the permanent collection of the San Francisco Museum of Modern Art.

Rashid was born in Cairo in 1960. His father painted sets for films and TV shows. His mother taught at a school. Raised in England and the US, Rashid studied industrial design in Italy and then worked in Canada. He speaks with a Canadian accent, is married to an American and won't call anywhere home. In 1993, he moved to New York, where he scored with innovative designs for ordinary objects such as a snow shovel and a plastic chair. He says:

I don't feel very culturally or racially attached to either England or Egypt… I jokingly say I'm nomadic. That's why I'm probably in America. You have an autonomy here that takes place nowhere else in the world. You don't have to have a [specific] heritage. This freedom allows me to be globally interactive. Because I don't feel I belong to a specific community, I feel I'm perpetually able to analyze it. So I'm always observing. That's the start of my work.

Outsider and yet insider, Rashid wants to turn design norms upside down. His fascination with plastic, a material that litters poor countries and represents tackiness in rich countries, reflects this. He favours what he calls 'casual engineering' of ordinary stuff, so that 'mass, everyday items gain the qualities of high design'. This vision leads him to question many preconceived notions:

I try to let go of mental baggage… Who told us that this is the way we have to sit? Who told us I should be seventeen inches off the ground? We have shaped our own behavior; we have created everything we do. There's nothing 'natural' or 'intuitive' about it. So I ask myself, can I imagine a world that's completely different?

Drawing on his own diversity, Rashid sees the world in unusual ways. One night at a restaurant, he sat in a flimsy and uncomfortable plastic chair. His back hurt so much he could hardly enjoy the meal. That night he had the counterintuitive idea 'to elevate plastic to a new plateau of quality and good taste. It was time to drop the idea that plastic was a cheap material'.

This insight led to his attempt to bring glamour to the lowly garbage wastebasket. He named his pail Garbo in a frank attempt to associate trash with glamour (the name of the Hollywood star shares the same prefix as garbage). And the pail's striking shape flowed from Rashid's curious practice of studying waste containers in malls, grocery stores and offices. He even visited plastic-moulding factories to learn the methods used to create his pail. Rashid comments:

We want rules and I'm trying to do the complete opposite...
To free myself from any preassociations. That's hard to do. A
lot of times I get angry with myself that I'm not thinking out of
the box enough.

His sense of life as a melding of the friend and stranger, the rooted and the winged, informs his designs with an unmistakably hybrid quality. They embody the sort of surprising juxtapositions that result from having crossed signals intelligently. In an arena where hype and high prices are the norm, Rashid's designs are appealing, original, practical and priced for the masses.

His aesthetic flows from cultures he knows well. Whereas others look for ways to make the expensive in a cheaper guise, he studies cheap things in order to find ways of endowing them with richness (Zachary, 2003).

HYBRID INNOVATORS IN THE UK

The UK's history is littered with examples of migrants reaching these shores with little or nothing yet leaving a lasting legacy. One particularly intercultural example is Guglielmo Marconi. He was born near Bologna, Italy, the second son of an Italian landowner, his Irish wife, Annie Jameson, granddaughter of the founder of the Jameson Whiskey distillery. Marconi was educated in Bologna, Florence and later in Livorno. As a young child Marconi didn't do very well in school. Baptized as a Catholic, he was brought up Protestant by his mother and was a member of the Anglican Church. He formally converted to Catholicism after his second marriage. Fascinated by the emerging science of electronics and a burning desire to make something widely usable from it, he was dismayed by the Italian government's indifference to his appeals for support. In 1896 he travelled to London and demonstrated his new 'radio' on the roof of the post office in St Martin's Lane. It attracted the attention of two important customers, the Admiralty and the Post Office itself, and both he and his idea were launched, earning Marconi a Nobel Prize for Physics in 1909 and a place in the pantheon of British engineering (Winder, 2004).

Nineteen-year-old Michael Marks left Slonim in Polish Russia in 1878, in the face of increasing anti-semitic repression. He washed up in Hartlepool and then scoured the northern counties as a pedlar, and later as a sales rep for clothing entrepreneur Isaac Dewhirst, before drifting to Leeds where he had a twice-weekly pitch on the Kirkgate open market. He soon attracted attention with his snappy slogan – 'Don't ask the price – it's a penny' – and quickly spread his penny bazaar to other markets around the north. Eventually, he teamed up with Dewhirst's old cashier, Thomas Spencer, and in 1894 Marks & Spencer was born. By the time he died there were 60 branches and M&S was well on the way to becoming a British institution. At about the same time, another Yorkshire Jew, an ex-Lithuanian tailor, changed his name from Montague Ossinsky to Burton. By 1913 he established Burton & Burton in Leeds and by 1925 had turned it into the biggest retail empire in Europe. On the eve of the Second World War, this immigrant who reached the UK impoverished at the age of 15 was the owner of 600 stores as well as textile factories employing 20,000 (Winder, 2004).

Moving forward to the present day to a study we commissioned of migrant business in the UK, we looked at three successful entrepreneurs (Ghilardi, 2006). Stelios Haji-Ioannou (he prefers to be called by just his first name) is the founder of the low cost airline easyJet. He was born in Greece to a family of wealthy industrialists, was educated in Athens, and then attended the London School of Economics and City University Business School, where he gained an MSc in Shipping Trade and Economics. He set up Stelmar Shipping at the age of 25 and the low-cost airline easyJet at the age of 28. Since then he has rolled out the 'easy' brand, which offers value for money and no frills products, to many other areas, from travel to leisure, telecoms and personal finance. Using his private investment vehicle, the easyGroup, he owns the 'easy' brand and licenses it to a variety of other entrepreneurs.

Stelios has revolutionized air travel, making it much more democratic and classless, and into the bargain has helped the regeneration of those cities whose airports accept his airline. As well as uniquely offering access to everybody, his airlines have also appealed to business people who claim that this way of travelling not only allows them to save on business trips, but also gives them more flexibility and faster access to their clients and markets.

Chai Patel, the mind behind the mental health and neuro-rehabilitation centres under The Priory name, was born in Uganda from a poor Indian family. They left for India before Idi Amin expelled the country's Asians and Patel lived there until 1969 when his family came to the UK in search of work (his father was a postmaster and his mother a shop assistant). In London, he was educated in a comprehensive school and later gained a place at university to study medicine. After qualifying as a doctor, and following a brief period working in the National Health Service, he embarked on a career in merchant banking. This brought him into contact with some of the wealthy individuals who backed his venture into private health care. Patel created The Priory Group by merging Priory Healthcare with the Specialist Healthcare Services Division of Westminster Health Care in 2000. Some of its services are free at the point of use but supplied by private companies. At present, The Priory Group consists of 15 psychiatric hospitals, seven schools, two therapeutic community assessment services, five brain-injury rehab units and five secure and step-down units.

Alan Yau, the creator of the noodle bar chain Wagamama, was born in the New Territories outside Hong Kong. When he was 12, his family moved to King's Lynn in Norfolk. His father, a tailor, was attracted to Norfolk because friends from the same community had already settled there. As economic migrants, the Yaus were determined to build a better life in the UK and soon set up in the Chinese restaurant business. The eldest of six children, Alan Yau attended London's City Polytechnic graduating in Politics and Philosophy. In the late 1980s, after opening a Chinese takeway in Peterborough with his father, he raised enough funding (through his family) to create his first 'fast-food' new idea, the Japanese-style noodle restaurant Wagamama, which opened in London's Bloomsbury in 1992. Since then, he has diversified into several other London restaurants, including Yauatcha, Hakkasan and Busaba Eathai, and has expanded internationally.

All three global entrepreneurs were happy to talk to us (Ghilardi, 2006) about their origins and why they think Britain provides the best environment for their business. Stelios says:

> *I am an economic immigrant myself, albeit one who is a graduate of the London School of Economics and who has a rich father. I found British society much more open than even some Brits would admit, accepting someone with an unpronounceable surname and a Greek accent to launch an airline which they are happy to trust with their lives. More than 70 million passengers later, easyJet, now a PLC run by professional management [of a mixed cultural and ethnic background], is still struggling to be perceived as a local airline [as opposed to a British one] in both France*

and Germany, despite our significant investment in those
markets.

As opposed to Continental Europe, he sees the UK as a much more newcomer-friendly place.

For Chai Patel, commerce and caring have as high a status as business values, and The Priory Group is the embodiment of such values. In reply to the question of how he managed to place these values at the heart of the UK health sector (notoriously under pressure to meet targets and outcomes), he replies, 'I increasingly bring it back to my cultural origins. In Indian culture, caring plays quite a critical part. It is a very important part of your spiritual life' (cited in Ghilardi, 2006).

He believes he is more of a hybrid than others because he went to school in the UK and his family did not pursue any particular isolationist approach. As newcomers, they were not afraid of assimilating into the local culture. What he preserved is what he chose to preserve, rather than what he has been forced to preserve:

> *We draw from where we come from but that's not where*
> *we are living. We are living here, we live here in a modern*
> *fusion world, but it is a world which draws certain values*
> *that can be traced back to our origins.* (Chai Patel cited in
> Ghilardi, 2006)

As so often in the intercultural world, fusion is the key.

Yau's background plays a key role in the development of his business. Being the eldest of six children, says Yau, 'carries certain responsibilities in Chinese culture'. But although he worked for his father from the age of 16, he says he:

> *detested the whole [Chinese take-away] industry. The*
> *way they operated family businesses with no level of*
> *professionalism and very limited reward, and the racial*
> *abuse. I couldn't stand the whole package.* (Cited in
> Ghilardi, 2006)

This is what made him want to start something that was unique and different from what his parents (and the members of his community) had already done.

These global entrepreneurs have learned lessons from their experience of doing business the intercultural way. Stelios, for example, is well aware that not everything is rosy in the UK and that certain negative attitudes persist:

> *Gordon Brown, the chancellor [now Prime Minister], has said he might change the law to destigmatise non-fraudulent business failure, and I applaud that. But it will take more than that to alter the nation's attitude to business failure. The problem lies deep in the British psyche: what will always stand in the way of entrepreneurship is that Brits all love the underdog until he or she succeeds and then they love to shoot them down. This will not change.* (Cited in Ghilardi, 2006)

But, having created 12 companies in 12 years in industries that trade in as many countries, he remains convinced that Britain is still the best place to do business in Europe because, as he puts it, 'There is nobody out there that is more receptive to foreign entrepreneurs than the British'.

Each of these entrepreneurs borrows some aspects from their original culture and applies it to the identification of new niches where they can innovate and leave their mark. Each builds on the social, economic and cultural strengths of their original community, but then departs from it and creates something that at times is alien, or in conflict with their community. However, it is precisely this tension and this need to break with tradition that gives them strength and the impetus to expand into new ventures. It is usually at this stage that they seek like-minded people to work with. And this is also why they prefer to employ people from diverse backgrounds, rather than from their own. It is the talent, the flexibility and the capacity to adapt that they seek in colleagues and employees from other backgrounds and not the security of family ties, or the cultural understanding of the ethnic group. Increasingly, but not uniformly it would seem, the UK is providing the right climate for this.

There is one thing that links most of the examples we have given so far, however. Their sphere of operation tends to be national or international and their connection with a particular place is difficult to discern. As we are concerned with the benefits that diversity and mixing could bring to the *city*, we need to dig a little deeper.

We earlier looked at the success of M&S and Burton and their association with Leeds was no doubt important to the prosperity of that city, without it being particularly explicit. We also looked at Marconi whose dual heritage no doubt contributed to his enquiring mind and drove him to leave one homeland for another in search of opportunity. However, it is another towering figure from the 19th century who perhaps best exemplifies the convergence of these two trends of intercultural exchange for the advantage of a specific city.

Marc Brunel fled revolutionary France at the end of the 18th century, coming to Britain where he met and married Sophie Kingdom. Their son, Isambard Kingdom Brunel, was born in 1806 and showed early signs of wishing to follow his father's trade of engineering. Not trusting the British system of education, the father sent his son to the most demanding school in France, the Lycée Henri-Quatre in Paris, and on to the University of Caen, giving him the best grounding in engineering available. The boy was not only good, but exhibited genius, and left college keen to put his ideas into practice, but such was the climate in France that no one was prepared to take a risk on this unproven graduate and his apparently madcap schemes.

It was therefore to a more entrepreneurial Britain that Brunel had to move where he found people prepared to back him. Starting with bridges, his crowning achievement in this field was the Clifton Suspension Bridge in Bristol, which had at the time the longest span of any bridge in the world. This association with Bristol continued with his building of the Great Western Railway from London, including Box Tunnel, the longest railway tunnel in the world at that time. Not satisfied with connecting Bristol with London, he saw no reason why a link between the city and New York should not be possible, so he built the Great Western, the largest and fastest steamship in the world. Brunel achieved many other feats in other places, but as a symbol of how one person can embody the best of two cultures and focus them to the enormous benefit of a particular city, Bristol's Brunel is the exemplar.

PRECONDITIONS OF DIVERSITY ADVANTAGE

The London Development Agency (LDA) promotes the 'business case for diversity' and pronounces that 'Diversity provides opportunities for business growth, and diversity is one of London's greatest strengths'[2], pointing out that:

- *Londoners speak over 300 languages and belong to at least 14 different faiths.*
- *Nearly a third of the city's population is from black, Asian or other minority ethnic (BAME) groups and over the next 10 years they will account for 80 per cent of the increase in London's working age population.*
- *By 2010, 40 per cent of the workforce will be over the age of 45.*
- *London's BAME communities have enormous spending power, with an after-tax income of around GB£16 billion.*
- *At least 5 per cent of London residents are gay or lesbian – the economic value of the 'pink economy' in the UK is estimated to be around GB£95 billion.*
- *BAME-owned businesses generated a combined sales total of GB£90 billion in 2004, and made a significant contribution to the London economy in terms of job creation, GDP, income and wealth creation.*

It leaves one in little doubt where London's diversity advantage lies.

The LDA launched the Competitive Advantage of Diversity initiative in 2004 to explore the relationship between ethnic and linguistic diversity and urban competitiveness. The resulting report (Smallbone et al, 2005) shows that involvement of ethnic minorities in entrepreneurship varies considerably between groups. The Chinese, Pakistani, Indian and white Irish groups, for example, have the highest rates of self-employment in London at over 20 per cent of those in work in each group. This contrasts with black Caribbean, black African and black other groups, which have among the lowest rates at between 10 and 13 per cent. In each ethnic minority group male self-employment is considerably higher than female, but Chinese women have the highest self-employment rate among women. Almost one in four businesses in London (22.6 per cent) can be categorized as BME. Collectively, it is estimated that they employ some 504,700 people or 19 per cent of total private sector employment in London. Asian owners comprised 10.7 per cent of the total, while black owners represented 4.6 per cent. The remaining businesses are made up of mixed-race (4.3 per cent) and 'Other' (3.0 per cent) ethnic groupings. The report also highlights that in London there are around 10,000 Indian-owned businesses turning over GB£20 billion each year, 4000 Pakistani-owned businesses and 900 Bangladeshi-owned businesses. In addition, there are approximately 16,000 black Caribbean and black African business owners, turning over around GB£10 billion.

Smallbone et al (2005) offer the basis for a diversity advantage strategy for London comprising:

• business start-up, business development and competitiveness;
• workforce diversity and competitiveness;
• linguistic diversity and competitiveness;
• ethnic diversity, creativity and competitiveness;
• supplier diversity and competitiveness;
• ethnic diversity, diaspora networks and competitiveness.

The strategy is now in its early stages of implementation. What is not yet explicit in London's approach, however, is the sense that it is seeking to encourage intercultural engagement, leading to new hybrid entrepreneurs and business models.

What is equally interesting to us, of course, is the interplay of immigrants with each other and their host community because it is an intercultural process that appears to support innovation. One has to look much harder to find examples from other parts of the world because very few places outside the US have yet begun to think about this, even in the UK. Hence in our 2005 study of the Tyne and Wear region of the UK (Comedia, 2005) we found rather more examples of how the region was missing out on the opportunity to find advantage in immigration and intercultural exchange.

On 19 May 2005 it was announced that a team working at the Centre for Life in Newcastle had become the first in Europe, and only the second in the world, to clone a human embryo based upon stem cell research. The breakthrough gave the UK, and Tyne and Wear city region in particular, an enormous advantage in the emergence of a new technology that promised to lead to lucrative new industries and economic spin-offs in areas ranging from human fertility to the treatment of Alzheimer's and Parkinson's disease.

The Centre for Life team was jointly led by a migrant who first came to the UK in 1991 and arrived in Newcastle in 2001. Miodrag Stojkovic was born in Leskovac in Serbia, the son of a kitchen maid. He trained as a veterinary scientist and was working in a pharmaceuticals company when, with the outbreak of the Yugoslavian civil war looming, he decided the only way of fulfilling his research ambitions would be to move to the West. Finding a research position in the UK, he then started looking for a place with the combination of expertise, facilities, ambition and financial resources to enable him to expand his interest in one of the most promising but also controversial of emerging technologies, stem cell research.

Centre for Life provided the ingredients to enable him to realize his ambition. He subsequently married a colleague and settled in the region as its most accomplished and celebrated knowledge migrant. Sadly, only a few months later in early 2006, he suddenly quit Newcastle to take up a post in Valencia, Spain. Apparently he was angered at the decision of the Centre for Life to publish findings of the study before a full account had been reviewed by experts and published in full in a scientific journal.[3] It is suggested they were trying to gain a publicity coup over a South Korean rival, but the British penchant for 'news management' was clearly not to the liking of the Serbian.

What this example teaches us is that while cities and institutions may now be aware of the potential advantage of high skill migration, they do not perhaps devote sufficient effort to building the cultural literacy that will enable them to hold onto and nurture diverse teams.

We found further evidence of British inability to create an inter-cultural and integrational environment for knowledge migrants in our study. We spoke to a professor (who wished to remain anony-mous) at the University of Newcastle. British by birth, she had orig-inally moved to Australia some 20 years ago for employment and has now returned, with her Australian husband, for a senior post at Newcastle University. Moving back to England had proved much more difficult than she had expected. A host of minor niggles had the cumulative effect of making her feel quite unwelcome. Problems ranged from her bank account to even renting a van to move her belongings. Her husband, who used to work as a chief planner in Australian local government, had to take a significant step down as a team member in Darlington because his Australian qualifications were not fully recognized in the UK.

On first arriving in Newcastle he was unable to rent a removal van with his Australian passport and driving licence. His passport stamp said 'Spouse Visa' so his wife needed to accompany him, with her passport, whenever he confronted officialdom. Her bank account had been declared 'dormant' so she could not apply for facilities such as debit or credit cards until it was brought back to active status again. Her husband had no rights to open a bank account at all until he had a job, or to open a joint account with her. She explained, 'When I first went to Australia, I told them, I am new here and I want to open a bank account,' and within few minutes she had it. It seems that even 20 years ago Australia was more equipped than the UK is now to handle new immigrants.

Meanwhile, Zhang Wei (from China) recently graduated with a Masters Degree in Transport Systems Engineering from Newcastle University and had been offered a job in a company called Serco, who agreed to sponsor her work permit. The Home Office rejected her application without a reason and further sent notices to the company that if they were to employ her, they would be in violation of immigration regulations. 'I am very disappointed. I spent so much time preparing for the application and waited for their decision to come,' Wei says. One of the directors at Serco commented:

> *I cannot think of a reason why they would refuse her a visa. We wanted someone with Mandarin speaking abilities as we are planning to expand our transport business to East Asia. The paperwork was extremely difficult to go through and we even had to submit proof of our existence, which is interesting as Serco is one of the largest suppliers of speed cameras to the Government (Department of Transport).*

(Cited in Comedia, 2005)

BEING INTERCULTURAL

Box 6.3 The Fresh Talent initiative, Scotland

This is a direct response by the Scottish Executive to the projected decline in Scotland's population to below 5 million by 2017. It is the first attempt in the UK to consider the regionalization of immigration.

It sets out to attract and retain within Scotland highly skilled workers from overseas, both foreign and expatriate. It aims to do this through a combination of aggressive place marketing and the streamlining of the migration experience in order to make it as easy as possible for migrants to settle. It is unique in the UK in that it has been granted permission by the Home Office to waive significant sections of immigration regulations.

Prominent within this is The Fresh Talent: Working in Scotland scheme that will enable non-EEA nationals who have successfully completed an HND, degree course, Masters or PhD at a Scottish university to apply to stay in Scotland for up to two years after completing their studies to seek and take work.

To be granted leave under the Fresh Talent: Working in Scotland scheme applicants must:

- have successfully completed a course at a Scottish institution of higher or further education;
- have lived in Scotland while studying;
- intend to work during the period of leave granted under the scheme;
- be able to maintain and accommodate themselves and any dependants without recourse to public funds;
- intend to leave the UK at the end of their stay, unless granted leave as a work permit holder, highly skilled migrant, business person or innovator.

Scheme participants will subsequently be eligible to qualify for leave to stay as one of the following:

- work permit holder;
- Highly Skilled Migrant Programme (HSMP) participant;
- business person;
- innovator.

The scheme includes the establishment of a 'one-stop-shop' Relocation Advisory Service, which opened in October 2004 with five staff to handle enquiries on a range of issues including immigration, legal and financial matters, housing, education and leisure. The advice service is not only available to potential migrants but also to employers seeking to employ migrants.

Research programmes are under way, for example a mapping of foreign qualifications to provide guidance to Scottish employers who may be confused with the credentials of job applicants. There is also a study of migrants who have already made a successful transition to Scotland, to act as exemplars for the scheme.

The other main strand of the Fresh Talent initiative is the joining up of all the agencies with a responsibility for projecting Scotland's image abroad. Where previously there was little liaison between responsibilities for business and export, inward investment, tourism, education and Scottish diaspora networks, all now work in close cooperation.[4]

While our research focused on the Tyne and Wear area we suspect most other regions in the UK and around Europe would fare little better (although Scotland now seems to be making a determined effort). There is still much to be done if cities and regions wish to realize the diversity advantage.

We conclude with an example from Leicester.

BOX 6.4 PARVIN ALI: FATIMA WOMEN'S NETWORK, LEICESTER

Parvin Ali was born in Malaysia and came to the UK at the age of two. Her father was an entrepreneur who worked in textile manufacture, distribution, travel agencies and social clubs. Her family also founded the first private bus company in Malaysia. She attended grammar school in Leicester and initially wanted to be a teacher but changed her mind and early on decided to join her father in running a company in the textile sector. At the age of 20, she set up her own company to make and sell textile trimmings, and then married a man who also worked in the textile business. As her father retired, she took over his business and ran it for ten years. In 2002 she did an MBA at De Montfort University, Leicester. Then she founded the UK-based FATIMA Women's Network in Leicester in 2003.

Ali's FATIMA network works for the economic empowerment of women, particularly those from disadvantaged backgrounds. Its distinctive feature is that it provides education, training and employment across communities to make women financially independent. To raise funds, FATIMA undertakes research work on gender and diversity for the national and regional governments in the UK and provides training for the Learning and Skills Council.

Ali traces her entrepreneurial spirit to her teens:

At the age of 14, I already wanted to work – as an Avon representative – and in fact my mother took this part-time job to allow me to help her and to keep some of her earnings as pocket money.

This incident underlines the importance of family to her development of business skills. She says:

> *It is something that is really in your genes. Business and investment was one of those things that you live and breath in the household and this makes a difference to your outlook on life.*

Being able to use her own initiative was also a key to success. Her family also influenced her attitude to risk:

> *We often talked about enterprise as if it was an everyday thing. The culture in which enterprise is absorbed in the psyche is influenced by the people with whom you are involved and if it is your family then you think risk is the norm and risk does not seem so risky, but something you just do.*
>
> *At the same time, being a newcomer was also a spur to action. There is also the point that being an outsider you always expect obstacles and you always think that you have to be that much better and that's what you do, you work much faster and think quicker.*

Overcoming this meant concentrating on soft qualities such as trust: 'The main thing is building relationships of trust, which means really building sustainable relationships: when it comes to business at our level everything has to do with trust (with suppliers and customers)'.

She found that she never fitted into any dominant community, but that barrier could also be a strength:

> *My father used to go to any mosque, wherever it was convenient, to say his prayers and in that respect he was given a lot of respect from the community because he never took sides with anyone and, up to a point, that worked in our favour.*

Ali's cultural background was both a problem and an opportunity:

> *The textile business environment tends to be very Indian-dominated and they don't see us as belonging to the community: we are Malaysians and we are outsiders. They also look quite resentfully at a female coming in because they belong*

> *to an old-style Asian work culture. They are quite happy to have women behind the scenes but not in positions of power. But, ironically, every single one of them were our customers because when they needed something no one else could supply them.*
>
> In this way, business can help overcome prejudice (Ghilardi, 2006).

The case study of Parvin Ali shows that intercultural entrepreneurs are successful (and innovative) because they identify niche and alternative markets where they can flourish. The particular forms that these enterprises take are dictated by a need to move away from saturated 'traditional ethnic business' sectors (that is, food, retail or the provision of services to minorities) in order to create distinctive 'transcultural' products, or more cross-cultural bespoke services to diverse communities. Here, too, elements from individual original cultures are mobilized and combined with the local culture, with the result of generating interesting new hybrids. The example also shows that the success of niche businesses depends greatly on the ability of each entrepreneur to transcend both their original culture and local stereotypes and institutional constraints.

And so who will be the Brunels of our own era? And beyond civil engineering, who will be the risk-taking bridge-builders in economic, social and cultural fields? It is a question no city should ignore or leave to chance.[5]

NOTES

1 Tom Petzinger quoted in Zachary, 2003.
2 www.lda.gov.uk/server/show/nav.00100200300f004
3 *The Sunday Times* (2006) 'Cloning expert quits country in row with partner', 15 January.
4 www.scotlandistheplace.co.uk
5 For further reading on this topic see Scott E. Page's new book (Page, 2007), which emerged as our book was going to press but which looks fascinating.

7

The City Through an Intercultural Lens

For cities to unlock the benefits of cultural diversity – to realize the diversity advantage or dividend – they need to become more intercultural. They need to become stages upon which the free interplay of different skills, insights and cultural resources may take its course. But they also need to be seedbeds in which the new social, economic and technological ideas that ensue can be nurtured and grown.

This chapter explains how cities can make themselves more intercultural by taking a fresh look at the things they do, taking aspects of the living and running of cities and looking at them again *through an intercultural lens*. We ask the question, if the primary intention of policy was to achieve innovation, advantage and happiness through greater intercultural activity, how would things be done differently? We take as our starting point the belief that cities are, in part, formed and reformed by the interplay of different groups and interests – politicians and policy-makers, practitioners and professionals, and residents who all act in their own way as *place-makers* – as well as economic forces. As such, the knowledge each group or interest has, and the interpretation that they place upon it, can become extremely influential on the way in which the city develops.

We follow Leonie Sandercock (1998, 2003a) in believing there are multiple ways of knowing a place. She identifies six:

- knowing through dialogue;
- knowing from experience;
- learning from local knowledge;
- learning to read symbolic and non-verbal evidence;
- learning through contemplative or appreciative knowledge;
- learning by doing, or action planning.

We believe that a city based upon intercultural principles will require its place-making groups and interests to have access to as many of these forms of knowledge as possible and the capacity to apply them. Having established in the previous chapter the requirement for openness as a precondition, we now look at what would be the specific competences and tools for the creation of an intercultural city. *Cultural literacy* is the capacity to acquire, interpret and apply knowledge about cultures. This creates the possibility to take an apparently familiar issue or discipline and to look at it afresh through an *intercultural lens* – a new idea that we propose here for the first time. Finally, we have taken a series of themes that characterize contemporary urban life and subjected them to a re-evaluation through an intercultural lens. This has produced findings with implications for policy.

CULTURAL LITERACY[1]

People behave in the way that they behave because of the culture they have assimilated. It may be an ethnic culture though it could equally be an organizational or professional culture that influences their reading of and responses to the world. Without an understanding of this, urban place-makers are lost. Our question here is not so much, how can the place-making professions do their job while taking culture into account? But instead, the real question is, how have they possibly been able to do their job for so long without taking culture into account?

Only through being culturally literate we can understand and read both the surface of any situation but also its deeper meanings and wider context. We take as our starting point an anthropological definition by Ogbu (1995) of culture as a way of life with five core components:

- *Customary ways of behaving: of making a living; eating; expressing affection; getting married; raising children; responding to illness and to death; getting ahead in society; and dealing with the supernatural;*
- *Codes or assumptions: expectations and emotions underlying those customary behaviours;*
- *Artefacts: things that members of the population group make or have made that have meaning for them;*
- *Institutions: economic, political, religious and social so as follow through things in a fairly predictable manner; and,*
- *Social structure: the patterned ways that people relate to one another.*

In the context of the contemporary city with its highly diverse cultural mix, it is clearly impossible for individual urban professionals to accumulate an in-depth cultural knowledge of every group represented in their city. We therefore need to encourage intercultural dialogue to ensure that knowledge about and between cultures occurs more seamlessly on a day-to-day basis. The task is to bear a series of questions in mind such as:

- Are my expectations different?
- Are my assumptions valid in this different context?
- Are people interpreting what I say differently from how I think they are?

From this comes the awareness that in all forms of human communication, the information is making a journey through several filters. First, the communicator is inscribing their message with meaning derived from their own cultural preconceptions (that is, they are *encoding* it). Second, the addressee is receiving the information

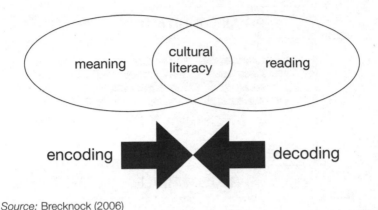

Source: Brecknock (2006)

Figure 7.1 Cultural literacy

and reading it according to their own cultural preconceptions (that is, they are *decoding* it).

In the case of urban planning and development, this entails engagement by the professional with a community, exploring its history, cultural institutions and current cultural values through its forms of artistic expression, skills, crafts, media of communication, oral history and memory. The value of such processes is that they uncover multiple stories, values, origins and often contradictory aspirations. It can therefore be as much an experience of community bonding as a research tool. Once these layers have been uncovered, it becomes possible to design physical, social and economic environments that are attuned to these deeper cultural meanings. As Edward Hall in *The Hidden Dimension* (1990) reminds us, 'people from different cultures not only speak different languages but, what is possibly more important, *inhabit different sensory worlds*'.

To understand these layers of complexity requires a process of analysis through a series of cultural filters that can be applied to planning, community development, urban regeneration and the physical aspects of local economic development. Figure 7.2 explains how this might translate into a process of engagement between city planners, a developer and the community in a culturally diverse neighbourhood.

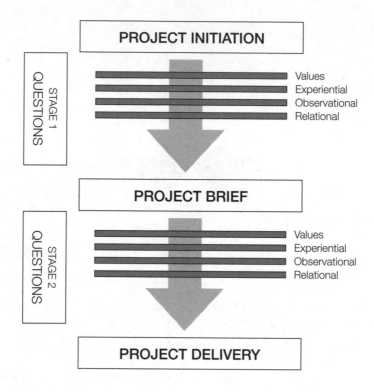

Source: Brecknock (2006)

Figure 7.2 Cultural filters

The four proposed filters are values, experiential quality, observational quality and relational quality:

- The first filter asks, what values should inform the project?
- The second teases out the nature of the experiences the project aims to create. With a building project one could ask, does the building provoke a feeling of welcome or inspire awe?
- The third filter concerns the visual impact of the project and asks, what visual signals will it convey?
- Finally, the filter of relations asks, what linkages will a project enable or prevent?

Box 7.1 Sense of Place, Manchester

Manchester City Council has launched the Sense of Place campaign to explore what the city means to people. In a 12-month programme it aims to speak to as many people as possible. It is going far beyond the usual limitations of public consultation to engage with the deeper and even subconscious feelings that people have about the place where they live and those they share it with. Participants are asked to talk about their neighbourhood and the city as it impacts upon their senses: what it sounds and smells like; what their own personal and family stories of the place are; and how differently it might feel through the eyes of different people such as a woman with a child or someone in a 4×4 car. In the process, better understandings are gained of, for example, the journeys people make, how different locations develop meaning and reputation, and how local stories and/or myths develop.

The research has so far thrown up a vast range of responses. For planning and built environment professionals it is enhancing the palette of possibilities by which they can understand the potential impact a piece of work might have upon a group of citizens – and they on it.

Manchester already has a Community Engagement Toolkit but is now enhancing this with its 'Forty concrete ideas for developing Sense of Place'. This is proving particularly helpful around two issues that might previously have been considered difficult: first, in the building of greater trust and understanding between refugee and host communities; and second, in joint working between the city and its neighbours, for example in the joint planning of the Irwell Valley with Salford.

Sense of Place works through:

- Sense of Place workshops;
- meta-data analysis of recent community engagement work;
- research into the city's history and present make-up;
- community arts workshops;
- working in partnership with specialist agencies such as the refugee network;

- devolution of budget to community radio across Manchester to run programmes exploring local identity;
- use of community comics[2] to explore the meaning of belonging and placelessness;
- working with allotment groups and using fruit and vegetables as a means to enable people to express their feelings about places and situations.

A budget has been created to facilitate different council departments and voluntary and neighbourhood organizations to initiate events (Comedia, 2006).

Following these steps may seem cumbersome at first. However, as with issues such as the environment or gender, the habit of asking the questions turns cultural literacy into a familiar idea, a sort of common sense.

Cultural literacy is then the ability to read, understand and find the significance of diverse cultures and, as a consequence, to be able to evaluate, compare and decode the varied cultures that are interwoven in a place. It allows one to attribute meaning and significance to anything seen and produced. It is a form of cultural capital that enables us to act sensitively and effectively in a world of differences. It is as crucial for survival as is the ability to read, write and count and fostering this culture of sharing knowledge across perceived boundaries is going to be a major challenge for the education system and professional practices in the years to come.

SEEING THE WORLD THROUGH AN INTERCULTURAL LENS

The intercultural city will be one in which cultural literacy is widespread so that people can understand and empathize with another's view of the world. This may be an ideal concept, but the road towards it begins with the agents and the processes that make our cities. If city institutions, policy-makers, planners and professional practitioners could begin to reconceive their role through an intercultural lens, the ideal could become reality.

Below we take three themes germane to urban place-making and subject them to a rethink on intercultural lines: public consultation and engagement; urban planning and development; and education. Readers from other disciplines might wish to subject their own professional principles and practices to a similar exercise.

A capacity to listen and consult

Modern cities should be seen less as places of distinct communities marked by clear and fixed boundaries but rather as local public spheres with multidimensional connections that overlap and conflict. As such, citizens cannot easily be ascribed to one homogeneous group but may be part of several. How then can policy-makers and planners try to understand what a community of this kind really thinks and wants? To be intercultural means being able to listen to and understand other cultural perspectives, and in the process of place-making, therefore, consultation cannot simply be a one-off and standardized exercise but a continuous process of informal discussion and engagement.

The orthodox multiculturalist approach to public consultation requires that communities are defined by their ethnicity and consulted in isolation (e.g. 'the African Caribbean community', 'the Asian community', and so on) as if ethnicity is the only factor influencing the way in which people will lead their lives in the city. Such an approach is increasingly flawed. Our research in numerous culturally diverse settings has identified a set of problems that often characterize (either singly or in combination) consultation processes.

We have found that consultations are often based upon a crude understanding of ethnic difference, with small numbers of 'community leaders' accepted as the voice of specific ethnic communities, overlooking the internal diversity of such communities. As a corollary to this, methodologies can be standardized to elicit views on a 'community by community' basis rather than exploring overlap between communities and, more significantly, the combinations of perspectives of intercultural communities where ethnicity and race are not the determining factor. Consultation processes can also be limited by a perspective that recognizes the views of the white population as the cultural norm and the views of ethnic minorities (or in some places ethnic majorities) as inevitably different or aberrant – while hybrid identities and complex intercultural views are not anticipated, and therefore not sought. In short, consultation and participation strategies are often disconnected from the complex intercultural relations that actually exist between people.

In this sense, the pursuit of consultation solely with neatly identified 'ethnic minorities' in mind is misguided. Markers of identity are proliferating and reconfigure sense of community and place in the contemporary city. Notions of the 'Bangladeshi' (or any other) community can clumsily ascribe individuals to a notional 'community' without appreciating that individuals have affiliations with a number of communities simultaneously and that ethnicity or 'race' might not be the primary basis of those ties.

The process of intercultural consultation and engagement was explored in a case study of the London Borough of Tower Hamlets. The Council is acknowledged as a leader in this field.[3] The policy implications of our findings relate to techniques that other cities might employ in future intercultural consultative exercises (Fleming, 2006).

We found that there is a need to think beyond ethnicity per se. This can be achieved by conducting more consultation in 'intercultural spaces' rather than ones that are ethnically homogenous. These spaces might be found by using intermediaries such as health professionals, refugee organizations and civic associations and by exploiting Internet networks. Consulting in more 'random' contexts such as on the street, in bars, at health centres, in schools, libraries, swimming pools and parks – that is, in intercultural spaces and places – will ensure a more varied, though just as pertinent, response. Further, our lines of inquiry should be framed around questions that require the respondent to think beyond the needs of their co-ethnics in formulating answers. Indeed, the networks of communities that

Box 7.2 Intercultural community engagement: Leeds

Although adjacent to Leeds' thriving central business and retail district, Holbeck's 19th century industrial fabric had until quite recently remained largely untouched. Plans to create Holbeck Urban Village (HUV) comprising new residential, business and retail development were seen to be necessary, but at the same time there was concern not to overwhelm the delicate ecology of the original community. There was also awareness that Holbeck sits across the route that links the city centre to the suburb of Beeston – a place made notorious as the home of two of the 7/7 London bombers – and a sensitivity of the need to not reinforce that community's apprehensive relationship with the outside world.

The city council's Development Department decided to go far beyond its accepted standards of community engagement and committed extensive resources to involving its own staff and several outside consultancies and arts organizations. This culminated in a month-long exhibition entitled 'What Kind of Place?' to generate debate and discussion around proposals for the area. This was launched with a two-day 'festival' of high-profile engagement events. These included 'Secrets and Lights', a series of light installations by the Culture Company exploring the theme of 'hidden Holbeck'.

There was a concern that the consultation would be perceived to be only of relevance to the newly arrived businesses and loft residents so Multicultural Urban Design were engaged to ensure there was targeted engagement with the white working class and BME resident communities of Holbeck and Beeston. This involved persistent attempts at grassroots community involvement, presentations to women's groups, door-to-door business and shop discussions, use of SMS technology, presentations in schools, signage across Leeds, and visits to mosques and churches.

The shadow of the 7/7 bombings had created a serious climate of fear in the Muslim communities. For example, one mosque refused entry to the engagement team altogether and another expelled a team member who was distributing leaflets, mistaking him for a political activist. This encouraged the team to be more ingenious in getting around the 'community gatekeepers' to engage with people directly.

The result was a procession of Beeston residents, led by musicians, who attended the exhibition launch to rub shoulders with IT executives and loft-dwellers to add their comments on the plans, swelling the attendance to over a thousand.

All groups in Beeston claimed that this was the first they had come to know about the plans in HUV. Kalsoom Bibi from the ASHA Group said after the event, 'Normally we wouldn't get asked to attend such an event and it was a real treat to be able to see what is going on in Holbeck Urban Village … the top officers were showing us around and taking us for a tour … it was brilliant and I learnt so much' (Comedia, 2006).

we engage should not even be defined in terms of ethnicity. Thus groups and workshops should be suitably and continually mixed across age, gender and income as well as faith and ethnicity.

By identifying the audience as intercultural, the consultation process itself can become a bonding exercise, strengthening community and civic responsibility. With this in mind we stress the need to promote the consultation process as part of a longer-term, iterative process of gathering opinion, asking direct questions and evaluating responses. Decision-making and implementation processes should be seen as part of a flow of engagement where the engagement itself is as important as the practical translation into policy action. Questions can then be reframed for future consultation rounds. If the council appears to respond to the various voices of the community then trust can be built. Short-term interventions can be made to show that the council is listening and responding, because without micro actions, engagement with macro issues will be unfulfilling and undermined by a lack of trust.

Consulting with new intercultural audiences calls for new and creative methods, employing a wider range of media and experimenting with them. Using different writing styles, for example, will result in a wider range of responses, while combining ethnicities and generations to engage with a physical proposal may produce previously unforeseen approaches. Artists and community workers can function as facilitators in a collaborative process that hands over ownership of the process to the intercultural grouping itself. And all the while, active participation on intercultural grounds means that the community itself is being subtly reconfigured. Meanwhile, existing norms that relate to notions of, say, 'aesthetically pleasing', 'safe', 'dynamic' (that may have been protected over many generations by the white majority), are questioned and not taken for granted.

For their part, officials will brush up on their cultural literacy. It is vital that officials work cross-departmentally prior to statutory consultation processes so that they can build their knowledge of the intercultural reality of the location they are seeking to plan for. It will be very difficult to establish trust if they enter the process in a state of ignorance.

Once an issue or a problem has been reframed as something that is shared and experienced across ethnicities, it becomes possible to conceive of solutions that are predicated upon a shared approach.[4]

City-making through an intercultural lens[5]

The built city is the most complicated cultural artefact humankind has invented. Cultural preferences and priorities are etched into the mindscape of the professional urban experts who determine what the physical fabric of our cities looks like: engineers, surveyors, masterplanners, architects, urban designers, cost accountants, project managers and developers do not make decisions that are value free and neutral. What, at first sight, looks like merely technique and technical processes – whether a building will stand up, whether traffic can flow, what uses should be brought together – are shaped by value judgements. The look, feel and structure of the places that planners encourage, help design and promote, reflect their assumptions about what they think is right and appropriate. This is etched into codes, rules and guidelines. Even the aesthetic priorities people choose themselves have their cultural histories. It is inevitable, therefore, that planners and designers apply their own cultural filters to their professional work, cultural filters based on their upbringing and life experience. Without a policy mechanism that requires the gaining of cultural literacy, the professions will remain locked in a very narrow understanding of culture and the built environment. Active cultural literacy programmes are needed that help built environment professions understand that every planning and design decision they make has a cultural consequence.

At a more fundamental level, the city is built to respond to landscape, weather, location, available materials, the function the city seeks to play, exploitable resources, the talents it can develop and attract, and how it makes its living; and the interplay of these continues through time. At each point, the choices the culture makes about what is important, valued and what seems right to them can be seen in the physical fabric. And, interestingly, our perception of things changes along the way. Inevitably the relatively cold, rainy, windblown UK builds with weather protection in mind. The trading city makes space for warehouses and the business services city hubs for offices. So much is obvious.

More interestingly we might ask, how do social values play themselves out? What is our view of being public and private? How do we display this? Do we promenade and hang about listlessly in idle conversation in public spaces or are we more coy? Is this different for women and men? For some, ambling in public places is an intrinsic part of life; for others such socializing takes place in greater privacy at home or in a club. In some cultures women are confined to the domestic realm; in others their role is more public. Do we hide behind net curtains or, rather like the Calvinist inspired Dutch, is private life displayed through large windows because you have nothing to hide? What is our view of learning? The older libraries projected themselves as temples of knowledge where you, the learner, entered humbly and with respect to explore a prescribed, given canon of knowledge. Today, by contrast, with our goal to democratize knowledge, we look for a more open, transparent and welcoming feel. So the look of libraries is different. Things change. The factories, especially 'the satanic mills' of old, are transformed into aspirational housing and loft living. What once was gloomy is now very classy.

What happens then when different cultures meet and coexist in the same space? There have always been borrowings and graftings; they have been there so long we cannot see them. For centuries building styles and fashions criss-crossed Europe: English and French baroque, or German and English gothic. Exceptions apart, the architectures of Arabia, India and China are not visible in exterior design; they have influenced the interior much more. One only sees the mosque, the gurdwara and Chinese gateway arches in Chinatowns. Can and should we learn from the great traditions of Arab and Indian architecture and their aesthetics?

Are the basic building blocks of the city the same when looked at through intercultural eyes? Think of street frontages, building heights, set-backs, pavement widths, turning circles, the number of windows and their size, how architects and planners deal with enclosure, privacy or sight lines. Think too of the materials used, colour, light and water. Are streets and the colour palette used different when produced interculturally? Should architects and planners structure space to reflect different cultures as they might see and use spaces in varied ways? Or should open-ended spaces be created that others can adapt to, such as the Kurds who gather around the steps of Birmingham's Chamberlain Square?

You already see day-to-day interculturalism in the sign and symbol world of every British city: Chinese-run takeaways that double up as fish and chip shops, or kebab/curry/burger houses. But imagine a city in the UK that had more than the foreign-sounding restaurant names or shop signs and the cultural aesthetics to match. What would the city look like? We know the experience of seeing restaurants with names like Lee Ho Fook, The Great Wall, Golden Dragon, Lakorn Thai, Aphrodite Taverna and Cantina Italia. All of these signs of multiculturalism and business diversity are predominantly superficial 'cultural cross-dressing' (Brecknock, 2006) that demonstrate the adaptability of migrant communities and their ability to work within the existing built form. But there is more to interculturalism than this.

Masterplanning interculturally

The question of how city planners can balance the seemingly contradictory cultural priorities of differing communities and how different cultural values should be reflected in space was the challenge explored in our case study of the London Borough of Lewisham on 'masterplanning through an intercultural lens' (Comedia, 2007). In surveying the built environment professionals and their national professional associations, it became clear there was great sympathy and desire to understand how different communities work. Yet the day-to-day procedures of the professional life of, say, the engineer or planner did not predispose them to understand the details of how diverse communities think about their space.

Within the local authority it is more often those dealing with issues such as social inclusion that require a better understanding of the texture of their communities. This highlighted the significant need for interdisciplinary approaches to urban planning to be developed, where social inclusion and land use planning might work collaboratively rather than in isolation. Breaking down the professional boundaries and silo mentalities of organizations is one of the most significant challenges of developing a truly intercultural approach to urban development and city management.

Part of this challenge is the need for increased cultural literacy. Our report, '*Knowing Lewisham*' (Comedia, 2007), proposed that a series of *knowledge questions* become part of the *listening and learning cycle* consultation procedure of any major projects. Our questions included:

• Do extended families share or wish to share houses?
• How well do existing houses meet the needs of community members in terms of family size, community gatherings and room layouts?
• What are the cultural, gender and generational sensitivities associated with public life that need to be understood by council planners?
• Are young people respected and catered for in the planning and design of public space?

The importance of these knowledge questions lies in the gradual build-up of cultural literacy among the council officers in planning and urban design. As a result of increased cultural literacy, officers are better equipped to understand cultural diversity in their communities and therefore make culturally informed decisions with an understanding of the possible impacts developments might have on existing cultural life.

Unfortunately, addressing these was generally regarded as a task best dealt with by someone else whose job gave them a better understanding of the texture of their communities.

A new skill set

The implication of the response of the professionals to these questions is that professional practice needs to be reassessed. This is timely given the recent Egan Review of New Skills for Sustainable Communities, which led to the setting up of an Academy for Sustainable Communities for the UK. This has been helpful in shifting the debate and setting out what new skills are going to be required in making modern cities work. These centre very much on understanding communities from a 360-degree perspective and applying a set of generic skills, behaviours and ways of thinking that are requirements for moving forward, such as inclusive visioning, team working, leadership, and process and change management.

Consultation means a continuous process of informal discussion and engagement with people, as opposed to formal discrete public participation required by regulation. Clearly a highly diverse cultural mix makes it impossible for individual urban professionals to accumulate an in-depth cultural knowledge of every group represented in their city. We therefore need to evolve new forms of intercultural dialogue.

Diversity in its many forms is the primary element of a vibrant place – diversity of business, diversity of activities and a diversity of built form creating visual stimulation. Taking street markets as an example, they often exist in unremarkable settings but their vibrancy comes through the interaction between the people and products. The most successful markets are those where there is a wide diversity of products and suppliers. Sadly, cities often seem to overlook these factors, being far more concerned with the physical form of public places. They put the responsibility on the urban designer to transform a place through cosmetic factors such as new paving, elegant street furniture and improved lighting, when the reality is that many places are unattractive or underperforming for other reasons such as failing business, traffic domination and anti-social behaviour.

The intercultural city depends on more than a design challenge. It derives from a central notion that people are developing a shared future whereby each individual feels they have something to contribute in shaping, making and co-creating a joint endeavour. A thousand tiny transformations will create an atmosphere in public space that feels open and where all feel safe and valued.

It also relies upon a deeper and richer knowledge on behalf of the city-making professions of the communities in which they work. In the Appendix we have designed an exercise that could be conducted to begin a process of intercultural masterplanning that we term the *Knowledge Questions*. The findings from these questions, as indeed the whole process of the inquiry, will gradually change the relationship between the professionals and the communities. Ultimately, there may even be the need to establish local 'observatories' to manage this process.

Making intercultural spaces

In our survey of residents in Lewisham and Bristol to identify popular intercultural spaces, the places mentioned with most frequency were not the highly designed or engineered public and corporate spaces but rather the spaces of day-to-day exchange such as libraries, schools, colleges, youth centres, sports clubs, specific cinemas, the hair salon, the hospital, markets and community centres. These are the 'spaces of interdependence and habitual engagement' where (what Ash Amin (2002) calls) 'micro publics' come together and where (according to Leonie Sandercock, 2004) 'dialogue and prosaic negotiations are compulsory'. In these places, 'people from different backgrounds are thrown together in new settings which disrupt familiar patterns and create the possibility of initiating new attachments' (Sandercock, 2004).

Where are the British cultural institutions or public spaces that achieve this kind of synthesis? The city-making professions of the UK face an enormous challenge to fashion a built environment that reflects the country's growing diversity.

Education through an intercultural lens[6]

School and formal education is, of course, only one aspect of a child's moral, intellectual and cultural upbringing but is a vital one and can have a profound effect upon an individual's as well as a group's capacity to be intercultural. It is also significant to us as an area in which cities themselves have the discretion to intervene.

Educational multiculturalism as practised in the 1970s, 1980s and 1990s has been subjected to recent criticism for being beneficial to some at the expense of others. Multiculturalism, it is said, celebrated an acceptable face of difference but excluded many, particularly young men. The white working class were often left to feel that multiculturalism was actually a celebration of the culture of everyone but themselves, while the notable underachievement of Afro-Caribbean and Pakistani young men has also been blamed on any number of things, from a lack of a clear disciplinary framework to racism.

Now, in a climate of increased intercommunal tension, as well as the increasing need for youngsters to able to communicate with people of all varieties in their future careers, there is an even greater need for schools to prepare pupils to be outward-facing; but what would an intercultural educational system look like? It would be predicated simply on the belief that the dynamic cultures of the various groups that make up the UK are a fundamental part of their identity and that the education service needs to know, understand and build upon the spiritual, moral, social and cultural backgrounds of all its pupils. All ethnic groups, including the majority 'white' groups, *of whatever social class*, would be encouraged to feel that their background, history and narrative are valued in the school context. It would also ensure that all groups are aware of the backgrounds of groups other than their own. This would need to be undertaken,

BEING INTERCULTURAL

Box 7.3 Intercultural education, Bologna

In 1992, the City of Bologna, together with other interested institutions at the provincial and regional levels and in collaboration with the University of Bologna, established a service to support teachers in receiving students with migration backgrounds and to promote their integration. The Centro Documentazione/Laboratorio per un'educazione interculturale (CD/LEI) (Centre for Documentation/Laboratory for intercultural education) aims at promoting the integration of pupils with migration backgrounds into the school system, carrying out activities to guarantee them equal rights in education and to improve their performance. Its purpose is to support Italian schools in creating intercultural school careers and in dedicating resources to the management of cultural diversity, as well as to involve teachers.

In addition the centre supports the exchange of 'intercultural good practices' between educational institutions at the local, regional and international levels and promotes links between interested institutions and associations in order to facilitate activities to receive and integrate pupils with foreign backgrounds. In 2004, the centre opened a 'counter of intercultural consulting' to school teachers, intercultural mediators and intercultural operators.[7]

---

however, in a framework of shared values so that all pupils had a sense of belonging.

Our research was based upon the city of Leicester. Although one of Britain's most diverse cities, the education service had done little to positively address it and this, alongside other factors, contributed to its failing of an Ofsted inspection in 1999. However, this created the motivation for innovations in policy and practices, not least in coming to terms with the new Community Cohesion agenda. This was acknowledged in 2002 when Leicester was identified as a Beacon council for its work on community relations, a designation that brought with it some extra funding. A decision was made to focus the Beacon Pathfinder funding (a special fund awarded by the government to 15 local authorities to take forward their work on community cohesion) on work with children and young people, the chosen themes being drama, sport, media and conflict resolution.

The drama strand is particularly notable. It comprised the twinning of schools from across the city (and over various ethnic divides) to work together with a resident South African arts group, Mighty Zulu Nation, to produce performance pieces. The pieces raised issues of difference, separation, oppression and the transition to adulthood. It had a profound effect on many who took part.

The conclusion of the Beacon Pathfinder was that creativity lies at the heart of building intercultural understanding in schools. The arts and creativity were seen as central to the work of developing interculturalism and improving community cohesion because they dealt with the deep issues of both personal and communal identity. At their best, they helped young people to see the world from another person's point of view, to stand in their shoes, as well as to work together with others to achieve a common purpose. It was found that the intensity of young people's experience was such that, even during the course of a single day, they could establish valuable connections with those from different communities that, in many cases, then developed into more long-lasting relationships.

From these experiences it became possible to imagine what a more intercultural form of education might look like. In Leicester it was suggested that the basis of an intercultural education agenda should be a commitment to instil the following key set of six competences in young people:

- *cultural competence* – the ability to reflect upon one's own culture and the culture of others;
- *emotional and spiritual competence* – the ability to be self-reflective, handle one's own emotions, empathize with others;
- *linguistic and communicative competence*;
- *civic competence* – the ability to understand and act upon rights and responsibilities and be socially and morally responsible;

- *creative competence*;
- *sporting competence.*

These intercultural competences would require schools and local authorities to develop structures and processes that would enable them to translate, adopt and adapt their existing practices to take account of the changing realities of their communities.

What then is the way forward? Experience suggests that the following are the key issues that need to be addressed with some urgency if the schools system is to contribute to making the intercultural city a reality in the UK:

- Social vision should drive educational practice. The essential premise of all educational thinking is the articulation of the kind of society that we wish to see in the future.
- The whole school curriculum needs to be reviewed through an intercultural lens. This is not proposing fundamental changes to the National Curriculum in terms of removing elements from what already exists and replacing them with new ones; but much could be progressed through looking at what exists from a different perspective, the migrant experience, for example.
- Multiculturalism needs to be redefined as being applicable to all communities, including the indigenous population. 'Multiculturalism' in practice should mean what it says, that is, applying inclusively to all communities. The narratives of indigenous white communities have been largely ignored in multicultural work that, again, has served only to erect more obstacles to community cohesion rather than helping to develop the intercultural city.
- The place of faith schools within the educational framework needs a fresh appraisal. It is difficult to conceive of them as being anything other than incompatible with an intercultural society.
- The practice of interculturalism needs to be integral to the work of key monitoring agents.
- A fundamental rethink is needed as to how best to develop citizenship in children and young people. Citizenship is developed through its lived practice in democratic processes so it requires

far more than the simple dissemination of information to make it a reality. The intention to involve children and young people in a much more proactive way, as signalled in the 2004 Children's Act, is an encouraging pointer as to how we might go forward.

NOTES

1 This section draws upon Brecknock, 2006.
2 See www.comicdemocracy.org.uk/.
3 London Borough of Tower Hamlets was designated Beacon status by government for 'Getting Closer to Communities' in 2005/2006.
4 For a more detailed analysis of this issue see Comedia, 2006.
5 This section draws upon original research for the Intercultural City conducted by Richard Brecknock and Andy Howell, 2005.
6 This section draws upon Coles and Vincent, 2006.
7 *CD/LEI Centro Documentazione/Laboratorio per un'educazione interculturale* (2006) www.comune.bologna.it/istruzione/cd-lei/index.php.
8 See also www.bwdbelonging.org.uk/.

BEING INTERCULTURAL

Box 7.4 The Belonging to Blackburn Campaign

The Borough of Blackburn with Darwen in northwest England set out to increase the proportion of residents who feel that their local area is a place where people from different backgrounds can get on well together and who feel that they belong. In its action plan, the Local Strategic Partnership declares that:

> *In the past, the emphasis was on celebrating diversity, but now this has evolved into highlighting the similarities that unite people from all walks of life and acknowledging the contributions that they all make to improving life in the borough and delivering a new approach to:*

- *strengthen citizenship by promoting pride of place and a sense of shared future amongst all citizens*
- *uniting all sectors and communities*
- *emphasising what we all have in common rather than our differences.*

The main elements of the Belonging work have been a poster campaign and a charter of belonging that has been promoted and signed within schools, by public and private sector partners and within the voluntary and community sectors. The poster campaign depicts a diverse group of local residents: disabled and able-bodied, from different age groups, occupational backgrounds and ethnic groups. The poster, with the strapline 'many lives ... many faces ... all belonging' is designed to promote an image of a community to which people from all backgrounds can belong, regardless of their differences.

In consequence a Charter of Belonging was drawn up, laying down a common set of civic values.

The Belonging theme has provided an ideal focus in particular for school twinning work, because it cuts across curriculum areas. One of the twinning projects that the Belonging Campaign has stimulated is My Home Town, led by the heads of citizenship from four schools in the borough. This project involved students debating the charter and considering what belonging to Blackburn with Darwen means to them personally. According to a teacher:

> We've looked at the charter, we've talked, we've had work-shops within groups and we've asked young people what does it actually mean to them?... We've asked them to come up with their own definitions and their own explanations and their own perceptions of what Belonging to Blackburn means to them. Ultimately they'll sign up to a campaign but we've deliberately not asked them to do that yet ... so it's not just a tokenistic gesture ... you'll get a real feel of what it does mean to them.

By acting as a focus and springboard for other projects, especially in education and children's services, the Belonging Campaign has aimed for this depth, as well as breadth of impact. The My Home Town Project has created opportunities for young people from different backgrounds to interact, while discussing the ideas raised by the charter. A Blackburn teacher commented:

I think the biggest achievement has got to be what the children and what the young people have achieved. You can ask them yourselves and they will tell you very clearly that they have met people that they would otherwise not have ever come across... Which I think reflects parallel lives very clearly ... they would probably be neighbours with somebody with a different background but would choose not to get to know that person in a more bonding way.

The major recent development of the Belonging campaign has been through a series of '100 Voices' discussion and consultation events, of which three have been held to date. This programme is now being extended to a local level, with the establishment of five Neighbourhood 100 Voices. These events are forums for open and honest debate around cohesion issues, as well as an opportunity for local residents to shape the direction of the campaign (Ipsos MORI, 2007).[8]

8

A New Intercultural Citizenship

Throughout the 1990s and even more so since the turn of the century, politicians and policy-makers alike have become increasingly concerned with the apparent loosening of the ties that once bound urban communities together. Evidence of diminishing levels of civic commitment (as seen through falling voter turnout), spatial segregation, the 'missing millions' who don't complete census returns or work in the legitimate economy, worries about the loss of respect between people of different generations and social classes, falling membership of voluntary associations, and particularly the spectre of rioting by marginalized groups have all served to arouse a renewed interest in what should and could bind a society together.

As Bhikhu Parekh (2006) has argued, complex modern society faces conflicting demands and must devise a political structure that can reconcile them fairly:

> *It should foster a strong sense of unity and common belonging among its citizens, as otherwise it cannot act as a united community able to take and enforce collectively binding decisions and regulate and resolve conflicts. Paradoxical as it may seem, the greater and deeper the diversity in society, the greater the unity and cohesion it requires to hold itself together and nurture its diversity. A weakly held society feels threatened by differences and lacks the confidence and the willingness to welcome and live with them.*

The need to resolve these demands has been met in different ways. Some states have always demanded conformity and assimilation into a monolithic national citizenship and culture, while others have taken a more pluralistic approach, acknowledging and institutionalizing the rights of minorities to retain their difference. However, since 9/11 in particular, the majority of Western nations, including some of the most liberal such as The Netherlands and the UK, have at the very least begun to reappraise their position and to toy with the idea of having stronger and more narrowly defined models of integration and citizenship.

It is not the purpose of this section to rehearse the debates surrounding rights and responsibilities in a multiethnic state. Parekh and many others have already done this very thoroughly. Our concern here is to ask the question, if our aim were to create a society which were not only free, egalitarian and harmonious but also one in which there was productive interaction and cooperation between ethnicities, what would we need to do more of or do differently? And in particular, what kind of leaders (political and communal) and citizens would this require?

A SYSTEM IN CRISIS

In the UK this renewed interest has been encapsulated within the 'community cohesion agenda' that emerged from the aftermath of the 2001 riots in northern English towns. In his report to the Home Office (Home Office, 2001), Ted Cantle identified five domains upon which policy would need to focus if greater community cohesion were to be achieved:

- common values and civic culture;
- social networks and social capital;
- place attachment;
- social order and social control;
- social solidarity and reduction in income disparity.

Cantle was suggesting that there were serious problems in the structures and value systems in some of the localities where the riots occurred. He was not, however, targeting his questions simply at the communities at the centre of the disturbances but more widely at the systems and cultures of local governance in those cities and, by implication, at the nation as a whole.

A more widespread scrutiny of multiculturalism as a policy orthodoxy has accompanied these enquiries and this in turn has been part of a wider questioning of what might be portrayed as the question of what will succeed the supposedly outdated value system of the industrial age. We see a crisis of leadership across society. The working class has lost many of the institutions – the manual workplace, trade unions, social clubs and friendly societies – through which new leaders were honed and through which structures of loyalty and reciprocation were built (Pahl, 2006). This has been accompanied by a straining of the bonds between generations, making it increasingly difficult for the old to demand respect from the young or to give it.

Paradoxically, these structures of leadership and solidarity lasted longer in many minority communities than they did with the whites, but there is growing suspicion that this was simply masking the process of change within. The charge of many after the 2001 riots was that leadership in many communities had ossified and was becoming a dangerous barrier to change, helping to reinforce the tensions that eventually exploded.

To summarize, traditional local government political parties and leaders had entered into alliances with (often self-appointed) ethnic community leaders in an arrangement that traded votes and compliance for status and access to resources. As the critics of multiculturalism point out, being and remaining ethnically distinct and separate proved to be the most effective way of retaining leverage in such a system and so there was little incentive to develop a new, more cross-cultural form of polity. This proved frustrating for those who did not feel part of it: the sections of the white working class who felt alienated and let down by their traditional leadership, and the second- and third-generation children of migrants who, often feeling neither part of their parental homeland nor wholly part of the UK, were struggling to find a new identity and a political voice that reflected this.

For many years, places remained stultified within the structures and the language of both formal and communal governance, neither reflecting nor even comprehending the changes and the tensions that were building below. In this period the *modus operandi* of local government and traditional leaders when faced by new questions or potential controversies was generally to turn a blind eye to or neatly sidestep them with the offer of a favour or palliative. Debate or conflict between ethnicities was to be avoided at all cost, which is why spatial segregation was seen as no bad thing, while conflict within communities was to be left to community leaders to 'sort out' internally.

That some cities exploded, while most did not, is down to certain local factors, not least higher than national average levels of poverty. Into this mix of intercommunal suspicion, the sudden and spatially targeted injection of large quantities of government regeneration funding generated resentment and created a winner/loser dichotomy that rapidly became racialized. Some other areas of the country that experienced the same levels of segregation and intercommunal in-comprehension were cushioned by more buoyant economies. But many other areas experience similar levels of poverty and exclusion and have perhaps been able to avoid communal strife by evolving new and more responsive forms of leadership, governance and communication.

OPEN SOCIETY UNDER THREAT

Clearly, however, the issue cannot be wholly explained with refer-ence to local factors. In the age of globalization, national and increas-ingly international factors play a powerful part. Although the UK disturbances took place a few months prior to 9/11, the radicaliza-tion of certain sections of Islamic opinion is clearly a factor, as has been reaction to the subsequent military responses of the UK and US. Indeed, never before, perhaps, has there been such an intimate interweaving of issues of foreign, state security and social policy together at the level of the street. One thing that has emerged is that as local leadership and allegiance has dwindled; it has been replaced by other supra-local forces, whether religious, political or cultural.

In this context we should also raise a note of caution. Because of the connection (actual or otherwise) that has been drawn between local communal unrest and international Islamist terrorism, it has become too easy to portray the crisis we are describing as a symptom of a clash of civilizations between the Muslim world and the West.[1] We vigorously reject this. We are also alarmed at the growing assumption that the main or indeed the only reason why local civic capacity and leadership matters in 2007 is to prevent the development of enclaves that might act as seedbeds of extremism (Department for Communities and Local Government, 2007). There are already worrying signs that secret security services in many Western countries are now exerting a growing influence on local governance policy.[2] Our argument is that while civic capacity, local leadership and sociability in the public domain are all under pressure, this is both the product of and the responsibility of us all, regardless of ethnicity. Stigmatizing a whole community for the outrages of a few is not only unfair and wrong, but it also lets off the hook the rest of society who, albeit in a more passive way, are contributing equally to the decline of social capital and intercultural engagement.

While we have given a British account of the strains of social change, many of these will be familiar in other states too. The question remains the same though – can a new form of local polity be forged that speaks to the new conditions on the ground? While national and supranational governments still set the tone on issues of border entry and the granting of naturalization, it is increasingly at the level of the town and the city that multiethnic identities and relationships are being defined. In the rest of this section we examine the issue of local leadership, governance and citizenship through an intercultural lens and ask what it would take to build a new workable model.

FORGING A LOCAL INTERCULTURAL CITIZENSHIP

The idea that the local matters, and might even have an active role to play, in defining citizenship and identity is a new and still quite radical one. However, in countries such as Italy or Greece where national governments have been reluctant to recognize cultural diversity as an issue requiring action, it has fallen to city governments to improvise as they see fit. Hence we find alarming disparities in policy between, for example, the progressive municipalities of Rome and Turin and the cold shoulder presented by Milan and the new walled ghetto builders of Padua. However, in countries (such as the UK) in which central government has long taken the lead on matters ranging from rights of entry and anti-discrimination legislation to the dispersal of refugees, it is difficult for the capital to conceive any role for the local other than the implementation of policy.

There are vocal challenges to this status quo. Perhaps the most radical is from Rainer Bauböck (2003) who argues that that because it is cities that bear the greatest responsibility for managing and ministering to migrant populations, and because they suffer from the ambiguities and inflexibilities of national naturalization policies, they should be given far more autonomy. He contends that instead of migrants waiting – perhaps interminably – to hear whether they will be granted nationality by the state, the city should have the powers to grant citizenship to those who fulfil certain criteria:

> *Cities should fully emancipate themselves from the rules of membership that apply to the larger state... Cities are political communities of a different kind [from the nation state] and they can assert this by granting full citizenship to all residents within their jurisdiction.*
>
> *[I]mmigrants from other parts of the country as well as from abroad would be made aware that they are now full members of the polity and are also expected to use their rights of participation; the native population would be*

made aware that they share a common membership in the city with the immigrant population; and the city would formally assert its distinct character as a local polity vis-à-vis the national government. (Bauböck, 2003)

One doubts whether the interior ministries of any national state on earth are quite ready to enter into Bauböck's subversive vision, but this is a challenging insight into one direction that some cities may choose to go if they start to calculate that their best interests and those of the state no longer coincide. It is not so far-fetched either and is now being discussed in transnational municipal networks. For example, a joint statement issued by the Congress of Local and Regional Authorities of Europe and the Council of Europe (COE/CLRAE, 2006) called for a challenge to the governments of the continent to bring about a redefinition of the rights and responsibilities associated with effective 'glocal civic citizenship'. They explain that:

Glocal citizenship means guaranteeing basic rights for everybody, based on the social bond of belonging to and participating in the local community, redefining the concept of nation (linking culture to the real social dynamics of people interacting in geographical space in a non-static manner), redefining validity periods (moving from a bureaucratic approach to a social approach better tuned to reality) and redefining geographical scope (international-local: glocal), with the emphasis on multilateral civic citizenship permitting participation and governance by all those living in a territory in whatever manner.

A different but no less challenging appeal for the importance of the local is made by Will Kymlicka (2003). He suggests that a model of a 'multicultural nation state' has been emerging in the Western world in recent years. It can be defined by three criteria (Kymlicka, 2003):

• That the state is not the possession of the dominant national group but belongs equally to all citizens.

BEING INTERCULTURAL

BOX 8.1 LIVING IN HARMONY PROGRAMME, AUSTRALIA

To help manage population change, the Australian government introduced the Living in Harmony Programme, which aims to promote mutual respect, Australian values, community participation and a sense of belonging for everyone. The programme includes:

- funding for community projects in localities;
- collaborative partnerships to address strategic issues;
- ad hoc discretionary grants for significant emerging issues;
- a public information strategy that includes Harmony Day.

Harmony Day, celebrated annually on 21 March, aims to bring people together to promote Australian values (respect, fairness and equality for all) and to celebrate the Australian way of life.

Funded community projects are designed to engage the whole community in promoting harmony, interaction and partnerships to build positive community relations. Several sets of funding have helped nearly 350 community projects to deliver cross-cultural activity.

Communities have responded by working together to translate what the national shared values mean to them at local level. These values include: respect for the individual, a commitment to the rule of law, equality, tolerance, fair play and compassion for those in need (Commission on Integration and Cohesion, 2007b).

- That assimilationist and exclusionary nation-building policies have been replaced by policies of recognition and accommodation.
- That historical injustice has been acknowledged.

Kymlicka (2003) says that some of the most successful of these states have been those that have developed as multinational federations, for example Canada that comprises Anglophone and Francophone parts, Belgium comprising Flemish and Walloon elements, and Switzerland with its French, German and Italian elements. He argues that these states have created legal frameworks that protect the rights and culture of all groups irrespective of relative size and asks how must we judge their effectiveness (Kymlicka, 2003):

> *From one point of view, they are clearly a great success. They are among the most peaceful, democratic and prosperous countries in the world. They have learned how to resolve their conflicts between different linguistic and national groups in a completely peaceful and democratic way. The absence of political violence is quite extraordinary... From another point of view, however, it must be acknowledged that these countries can also be seen as failures, or at least as disappointments. In particular, the lived experience of inter-group relations is hardly a model of robust or constructive intercultural exchange.*
>
> *[I]ntergroup relations are often highly politicized, as members of both sides are over-sensitive to perceived slights, indignities and misunderstandings. As a result, many people avoid inter-group contact where possible, or at least do not go out of their way to increase their contact with members of the other group. When contact does take place, it tends to reduce quickly to rather crude forms of bargaining and negotiation, rather than any deeper level of cultural sharing or common deliberation, reinforcing the underlying sense of 'solitude' between the groups.*

This is very interesting. Kymlicka is suggesting that even countries with highly advanced forms of recognition and protection of minority rights may not guarantee that people get on at the level of the street and that, indeed, a multicultural approach at the national level may even prove a disincentive to people behaving interculturally at the local level. Kymlicka's solution to this is to give far greater emphasis to the city and the local as the location in which to build a new form of cross-cultural polity and citizenship, and this adds weight to our own call for a distinct form of local citizenship.

Kymlicka does, however, sound one important note of caution. He suggests that many of the people who would be the first to describe themselves as 'intercultural citizens' may actually be more part of the problem than of the solution:

> *arguments for enhancing the intercultural skills and knowledge of individuals do not tell us much about which groups we should learn more about. In particular, they do not give us any reason to learn more about local groups living next to us within our own country, than about distant groups living in other countries or even other continents.*
>
> *This is precisely what we see in many multination states ... while French-speaking Belgians have become more cosmopolitan and intercultural, fewer and fewer of them know or care about the internal life of the Flemish society in Belgium (and vice versa)...*
>
> *Many people seem to prefer a form of global interculturalism, focused on learning about distant/world cultures, to local interculturalism, focused on learning about neighbouring groups.* (Kymlicka, 2003)

Kymlicka may be right that this applies to the multination states but if this test were applied to the UK, we suspect the same picture would emerge. So what can this tell us about the new form of local leadership and citizenship for which we are striving? If we were to take a sceptical view, we might conclude that the UK's culturally diverse towns and cities contain very many people of an open and liberal disposition, and who also possess qualities and energies that could make them leaders or active citizens, but that many of them behave like Kymlicka's Swiss and Belgians. They might work actively for, say, the restitution of Aboriginal land rights in Australia or the protection of traditional ways of life in Namibia, but have little or nothing to say to the Nigerian they pass in the street or the Bangladeshi in their corner shop. At worst we could say this is little more than a form of exoticizing the stranger who is at a safe distance, while making invisible the stranger who is too close for comfort.

So in our quest for a new local citizenship, we can say that while being of a cosmopolitan outlook is important, it is not the defining characteristic. It seems to us that to be a true citizen is not just about having the right attitudes or about having certain rights conferred upon one. Essentially there has to be a element of agency and proactivity. In order to be a citizen one has to do things that make one a citizen. The things that make one a citizen are also the things that build civic capacity, sociability, trust, inter-reliance and reciprocity and thus make a community.

HARMONY THROUGH CONFLICT

We talked earlier about one of the problems with many of the places that experienced riots in the UK; this was that the local establishment had settled into a pattern of governance that avoided or suppressed debate and conflict and denied the space and forums to enable disagreement to be heard. Ash Amin (2006) has argued that this has distorted our understanding of why these riots took place and may well distort our response to them. He says it is wrong to portray them as race riots – instead they were 'civic riots' initiated by a group who felt invisible and disenfranchised and who made a statement of its presence and its need for the state to respond to and accommodate it. While Amin (2006) would not advocate rioting as a regular expression of active citizenship he argues that:

> *The ultimate test of a good city is whether the urban public culture can withstand pluralism and dissent. This is not to provide licence for gratuitous protest or the violence of those bent on harm. Instead it stands for 'participative parity' in a public sphere, such that new voices can emerge, the disempowered can stake a claim, the powerful can cease to hold free rein and the future can be made through a politics of engagement rather than a politics of plan. On*

Box 8.2 Managing conflict:
The Block, Sydney

The Block is a disused factory site in the Redfern neighbourhood of Sydney, Australia. Blighted by many familiar inner-urban problems, particularly drug use, the area was designated for 'clean up' as part of the city's preparations for the 2000 Olympics. The potential for dispute arose from the presence of two resident communities with widely different views: a long-standing conservative white community whose vision was for a park with a police station at its centre, and the Redfern Aboriginal Corporation who wanted the site for Aboriginal economic and community purposes.

Embarrassed by protests at its plans, the city council called upon a social planning consultant, Dr Wendy Sarkissian, for help. Having listened to as many voices as possible, she decided that there were viewpoints that, no matter how toxic or painful, needed to be brought out into the open and heard. These included white suspicions that any Aboriginal project could only be a front for further drug trade activity and deeply held resentment against 200 years of white suppression of Aboriginal culture and land rights. Sarkissian's decision was to hold a 'speak out' at which all were encouraged to release their fears and concerns. It was an angry and potentially dangerous encounter in which all sides, including Sarkissian, came in for criticism but ultimately it led to the joint preparation of ten guidelines underpinning a new masterplan for the area that all sides were prepared to stick to.

The message from this is that the avoidance of controversy may be expedient in the short term but may cause longer-term damage and that conflict, while never a pleasant experience, may be a necessary and potentially positive part of the planning and development process. As such it needs to be part of the professional's toolkit of skills to be able to work with conflict and to manage it in ways that are not ultimately destructive or divisive.

While Sarkissian is doubtless a remarkable practitioner, she exhibits skills that others can and should be exercising on a more regular basis. The first of these is preparation – a painstaking process in which she spoke widely to all protagonists, being prepared to

listen without judgement, which ultimately built within her the
trust and social capital that enabled her to 'ride the tiger' of the
speak-out. Second, she had succeeded in creating a 'safe space'
in which unpleasant things could be aired without them becoming
explosive. More than this, she had succeeded by formalizing or
'ceremonializing' the disputation, and some people have talked of
the need to take deep seated conflict beyond a safe space to a
'sacred space', with the idea of moving everyone to 'higher ground'.
There are interesting echoes here of successful conflict resolution
in South Africa and Northern Ireland. Third, Sarkissian recognized
'the need for a language and process of emotional involvement
or embodiment' using a range of techniques such as story-telling,
drama, music and visualization to enable people of widely different
backgrounds to describe the world as they saw it (Sandercock,
2003a).[3]

*the part of civic leaders this requires a certain confidence
in the creative powers of disagreement and dissent, in the
legitimacy that flows from popular involvement, and in the
vitality thrown up by making the city available to all.*

So an intercultural city has to be an engaged, argumentative and
an essentially *political* place. Someone who has addressed this issue
head on is Chantal Mouffe (2000). She argues that since the early
1990s with the collapse of the Soviet Union, the so-called 'end of
history' notion, the triumph of individual consumerism over collective movements, the gradual migration of political parties in
many democracies towards the centre ground and the replacement
of policy by presentation, the orthodox view has been that political
debate and engagement is a thing of the past. It has been replaced by
a rational morality and disputes are now resolved not by debate but
by recourse to the law and the achievement of consensus through
deliberative procedures. This, Mouffe argues, has served to remove
passion and emotion from public life and that, finding no outlet
through legitimate political channels, these passions have had to be

expressed through other channels such as the radical right or religious fundamentalism. As well as passion, we have lost engagement. This has produced a denuded form of citizenship in which we are increasingly distanced from each other, and our relationships are increasingly mediated by private or public third parties such as the legal profession and the welfare state.

Mouffe (2000) argues for a more radical and engaged democracy. She dubs it agonistic pluralism and explains it as follows:

> Antagonism *is struggle between enemies, while* agonism *is struggle between adversaries... from the perspective of 'agonistic pluralism' the aim of democratic politics is to transform* antagonism *into* agonism. *This requires providing channels through which collective passions will be given ways to express themselves over issues, which, while allowing enough possibility for identification, will not construct the opponent as an enemy but as an adversary. An important difference with the model of 'deliberative democracy', is that for 'agonistic pluralism', the prime task of democratic politics is not to eliminate passions from the sphere of the public, in order to render a rational consensus possible, but to mobilize those passions towards democratic designs.*
>
> *One of the key theses of agonistic pluralism is that, far from jeopardizing democracy, agonistic confrontation is in fact its very condition of existence. Modern democracy's specificity lies in the recognition and legitimation of conflict.*
> (Mouffe, 2000, original emphasis)

This then provides us with the building blocks of a new form of local intercultural leadership and citizenship. Leaders need to be creative risk-takers, prepared to cope with the uncertainties thrown up when barriers are removed and openness encouraged, in the knowledge that the new ideas, energies and alliances also released will outweigh the negative forces. Leaders can appear in many guises, whether in conventional politics, street politics, business, faith or culture. They

Box 8.3 The creative management of conflict, Turin

The city of Turin has not only accepted that intercultural conflict is a reality that must be recognized and faced, but has positively embraced the 'creative management of conflict' as an opportunity to build active and integrated citizenship.

Through several separate but inter-related programmes of work in various parts of the city, the council and its partners have invested impressive levels of resource and skill in engaging directly at the points of fracture and flashpoint where public authorities in other cities fear to tread.

It begins on the street – a place that the project management floridly describe as bearing some comparison to the African savannah in terms of its 'survival of the fittest' mentality. But an accompaniment to this state of nature is a rich ecosystem of languages, cultures, skills and aptitudes that can be released and positively channelled through a sensitive and intelligent approach. The city trains and employs a team of intercultural 'mediators on the street' to engage directly with young people, street traders, new arrivals and established residents to understand emerging trends, anticipate disputes, find common ground and build joint enterprises. The first cohort of eight young people originated from Algeria, Congo, Morocco, Serbia, Peru, Brazil and Italy and began work in three areas: Porta Palazzo (the great market and zone of meeting, notorious for the sale of illegal or counterfeit items and petty crime), San Salvario (the zone near the station where there have been skirmishes between established residents and new arrivals) and Barriera of Milan (a large area of flats where new arrivals are often first housed).

One illustrative example of the anticipatory skills of the mediators is given by a recent incident in Porta Palazzo. The police department initiated a crackdown on street crime that, superficially, produced the desired effect of making the area feel safer but actually displaced criminals into an adjacent public park used by parents and young children. The mediators were able to intervene quickly to prevent a possible clash and to engage some of the disaffected youth in community activities.

One step beyond the street, the city – in association with agency Gruppo Abele – has set about a programme of creating spaces where intercultural conflict can be addressed. It has opened three Casa dei Conflittl (or Homes of Conflict) that are staffed by ten skilled mediators plus volunteers. They are not designed primarily to solve specific problems but to 'receive' the warring parties and to instil a culture within the neighbourhood that conflict can be managed. If appropriate they will then refer people on to specialist problem-solvers but the primary factor is that communication dealt with quickly and locally is the best way of building an interdependent community.

A further step is the negotiation of 'neighbourhood contracts'. An example of this is Via Arquata where 24 voluntary organizations and public authorities have formed a 'tavola sociale' to anticipate and manage intercultural conflicts.[4]

need to be courageous in challenging myths, stereotypes and mendacity and to lead and shape alternative images and narratives.

The intercultural citizen is not necessarily a person who is sitting on neighbourhood committees five nights a week but is someone who is prepared to act in order to explain their own position and to understand the position of another. Citizenship to us is not waiting upon decisions on everything to be handed down from above, whether in the form of legal edict or religious judgement, but is being prepared to find a solution through argument, mediation and creativity. The intercultural citizen is someone who recognizes the 'Other' in their midst and is prepared to engage with the 'Other' as an adversary in order to find a solution.

The intercultural city is not always an easy or a stable place and demands high levels of maintenance in order to prevent some of its virtues turning into vices. It is worth working for, though, because:

> *The city of open rights can become a place of violence against those least able to defend themselves or a place of self-centred advancement ... placed within the context*

> *of a vigorous and confident urban public culture, the open city is better equipped to channel antagonism towards deliberative and agonistic disputes in the public arena capable of some degree of reconciliation or mutual recognition.* (Amin, 2006)

We cannot emphasize enough the importance of restoring the political (both formal and informal) to the heart of civic life. Interculturalism without adversarial engagement runs the risk of becoming simply a modern, corporate 'third way' version of the discredited cronyism that gave local multiculturalism a bad name. Because the city of Amsterdam has been one of the pioneers of local intercultural city policies, it has proved a fascinating guinea pig for some of the opportunities and challenges that can be encountered. One group of observers, while approving of much that has been achieved, are critical that in their zeal to drive change quickly and efficiently, the authorities have closed down the space for 'agonistic dispute in the public arena':

> *One important consequence of the stress on immediate results ... is that ethnic organisations are forced to neglect their role as vehicles for political socialisation: they are encouraged to view themselves as service providers with a short term perspective... [It also has the effect of] depoliticizing societal problems ... organisations that aim to structurally improve the position of ethnic minorities through political struggles have no role to play.* (Uitermark et al, 2005)

Enough of the theory though. Comedia has commissioned research in numerous international locations to test whether these ideas reflect the lived experience of people striving to make an intercultural polity and community in diverse cities and neighbourhoods.

BRIDGERS AND MIXERS: INTERCULTURAL CITY LEADERSHIP

Comedia commissioned two pieces of research designed to identify new forms of intercultural leadership and citizenship. Our first study (Zachary, 2005) compared the approaches taken by several US cities to the attraction and accommodation of overseas migrants, and particularly the role played by civic leadership. It started from the recognition that it is almost a *sine qua non* of US urban policy that cities must grow and that in order to do this they must primarily attract migrants, internal and international. The study analyses the varying success with which each city has accomplished this.

An impressive story emerged from Oakland, a city in the San Francisco bay area. Traditionally a blue-collar city, it followed a familiar pattern in the 1970s of industrial restructuring and white flight, leaving the inner core largely populated by African Americans and the threat of bipolarity exacerbating decline and attempts to revive it. Despite proximity to San Francisco, the city was not a natural stopping point for foreign immigrants, and experience across the US suggests that cities with significant or majority black populations are not known for being proactive about immigrant attraction (with the possible exception of Atlanta). Oakland, however, has bucked this trend as a city of 400,000 people of which 40 per cent are now foreign-born, mainly from Mexico, China, Philippines, Yemen and Nigeria. From 1980 to 2000, the foreign-born population of metropolitan Oakland rose by 206 per cent and the result is a vibrant and dynamic city with a diversified economy and GDP growth. The success is attributed to a strategy adopted by the black middle class ascendancy of the city. One notable initiative has been investment in the public education system to fast-track new arrivals into skills and jobs. The so-called community college provides a valuable stepping-stone to university and middle-class entry in the American system.

The city's mayor for most of the 1990s was an African American, Elihu Harris, who undercut his affirmative alliances with blacks by forging effective links with new Americans. Also important was the mayor's appointment of a chief of staff, Jeanette Dong, from the Chinese community and the encouragement to all ethnic groups to register to vote and elect co-ethnics onto the city council. This inevitably created political tensions but was, in the view of Dong, a positive rather than a negative sign – evidence that the city is vibrant and is attempting to make a future through interaction and dealing with difference, rather than through segregation and mutual indifference.

The case of Oakland contrasts starkly with the experience of Pittsburgh. Our research suggests that while Pittsburgh has not been negligent of its demographic problems, as a classic black/white bipolar city, it has preferred to seek to supplement its population through black and white migrants from within the US. Unlike our first example, the city has not launched campaigns either to promote the city to international migrants, nor has it tried to raise awareness of migrants in its own citizens with a view to making them more receptive of strangers. There has not been the same investment in language services or public education. Interestingly it seems that Pittsburgh has been engaged in a familiar campaign to attract a share of the highly skilled and talented elite of international migrants, in which it has had some limited success, but has completely failed to recognize the value of also attracting larger numbers of low and intermediary skilled people to fill the gaps left by out-migration.

The conclusion of our findings in the US is that most American cities now consider a constant replenishment of new foreign-born migrants as part of their economic and social lifeblood. Many also see increased diversification as a route out of the racial segregation and strife that characterized bipolar US cities of the past. With Americans of mixed race now numbering over 7 million and rising fast, increased hybridization of the population is also seen as a new stabilizing influence in a society that has had such trouble in the past with miscegenation.

But while Pittsburgh preferred a strategy of cherry-picking the migrants it felt would add greatest value to its economy, with little regard for wider issues of citizenship and community relations, Oakland has shown that a determined city, strongly led and clearly

BEING INTERCULTURAL

BOX 8.4 INTERCULTURAL LEADERSHIP IN BOSNIA

This is the story of not one but two remarkable leaders who defended and then rebuilt a historic intercultural city in the most difficult of circumstances. If the city of Tuzla is known around the world it is possibly as the location of the last but one of the bloodiest atrocities of the Yugoslav war when, with the ceasefire looming in May 1995, Serb gunners fired a shell into a market place full of teenagers, killing 71 of them.

For most of the war, Tuzla had kept it at bay and, more importantly, held together as a multifaith community of Catholic Croats, Orthodox Serbs and Bosniak Muslims. It is said that throughout history Tuzla's greatest attribute had been its internal cohesion in the face of external invaders and, even more than most Bosnian cities, its economy and social structure had resisted segregation on ethnic lines. Nevertheless the massacre placed enormous strain on this equilibrium and post-war recriminations threatened to tear the city apart. Into this crisis stepped Selim Beslagic, President of the United Bosnia and Herzegovina Social Democratic Party and between 1990 and 2000 the mayor of Tuzla. Following the war, Beslagic was determined Tuzla should be a place resilient to further conflict and so established processes of reconciliation and capacity building. One of his first moves was to found the Citizen's Forum, one of the first multiethnic NGOs in the Balkans, dedicated to the promotion of civil rights. He also supported the creation of the Centre for Peace and Non-Violence. He also cleverly developed a symbiotic model that persuaded citizens that if they exhibited peace and cooperation to the outside world, foreign investment for reconstruction would flow in; and he persuaded foreign investors that if they supported Tuzla, the cause of intercultural cooperation would be reinforced. Beslagic has received much recognition for his work, including a nomination for the Nobel Prize.

In 2000 Beslagic was succeeded as mayor by Jasmin Imamovic, a charismatic lawyer as well as best-selling poet and novelist. Where the older man established the solid foundation of intercommunal cohesion, his protégée has followed up with astute and inclusive political skills designed to prevent the emergence of factionalism. Imamovic embarked upon a two-year process of public consultation on a scale previously unknown in the former Yugoslavia. This involved ongoing engagement with 40 local communes and voluntary organizations in which views on a wide variety of issues were canvassed. It has also seen the creation of a Mayoral Advisory Council of 25 unelected advisors representing the ethnic, religious, cultural, age, sexual and professional diversity of the city. He has also initiated a regular six-monthly city-wide survey of public opinion that appears to have the equivalent power to a referendum on key issues. He also personally engages in a lot of local meetings and informal debates in the city's coffee houses and youth clubs.

But Imamovic has also exhibited a remarkable talent for civic entrepreneurialism and the iconic gesture. Tuzla translates as 'salt' and it was from mining this staple of life that the city was built. In doing so, however, the city had over the years quite literally eaten away its own foundations and by the time of Imamovic's succession large areas of the city centre were sinking. In a stroke of brilliance, the mayor declared the city's greatest weakness would be turned into its strength by transforming the sunken land into a great Salt Lake. Now surrounded by beaches and a beautiful park commemorating the victims of the war, it has become one of Bosnia's most popular resorts and is a place for people of all cultures to come together to relax and celebrate.

Mayor Imamovic has also shown great understanding of how cities must position and brand themselves in the competitive new economy. He has carefully cultivated a series of international links and relationships with cities that share a common bond including Barcelona, St Denis, Ravenna, Antalya, Bologna, Gothenburg, Osijek and Pecs. He has also gained membership for Tuzla of several pan-European and international networks. One clever way of building international links, while also sending out clear messages of the city's intentions and also improving the streetscape of the city centre, is his public art programme. He has identified a series of great symbols of humanity (for example, Mozart, Mandela, Shakespeare, the Beatles) and has invited their cities of origin to donate busts or sculptures to be displayed in the city streets. He also scans the world for important new pieces of public art and then asks the cities whether they would donate a copy or allow access to the cast. Through such cultural links, he believes business and investment relationships will follow. Tuzla has led the way among Bosnian cities in demonstrating that city development goes hand in hand with openness and interculturalism.[5]

focused, can realize the diversity dividend through making it easier for people to mix than to avoid each other.

Comedia has made a special study in the UK of people who in our opinion embody the intercultural ideal in practical day-to-day ways.[6] We looked at people in a variety of UK cities from many walks of life who move between different ethnic groups and in the process build greater communication and understanding. We described them as intercultural innovators because they often carve out paths not explored before or they create something new as a consequence of the mixing of two or more cultures. However, many would modestly claim that they are not deliberately setting out to be either leaders or active citizens, but are simply leading their lives in the way that seems most natural considering the hand life has dealt them.

Whether self-consciously or not, we have found in many of these people the building blocks of new intercultural forms of leadership and citizenship and, by extension, a new intercultural polity. Take, for example, Elaine Appelbee, the dynamic director of Bradford Vision, the city's leading partnership body for economic and community regeneration. She describes her revelation when participating in Bradford's Urban Hearings that all ethnic groups in the city had far more concerns in common – poverty, crime, their young people, race, culture and religion – than things that divided them:

> We can all tell you in Bradford how different we are from each other. What this was showing was that the issues, or rather sets of issues, were the same so there was a lot of commonality.[7]

She explains her role in the city as creating a framework for 'letting people define who they are, then bringing them together', and then a third stage of 'looking at the institutions to make them fit' to respond to the demands of engaged communities. This has led her to put the full weight of her organization behind such groundbreaking initiatives as the establishment of an Intercultural Communication and Leadership School in Bradford.

David Faulkner is a senior politician in the city of Newcastle. The city has not been one of Britain's traditional migrant-receiving areas and this meant that political awareness of the issue was very low profile. As migration in the 1990s began to grow there was little consciousness or response from the local policy community, overlooking the fact that the northeast of England was beginning to become a far more diverse region. Politically there is probably little to be gained and many potential pitfalls for a politician who takes a high profile stance on issues of ethnicity and migration but Faulkner felt he had to. Partly, he observed that race relations in the city had become stagnant and stereotyped (in the way we have described

BEING INTERCULTURAL

Box 8.5 The Intercultural Communication and Leadership School

The Intercultural Communication and Leadership School (ICLS) is an international organization that aims to promote community cohesion and prevent local and global conflicts. It gives young people from different cultural, religious and ethnic backgrounds a safe and neutral place to meet and discuss issues important to their area. In addition, it trains young people in conflict resolution and teaches them leadership and media skills, which they can use to influence their local areas. In this way, the programme encourages the development of mutual respect, peaceful contact and long-term cooperation within and across different faith, cultural and ethnic communities.

The seminars arranged by the ICLS run for five days and after they are over, the participants are expected to use the knowledge and experience they have gained to benefit their local communities. The ICLS has held seminars across Europe and Asia since 2002. So far, ten seminars have taken place in the UK including Bradford, Leicester and Walsall with over 100 young people participating in the programmes.[8]

above) and there was little recognition of the newer communities who were arriving in the area, nor of the new cultural hybrids that were emerging. He helped to found an organization, Shakers and Movers, that now provides a hub and an interface for the region's many different communities. He has also developed an expertise in the use of drama as a means of addressing racial harassment and bullying and for finding common ground, and has pushed hard to have this introduced into the city's schools.

Also taking the route of leadership through electoral politics has been Hawarun Hussain. We have already encountered her earlier in this book, coaxing parties of Asian women from Bradford onto the Yorkshire moors often in slingbacks, hijab and burka. This has been a remarkable act of intercultural leadership as it in effect opens 'doors of the mind' to new areas – both spatial and symbolic – that were formerly closed. She set up a Gardening for Health project to counter heart disease among Bangladeshis from rural Sylhet by getting the women to grow vegetables, taking advantage of their rural knowledge (they had stored seeds from the imported vegetables they bought locally) and applying it in an English context of allotments. She is the first Bangladeshi woman councillor for the Green Party and embodies a new style of community politics.

Another who leads people into new, formerly unwelcoming, territory is Parvin Ali. In her case she has set out to demonstrate that Asian women can play an equal part in the world of business through setting up and running the Fatima Women's Network in Leicester. While doing all the things that any business support organization might be expected to do, Fatima also explicitly sets out to 'Facilitate cross-community networking and encourage inter-racial and inter-faith harmony in learning and working environments'.[9] As a Muslim woman who came from a very diverse background – third-generation Malaysian, with an Indian mother and Iranian forefathers, and herself married to a man with Turkish and Pakistani parents – she never felt she set out to demonstrate that Islam is an inherently intercultural faith. The milieu her parents had grown up in of Chinese, South Asians and indigenous Malaysians she defines as 'more in keeping with the way of Islam', in contrast to some Muslims in this country who she finds can be aloof and elitist 'looking down on other people's different ethnicity'.[10]

Maza Dad believes quite literally in getting his hands dirty to bring about ethnic interaction and understanding in the city of Birmingham. He uses football as the way to communicate and bring together young men who may be at risk of falling into crime or forms of extremism. He recalls the first 15 young men:

> *Misfits if you like ... black, white, Asian. The beauty of it is that by the time I finished with these kids they understood that the team they belonged to should mean everything to them ... that the whole team should be there ... I can proudly say that these youngsters ... you'd say Winsome Green [i.e. the local prison] but everyone of them bar one ... has gone to university and on to fantastic jobs.[11]*

Out of a million such small victories is an intercultural citizenship born.

NOTES

1 That is, in the tradition established by Huntington, 1996.
2 See, for example, HM Government, 2006.
3 Further information at www.sarkissian.com.au.
4 URBACT at http://urbact.eu/themes/citizen-participation/tools-and-methods.html.
5 Interviews with the author (PW), Tuzla, November and December 2003.
6 The Comedia study of Intercultural Innovators was conducted by Jude Bloomfield during 2005 and early 2006. An outline of the study and findings can be found at www.interculturalcity.com/inter_innovators.htm. A full account of the research is to be published in book form by Comedia.
7 www.interculturalcity.com/inter_innovators.htm.
8 www.intercivilization.net/.
9 www.interculturalcity.com/inter_innovators.htm.
10 www.interculturalcity.com/inter_innovators.htm.
11 www.interculturalcity.com/inter_innovators.htm.

9

Indicators of Openness and Interculturalism

Our aim is to find out more about whether ethnic diversity and intercultural mixing are a source of dynamism for cities. To do this we need to pose certain questions that are not normally asked of a city because, we suspect, they have proved too difficult to measure or evaluate.

We might ask how ethnically diverse a city is, and this (as we have seen earlier) is easily answered with reference to statistical data derived from a census and other sources. But there is another set of questions including:

- How easily or frequently do different ethnicities mix?
- How open is the city, that is, how easy is it to enter and move between different communities or institutional networks?
- To what extent do people of different ethnic and cultural backgrounds actually cooperate and collaborate?

It is no surprise that such questions are rarely asked as it is very difficult to envisage how they could be answered, at least in ways that would enable the comparison of findings over different periods of time or between different places. This chapter sets out a new way of thinking about these and related questions and suggests practical steps that policy-makers and practitioners might take to systematically answer them. We propose a new toolkit for better understanding and planning of cities: *indicators of openness and interculturalism.*

APPLES WITH PEARS? COMPARING THE APPROACHES OF INTERNATIONAL CITIES TO DIVERSITY

The first stage is to appreciate that even in the Western world, cities operate within widely varying national and local jurisdictions and value systems and that these influence the way they may respond over time to demographic change and cultural diversity. We have already noted earlier that even between the US, UK, France, Germany and Italy there are considerable and even diametrically opposite approaches at the level of national policy. We have also considered briefly the tension that can emerge between national states that jealously guard their prerogative to regulate borders, security and citizenship, and cities who are in the frontline of actually trying to make heterogeneous communities work.

In this regard we review some important research undertaken by Michael Alexander (2001, 2003, 2006). Based upon a study of 25 European cities in 12 countries, Alexander has assessed mission statements and practical actions (or lack thereof) to gauge the attitude of local authorities to the increasing cultural diversity of their cities over a 30-year period, within the context of key policy domains such as employment, housing, education and policing. From widespread comparison, he identifies five broad categories of policy approach that can be summarized as:

- Non-policy – migrants are regarded as a transient phenomenon with no impact upon the city.
- Guestworker policy – migrants are regarded as a temporary labour force that will eventually return to their countries of origin.
- Assimilationist policy – migrants are permanent but their Otherness will be encouraged to disappear as they are absorbed.

- Pluralist (or multicultural) policy – migrants are permanent and their Otherness should be encouraged.
- Intercultural policy – migrants are permanent though their Otherness should not be overemphasized.

Drawing upon actual examples from cities, Alexander then draws up a typology of different policy approaches adopted by local authorities. We have adapted the main points of it to form Figure 9.1.

This raises several interesting questions. For instance, Alexander reminds us that urban policy is not static and can evolve over time in response to local and external factors. So, for example, while Amsterdam or Berlin might have had policies in the guestworker category in the 1970s they are now generally pluralist or intercultural. Meanwhile Athens for much of the period remained in the non-policy category, while Lille has been largely assimilationist throughout. It would be easy to draw a normative conclusion from this that there is a naturally progressing trajectory from the left of the table to the right as cities become more sophisticated, but this would be misleading. Certainly it is increasingly difficult for places to ignore migrants or to assume that they will not become permanent but there remains a strong commitment to assimilation in some cities. Nor should it be assumed that the intercultural stage is considered the highest level of attainment or the final resting place for a city. For example, one study of Amsterdam has described the profound debates and extensive opposition to the city's express intention to move from a multicultural to an intercultural approach, which is seen as a cover for the return of policies of incorporation and assimilation (Uitermark et al, 2005). This might be partly explained by the fact that many cities do not necessarily exhibit a uniformity of policy statement and deed across all domains, with perhaps one or two agencies or departments racing ahead or lagging behind the others, leading to some strange inconsistencies.

Nevertheless, Alexander provides a valuable model for understanding where cities lie in absolute and comparative terms, and what possible trajectories they might follow. This gives us the foundation upon which to think about how cities might begin to take a more

	Non-policy	Guest worker policy	Assimilationist policy	Multicultural policy	Intercultural policy
Minority group organizations	State ignores them	Informal cooperation on limited issues	State does not recognize them (Lille)	State supports them as agents of empowerment (Rome)	State supports them as agents of integration (Cologne, Zurich)
Labour market	Ignore. Turn a blind eye to black market activity	Minimal regulation – limited vocational assistance	General vocational support – non-ethnic criteria (Lille)	Anti-discrimination policy; affirmative action on training and hiring (Amsterdam 1980s)	Anti-discrimination policy; intercultural competence and linguistic skills emphasized
Housing	Ignore migrant housing. React to crisis with temporary shelters (Rome 1960s)	Short-term housing solutions; minimal regulation of private rental sector (Amsterdam 1970s)	Equal access to social housing – non-ethnic criteria. Ignore ethnic discrimination in housing market	Anti-discriminatory lettings policy. Affirmative access to social housing	Anti-discriminatory lettings policy. Ethnic monitoring. Encouragement for ethnic housing mix
Education	Ad hoc recognition of migrant children	Enrol migrant children in schools (Berlin 1970s)	Emphasis on national language, history, culture. State ignores or suppresses supplementary schooling (Amsterdam 1980s)	Special support for diverse schools. Mother tongue language support. Religious and cultural education (Birmingham)	National and mother tongue/culture teaching. Intercultural competence for all. Desegregation.
Policing	Migrants as security problem (Rome 1980s)	Police as agents of migrant regulation, monitoring, deportation (Athens)	High profile policing of migrant areas	Police as social workers. Proactive anti-racism enforcement (Leicester)	Police as agents of inter-ethnic conflict management (Stuttgart)

	Non-policy	Guest worker policy	Assimilationist policy	Multicultural policy	Intercultural policy
Public awareness	Migrants as a potential threat	Migrants as economically useful but of no political, social or cultural significance	Campaigns to encourage tolerance of minorities, but intolerance of those not assimilating	'Celebrate diversity' festivals and city branding campaigns (Berlin, Frankfurt)	Campaigns to emphasize intercultural togetherness
Urban development	Ignore emergence of ethnic enclaves – disperse if crisis arises (Rome 1980s)	Ethnic enclaves tolerated but considered temporary (Berlin 1970s)	Ethnic enclaves considered an urban problem. Dispersal policy and gentrification. Oppose symbolic use of space (Brussels, Paris)	Recognize enclaves and ethnic community leadership. Area-based regeneration. Symbolic recognition e.g. minarets (Amsterdam, Frankfurt)	Encouragement of ethnically mixed neighbourhoods and public space (Stuttgart)
Governance and citizenship	No rights or recognition	No rights or recognition	Facilitate naturalization. No ethnic consultative structures (Lille)	Community leadership, consultative structures and resource allocation ethnically based (Amsterdam)	Encouragement of cross-cultural leadership, association and consultation. Acknowledgement of hybridity. Emphasis on functional not symbolic use of space (Stuttgart)

Figure 9.1 Policy approaches

Source: Based on Alexander (2001, 2003)

strategic approach to the way they move forward, and how they might start to understand the factors that influence performance and how to monitor and assess them.

THE NEED FOR NEW INDICATORS

If we wish to understand how an intercultural city can be measured then there is a need to move beyond a simple understanding of demographic quantification and the degrees of physical proximity of ethnicities to getting to grips with the quantity and quality of interaction between different people. Thus we have to ask different questions of the data already available to us and gather new forms of data; and we then need to establish a set of indicators that are readily comparable across different periods of time and jurisdictions.

Indicators comprise key variables and provide snapshots of moments in time. Compared over time they give an idea of direction and the scope of change. Inevitably they provide an incomplete picture because of the pragmatics of data collection and its limitations, the criteria selected, the vagaries of quantifying things and the social limits of perception of qualitative measures. The indicators may be purely documentary (for example, does a policy or law exist), quantitative (can it be counted?), or qualitative (concerned with opinions and perceptions). So while some indicators are tangible and measurable, others are intangible and record peoples' perception of openness, such as, 'Do you feel the city is open and welcoming?' or 'Do you experience intolerance in your workplace or in public?' Some data can be established through existing sources, such as the census, while other data will need to be garnered through research or interviews.

Below we have produced the basis for a methodology. Two grids outline the possible indicators that might be adopted to determine the extent to which a national state or a city is moving towards a greater level of understanding of its own diversity. We argue that places need to start measuring more of these *indicators of openness* because the very process of gathering data in this way, and the findings that ensue, will make a place begin to think differently about itself.

INDICATORS OF OPENNESS

To address the question, 'How open is a city?' we have identified four principal spheres of influence:

- the institutional framework;
- the business environment;
- civil society;
- public space.

We outline below the kinds of questions that should be asked and the places one should look in order to determine the degree of openness.

The openness of the institutional framework

This will be determined principally by the regulatory and legislative framework within national or local government.

At a national or federal level, *easy access to citizenship* is, for example, an indicator, and the means of measurement would include: the naturalization rate; provision of language classes to learn the new language; and access to health and social welfare for refugees. Another indicator would be *respect for international human rights or law*, and the means of measurement would include: the recognition of right of family reunion; the recognition of the Geneva Convention on refugees; and the existence of an anti-discrimination law.

Moving into policy areas such as education, the presence of an *intercultural/multicultural citizenship curriculum* is an indicator, as would be the take-up by students of programmes to study abroad for a year or the number of school kids going abroad on exchange schemes (and the number coming to the UK) and the number of interpreters employed by the health and social services

At a city level an indicator and measure would be the existence of an intercultural strategy, the framing of intercultural planning regulations and guidance, and cultural awareness training in public institutions. More complicated, but achievable, would be the drawing up of a *power map* of the people of real influence in the city and an assessment of their ethnic diversity.

The level of cultural diversity represented by the composition of government bodies or elected members on a local government council, compared to the demographic make-up of the community being represented, can be seen as an indication of institutional openness.

The openness of the business environment

This refers to trade and industry, the job market and training. Indicators might be drawn from the internal policy commitments of businesses on recruitment and training, and on anti-discrimination/racial awareness issues and consequent monitoring and evaluation of outputs. At a national or federal level this could mean asking whether key business associations, such as the Confederation of British Industry, address the cultural diversity of the workforce and the 'business case for diversity'. An interesting measure might be a comparison between the number of culturally diverse students in professional training within the tertiary sector as compared to the level of diversity in employment within those professions.

At the city level, one would look for a chamber of commerce that addresses these issues of ethnic diversity in employment practices. The means of measuring this might be the ethnic composition of staff and leadership positions and cultural awareness training in the major 20 companies and a random sample of 30 smaller companies. Other indicators that might be assessed include:

- the foreign trade of local companies and their diasporic links;
- the ownership of local businesses of various sizes;
- the recruitment of employees from the outside, the diversity of the retail offer;
- the destinations of airport and train traffic.

In terms of employment, one might research and assess the percentage of jobs requiring minority languages, such as call centres, banks and financial services, the import–export trade, interpreters in hospitals, community social workers, therapists, youth and community workers, and *intercultural mediators*, that is people who help 'translate' across cultures. Alternatively one could ask how many ethnic minority firms are winning tenders from the city? What is the density of links and trade of ethnic minority businesses with countries of origin? Or what is the ethnic breakdown of take-up of training under government supported schemes?

A set of subsidiary questions might also be explored through interviews or self-completion questionnaires. For instance, has the Race Relations (Amendment) Act 2000, or other relevant legislation in participating countries, shifted priorities, especially in private companies? For relocating companies that conduct foreign trade, questions might include:

- Why did you come here?
- What keeps you here?
- How do you evaluate your choice?
- What role, if any, did the existence of a diverse population have in your choice?
- What three things could influence you to be more committed to the city?

Research might uncover what has put some companies off locating to a place or why others might be considering moving out.

The openness of civil society

The extent to which the social fabric of a place is accessible and permeable can be measured. At the city level, indicators might include the diversity of representation on health, welfare, and education boards or management and community forums. The ethnic make-up of senior management tiers in the 20 top public and private sector organizations could also tell a story

Cross-cultural economic, social, cultural and civic networks could be measured from observation and interviews to establish whether there are any ethnically and culturally mixed business associations, social clubs, religious groups, political parties and movements. Positive cultural representations or images of the 'Other' in the media, the number of minority broadcast channels and minority programmes within mainstream public service broadcasting can also function as indicators of openness. In addition it is useful to look at projects that involve different ethnic groups.

Much of the openness in public attitudes is seed-bedded in schools, and aside from assessing the overall curriculum, relevant indicators could include: the number of school children learning foreign languages and going on foreign exchanges, or the percentage of UK-born minority ethnic students at university.

In the social domain, the range of questions to explore might include: incidents of racial assault or crimes against asylum seekers; and, through interview, the public treatment of refugees and the incidence of cross-cultural child adoption.

Looking at a city's internal and external place marketing, one could assess how it has decided to project itself to the outside world. Research might ask whether it actively engages in twinning networks and other international arrangements, or whether the city actively searches out best practice from abroad or has external 'critical friends'.

Our Auckland study found that the notion of openness can be a highly personal one (Brecknock Consulting, 2006). For example, there are places in many cities where even locally born residents might feel alienated and insecure. Feelings of openness can be associated with: interpersonal relationships; interaction with groups or organizations; attitudes expressed by social, religious, business or political institutions; and by the planning and design of cities. Alienation and isolation can be the result of both the physical design of the built environment creating places that say 'no', or by the attitudes experienced in dealing with people in the street or in positions of power.

To engage with others, people need to feel secure and accepted in their community and have access to the same opportunities as all citizens. This means feeling a sense of entitlement to partake in anything one wishes to. In order to participate in intercultural exchange and draw creativity and innovation from the encounter there needs to be a sense of self-worth. As an Auckland respondent stated, 'People need to find their own identity first, then renegotiate what their culture means in the new environment while maintaining their specialness'. The proposition is that an intercultural approach to policy and planning can assist in enhancing social cohesion and building an open and inclusive community through increased cultural awareness and understanding of others.

The openness of public space

This focuses on the extent to which people feel they have the 'freedom of the city' or whether there are spaces or whole neighbourhoods that feel closed or even hostile to one or more groups within the city. The indicators would measure the degree of mixing in housing and neighbourhoods, safety and mobility of ethnic minorities in all areas of the city based on crime statistics; participation in public facilities such as libraries and cultural venues in the city centre; perceptions of cultural inclusiveness in public space; and views on which city institutions are welcoming and which are forbidding. This could be measured by:

- evaluating how mixed public sector and housing association housing allocation policies are;
- audience research on the level of mixed use of city centre libraries, other public cultural venues and sports centres;
- evaluating the range of diverse cultural events/festivals in the city's artistic programme and whether they reflect the plurality of cultures in the city;
- the number of interfaith organizations/forums and meeting places to assess the level and density of contact between religions.

Much of this could happen by observation and interviews in colleges, swimming pools, parks, libraries, community centres, theatres and concert halls but should also include less tangible spaces such as the airwaves and cyberspace. In regard to spaces with a particular influence over the more general atmosphere of the city, it might be necessary to initiate the kind of detailed observational studies of individual and group behaviour we described earlier in the book (for example, Dixon et al, 2005b).

INDICATORS OF INTERCULTURALISM

Once a place starts to understand itself in terms of degrees of openness and the dynamic relationship between elements of its social, economic, physical and institutional framework, it will then be ready to gather and interpret indicators that will tell the story of its interculturalism. The indicators of interculturalism measure the results of openness, both of organized intervention and voluntary effort, and so reflect the lived experience of an intercultural lifeworld. Indicators would include:

- intermarriage and other forms of social and cultural mixing;
- crossover networks, intercultural businesses, jobs and new professions;
- products that embody cultural crossover or fusion;
- the presence of intercultural literacy programmes in public administration;
- training in and remuneration of bilingualism and multilingualism in the business environment;
- the presence of buildings or public art in the city centre that draws on culturally diverse histories and traditions.

NEW QUESTIONS AND ANSWERS

To explore openness and interculturalism at an urban level, and test the assumptions of our Indicators of Openness, we undertook a case study in Bristol. We asked many of the questions relating to the indicators above and refined ones that were more or less usable and explanatory.

BOX 9.1 AN INTERCULTURAL CITY OBSERVATORY, MADRID

In March 2005, Madrid's city council launched a strategic plan to elaborate 'a city for everybody', a 'city of neighbours' appointing mutual responsibilities for both immigrants and natives named the Plan Madrid de Convivencia Social e Intercultural (Madrid Plan for Social and Intercultural Coexistence). The plan constitutes the practical outcome of a debate on migration matters between governmental and non-governmental participants convened within the Foro Social, a social forum established in October 2003. The overall objectives are defined as fostering the institutional progress of immigrant reception at the municipal level, to provide better access to civil rights and resources for immigrants, as well as to improve coexistence between Spaniards and foreigners in order to create dynamic and harmonious neighbourhoods. The Plan Madrid is coordinated by the city's General-Directorate for Immigration, Cooperation for Development and Community Service, affiliated to the Agency for Employment and Citizen Services (Dirección General de Inmigración, Cooperación al Desarrollo y Voluntariado del Area de Gobierno de Empleo y Servicios a la Ciudadanía), which, until 2007, controlled a budget of €41.6 million.

The Plan Madrid contains a clear set of working areas and instruments to attain the goals cited above. The municipality is entrusted with the planning and development of activities and institutions affecting the areas of employment (with the focus on gender equality), social services, immigration and civil participation. Since Plan Madrid was adopted, the city has established the first of three information centres for the integration of immigrants (Oficina Municipal de Información y Orientación para la Integración); another two centres were due to open in October 2006 and April 2007. It has also founded a centre to facilitate immigrants' access to the local housing market called Agencia de Alquiler del Área de Gobierno de Urbanismo y Vivienda e Infraestructuras del Ayuntamiento – integration policy and practices at local level (Accommodation Bureau of the Municipal Office for Urban Housing and Infrastructure). The housing agency collaborates closely with the intercultural mediation services of the city. As regards active participation in city society, various institutions have been established on the basis of Madrid's plan for peaceful coexistence. Several institutions have been established, aimed at initiating an effective intercultural dialogue. In Round Tables for Intercultural Dialogues in the Districts (Mesas Distritales de Dialogo y Convivencia, launched in April 2005) topics of everyday intercultural understanding are supposed to be discussed; representatives of these Round Tables are requested to meet in the Foro de Madrid de Dialogo y Convivencia (Madrid Forum for a Dialogue of Neighbours), which functions as a communication and advisory body on relevant issues. In addition, once in a year the Social Forum (Foro Social) is supposed to take place, following the precedent of the first meetings of the city government in 2004, gathering some 400 people from non-governmental institutions and from among those involved in policy implementation at the local level. Two more instruments are supposed to complete Madrid's institutional setting to target migration issues: the city's programme Apoyo Asociacionismo, starting in April 2006, will promote the creation and establishment of immigrants' organizations, while Apoyo a los Proyectos de la Iniciativa Social para Favorecer la Convivencia Social e Intercultural is a programme, operating since 1995, to support initiatives of Madrid's civil society for the advancement of intercultural coexistence in the city.

In the wake of Plan Madrid a scientific institute, the Observatorio de las Migraciones y de la Convivencia Intercultural de la Ciudad de Madrid (Monitoring Centre for Migration and Intercultural Coexistence of the City of Madrid) has been created. Since October 2004 the centre has exercised analytical as well as practical functions: besides investigating different aspects of the migration phenomenon in the city, it coordinates the exchange of relevant information within competent municipal structures (publishing a monthly bulletin, Dialogos, etc.) (EFILWC, 2007).[1]

Institutional framework	Indicators of openness	Indicators of interculturalism	Means of collection
	easy access to citizenship		naturalization rate
	respect for international human rights		recognition of right of family reunion, government funding for language classes, support services on housing, jobs, (re)training, healthcare, legal advice
	recognition of Geneva convention on refugees treatment of asylum-seekers integration policies		legal recognition, habeas corpus, no discretionary powers or detention centres, right of appeal
	national plan for welcome and integration of refugees		access to health/social welfare by refugees, recognition of special needs, health care, language needs, retraining/ requalification, safe housing, individual caseworkers
	race relations and anti-discrimination legislation		
	promotion of culturally diverse planning		policy commitment and guidance
	compulsory citizenship education within a school curriculum embodying cultural diversity		
	foreign language learning and promotion programmes		take-up by students of programmes to study abroad for a year under Erasmus
	government promotion of ethnic minority training		ethnic breakdown of take-up of training under government supported scheme

Figure 9.2 Indicators of openness and interculturalism: The federal level

	Indicators of openness	Indicators of interculturalism	Means of collection
		national creativity and innovation through diversity strategy	
		promotion of cultural renewal through intercultural dialogue against integration of migrants into a singular national narrative	
Business environment	business association policies addressing cultural diversity of workforce and human capital		
	growth of ethnic minority self-employment		
		recognition, training and remuneration of skills of bi- and multi-lingualism, intercultural literacy and innovation	intercultural business start-ups new products, services and processes
		bursaries, competitions mentoring and funding of intercultural innovation	
		measuring and monitoring of intercultural innovation	
Civil society and services		incidence of mixed-marriages	via census
Public space		national promotion of an intercultural planning model	via census

Figure 9.2 Indicators of openness and interculturalism: The federal level (continued)

Institutional framework	Indicators of openness	Indicators of interculturalism	Means of collection
	existence of a cultural diversity/intercultural strategy		
	cultural awareness training in public institutions		interviews on qualitative assessment training
	public commitment to creating safe haven for asylum seekers and refugees		e.g. participation in 'City of Refuge' programme, Council of Europe Shared Cities or Intercultural City programme of training refugee welcoming or inclusive projects
	anti-discrimination and equal opportunities plans and monitoring of implementation in public institutions		
	culturally and socially mixed housing		socially and culturally mixed housing management policies observation/interviews via housing managers
	intercultural planning guidance		
	fostering cultural exchange and foreign language programmes		number of school children going abroad on exchange schemes and number coming in for language services

Figure 9.3 Indicators of openness and interculturalism: The city level

	Indicators of openness	Indicators of interculturalism	Means of collection
		intercultural literacy training in public administration and institutions	
Business environment			
	ethnic diversity in managerial and professional positions in local workforce		
		new professions of intercultural mediation, animation, programming throughout public services and cultural institutions	monitoring jobs and job briefs
Civil society and services			
	growing overlap between economic, social, cultural and civic networks		look at umbrella, inter- or joint associations, forums, consortia
	growing ethnic mix in leadership positions public, private, voluntary. minorities and mainstream		holders of senior positions in top public and private sector organizations
		cross-cultural economic, social, cultural and civic networks	from observation and interviews on ethnically and culturally mixed business associations, social clubs, religious groups, political parties and movements
		interethnic and inter-faith forums active role in shaping public services	

	Indicators of openness	Indicators of interculturalism	Means of collection
Public space			
	open access, mixed usage of city centre institutions		observation, audience research; favourite place research
	attraction of minorities to city centre cultural institutions		audience research
	growing mixed attraction to ethnic minority neighbourhood cultural institutions		observation and interviews
	growth of mixed estates and neighbourhoods		
	open access public spaces culturally programmed to attract mass public/ young people		
		mixed population usage city centre institutions	observation and interviews in city centre library, museum, swimming pool/leisure centre
		iconic intercultural public institutions	
		cultural diversity of built environment drawing on different cultural traditions	
		culturally inclusive public celebrations/ programming/ broadcasting	

Figure 9.3 Indicators of openness and interculturalism: The city level (continued)

We interviewed 20 people under the age of 40 and another 20 people aged 40 and over who are well known in their fields. The fields included business, public service, universities, political leadership, major media organizations, entrepreneurship, council departments such as planning or leisure, and art. Most of the interviewees had come from outside the city. We also assessed how 20 historical figures had viewed the openness of the city.

The core questions focused on:

- how welcoming the city was;
- the incentives and obstacles to achieve what they wanted in the city;
- the kinds of people they mixed with in terms of their age, cultural or socio-economic backgrounds and neighbourhood;
- whether they felt Bristol was an intercultural place or whether people mainly kept to their own group;
- whether the perception of Bristol was of an open place and what places and spaces in Bristol encouraged intercultural mixing.

The detailed findings are available elsewhere (Comedia, 2006a). In summary, though, the Bristol findings confirm experiences observed in other cities and lead us to the following general conclusions:

- There is a need to establish a city vision, backed explicitly by the leadership, which emphasizes the welcoming of outsiders and of projecting the city as 'the world in one place'.
- Most larger cities are passively tolerant of outsiders and people live side by side. But they are not actively promoting engagement with the 'Other' and crossing boundaries.
- Physical infrastructural barriers, such as road patterns, urban design and transport, are an under-explored arena that can encourage segregation and reduce the possibilities of mixing.
- The problems of poor white working-class estates are as significant as those of poor ethnic minority enclaves.
- The places of intercultural mixing are more likely to be mundane and ordinary like the shopping centre, going to the doctor's surgery or the swimming pool.

- The creative industries and arts sectors are significant arenas where mixing occurs. By their very nature, being activities at the 'cutting edge', they involve exploration and engagement with the 'Other'.
- For the young, especially second- and third-generation immigrants, segregation makes no sense. Day-to-day involvements from work to play mitigate against separation. For this reason the young express greater confidence in an intercultural future.
- In many cases, social class or income bracket will be a more powerful influence than ethnicity in determining who mixes with whom.

Our conclusion is that even though a city may not outwardly display any signs of ethnic tension or antipathy, a passive state of 'benign indifference' is not a sufficient or desirable state. Not only is this perpetuating a state of mutual ignorance that might easily be tipped into suspicion and antagonism by some unforeseen crisis, but it is an unproductive and wasteful situation ensuring the city misses out on untold opportunities for achieving diversity advantage that might arise from greater interaction. By employing the indicators, a city will be able to gauge how near or far it is from becoming intercultural and productively diverse.

NOTES

1 Further information at www.munimadrid.es/Principal/monograficos/ ObservatorioMigra/default.htm.
2 Further information at *Stabsabteilung für Integrationspolitik*, 'A pact for integration: The Stuttgart experience', 2003 available at www.stuttgart. de/sde/global/images/sde_publikationen/s-ip/a_pact_for_integration. pdf. See also *Statistisches Amt der Stadt Stuttgart, 'Einwohnerstruktur'*, 2006, www.stuttgart.de/sde/menu/frame/top.php?seite=http%3A// www.stuttgart.de/sde/publ/gen/7086.htm.

BOX 9.2 AN INTERCULTURAL CITY STRATEGY, STUTTGART

The Department of Integration of Stuttgart City Council states that 'successful integration is the glue for social cohesion and in order to be successful, endeavours of integration need the back-up of a strong partnership between the public sector, private sector and civil society'. To reach that goal the city of Stuttgart signed the 'Pact for Integration' in 2001, institutionalizing the cooperation to promote the social and competitive inclusion of its migrants.

Stuttgart's integration philosophy is defined as consisting of eight so-called 'milestones', embracing areas such as education, economic growth, equal rights and opportunities, political and social participation, pluralism and cultural diversity, spirit of mutual respect and solidarity, participatory communication and international cooperation. In the field of education, the city of Stuttgart emphasizes good German literacy, while encouraging simultaneously bilingual and multilingual education. German language training is provided at a very early stage of a child's life in order to prevent later social and educational exclusion. Moreover, parents with migration backgrounds are 'offered some help' in supporting the learning capacities of their children. Assuming that economic growth is the base of everyone's well-being, Stuttgart emphasizes the important role of migrant IT workers in fostering the competitiveness of Stuttgart and the economic benefits provided by migrants living in the city for decades who have successfully started their own businesses.

Relying on the policy of cultural mainstreaming, the city has implemented a number of instruments especially aiming at the promotion of girls and women in education and professional training. Special language courses have been organized, and this often marginalized group has been familiarized with the German social and educational system by 'getting around'. Following a 'modern strategy of integration', after-school groups for girls have been created to increase the acceptance by Muslim parents of after-school activities.

To foster political and social participation, the city of Stuttgart has established an 'International Committee', which is a local consultative body made up of elected migrant representatives, experts and city councillors. The International Committee meets on a regular basis to discuss matters of integration and other aspects of local life in Stuttgart, aimed at supporting and influencing processes of policy formulation and decision-making in the city council.

To promote cultural diversity and pluralism, the municipal libraries provide books and electronic media in various languages, and public and private organizations offer seminars on integration policy and practices at local level, intercultural understanding and management. The Institute for Foreign Relations and different cultural institutions such as theatres and museums are involved in intercultural education. The city further promotes activities in individual areas such as language and education, integration in the neighbourhoods, support for pluralism and diversity in all spheres of society, as well as strengthening the intercultural self-perception of the city.

In 1998, the Forum for Cultures was created, reflecting Stuttgart's cultural heterogeneity and fostering its self-awareness as an 'intercultural city'. As an umbrella organization, the NGO started with cultural associations, expanding rapidly to its current 62 member organizations, with over 50 different national backgrounds. Besides its direct funding by the city, all member organizations qualify for the city's financial support to promote cultural projects. In addition to its intra-administrative efforts to reflect cultural diversity, the city of Stuttgart also encourages private organizations and associations in civil society to open up and to adapt their services to migrants. The employment agency cooperates closely with local entrepreneurs in finding new apprenticeship and job opportunities for young adults with migration backgrounds, emphasizing their multilingualism and intercultural skills as key elements in a globalizing economy. Moreover, various institutions and projects such as counselling services with bilingual psychologists, social services of migrant organizations and adult evening classes receive financial support from the city.

Recognizing the need to foster social cohesion between people belonging to and identifying with different cultural backgrounds, round tables were established drawing together social workers, policy workers, teachers, the police and others to improve the quality of multicultural life in the various city districts and to fight discrimination. In cases of private conflicts with a cultural or ethnic background, there is a team of trained mediators to solve problems outside the city courts. To promote integration into the neighbourhoods, several community institutions have been established within the city. The 'House 49', one of the oldest community centres (founded in the 1980s), was set up by Catholic and Protestant churches with financial support from the Robert Bosch Foundation. Its intercultural approach and philosophy are the basis for many new centres in the city.

As far as the participation of Stuttgart's migrants is concerned, it should be noted that there are several shops in the city selling newspapers in a wide variety of languages and that some immigrant groups edit their own local papers in their native languages. Moreover, the Forum of Cultures publishes a magazine that encompasses all the intercultural organizations and ethnic groups present in the city.

Special emphasis is given to the transition from school to work life, focusing on the one hand on migrant students and on the other hand on adult newcomers who have not been brought up in the German education system. In addition to the already existing training programmes on the German language, a one-year preparation programme for regular apprenticeship has been established within the framework of the German 'dual system'. This consists of theoretical instruction and practical training for young people with migration backgrounds (EFILWC, 2007).[2]

10

Conclusions: The Ecology of the New Civics

A Journey to the Intercultural City

Distinction – identification, categorization, ordering, valorizing – is integral to the way in which we, both individually and collectively, make sense of the world. Distinctions help us negotiate life and discover our identities. Without them we are, effectively, paralysed. However, when we distinguish between people and then cultures and ethnicities, our distinctions can become foci for hatred and stereotyping, especially in times of crisis such as severe economic austerity. Differences then appear starker and groups polarize.

We have seen the global context of the movement of people: more people are moving between more places. Diversity is inevitable and with it the potential for conflict. Now despite the efforts of far right politicians and other fundamentalists to convince us that there are natural racial differences between groups, identity is in fact multifarious and fluid; individuals have affiliations with a number of communities simultaneously. As such, no set of distinctions will be the same, and so there has to be a social and political context that allows differences to coexist and indeed flourish alongside each other.

But the *raison d' être* of this book is not simply to advise caution against intolerance and extremism. Throughout, we have tried to demonstrate that diversity should be embraced because therein lie opportunity, resources and advantage. Diversity is not something merely to be tolerated because this is the right thing to do or because our lives will be less troublesome. Diversity makes economic, social and cultural sense.

There is plenty of wisdom to guide us on how to avert segregation and foster diverse environments. Early on we reviewed the wealth of literature on diversity. To recap, we identified five strands of literature.

First, there is literature on cosmopolitan cities and the factors that influence the direction they take. Often diversity is linked directly with success. Richard Florida (2002a, 2002b, 2003), for example, argues that a diverse milieu attracts and retains a 'creative class' of the more talented who in turn contribute to a city's economic growth. Others have looked at successful, often creative, businesses emerging from minority groups themselves. Such enterprises also ensure a more varied range of local suppliers.

Second, there are studies of how diversity impacts on the functioning of organizations. Here productivity has been positively correlated with diverse workforces and thus some authors have made a 'business case for diversity'. Briefly, companies that embrace change in terms of a varied workforce are likely to have a propensity for learning and to be flexible. They will also probably have a better understanding of global markets. Crucially a workforce of multiple backgrounds is a workforce of multiple perspectives.

Third, research has been conducted on innovation. Gisela Welz (2003) is one author who proposes that an intercultural context is a creative one. She highlights the collective nature of innovation: creativity thrives in a context of exchange, cooperation and difference.

Fourth, social psychologists have contributed to our understanding of how individuals and groups behave when faced with others who are different, and how through recognizing 'culture shock' we can form strategies to overcome it.

Finally, there is good work on public policy on diversity at national and local levels. We have learned that different countries have often pursued radically different approaches to cultural diversity ranging from strict assimilation to no policy at all. We have charted the story of the UK model of multiculturalism, and its supercession by a greater emphasis on integration and cohesion and also how some places are inching towards something we might call *interculturalism*. After our literature review, we looked at segregation and the ways in which ethnic separation or integration can express itself spatially. This may manifest itself in a ghetto in which one group has been excluded from the social and economic mainstream; but it may equally be a Chinatown or a Little Italy where cultural difference has been accommodated and branded for economic advantage. Some northern English towns and cities have suffered because of de facto segregation between equally disadvantaged white and Asian populations, each leading 'parallel lives'. It is argued that segregation is not always a bad thing and that a clearly defined and separate community can offer support to new arrivals and can cluster familiar cultural identifiers (for example, food outlets) that can ground communities. Nevertheless, when people are segregated from an early age, this may foster rather unhealthy and unhelpful attitudes to race, culture and social solidarity in later life. Further, as Dixon (2005a, 2005b) shows us, even when people appear to be occupying the same physical spaces of residence or leisure, they may be practising a casual routine of avoidance. We even find that in the supposedly colour-blind context of cyberspace, there is distinction and division.

Historically, successful cities, from Ancient Rome to Muslim Córdoba, have often been diverse. As we saw in Chapter 4, this meant not just toleration of minorities but also active embracing of difference, if only to encourage successful trading links with the outside world or to consolidate empire. Diversity was not just an incidental characteristic of these cities but was integral to their functioning. We could say, drawing an analogy with the psychology of individuals, that self-confidence and openness to outside suggestion went hand in hand. These cities were not necessarily secular and there was often a dominant religion. By the same token, we conclude that urban cosmopolitanism, tolerance and interaction do not derive their lineage exclusively from the Western Enlightenment tradition and nor should it be assumed that the intercultural cities of the future will be exclusively of the West.

Chapter 5 looked at cases for, and instances of, social mixing and living together. Social mixing is good for us: cultural advances can result from cross-fertilization between groups and a certain amount of social disharmony can mature societies. Since 1954, when Gordon Allport proposed his *Contact Hypothesis* in which given the right conditions, contact between different groups can challenge stereotypes and foster more favourable views of minorities, there has been a theoretical basis for the value of mixing over aversion.

Having looked at some of the theory behind social mixing and contact between groups, we took in turn different arenas where they might take place: housing, education, the workplace, markets and shopping, friendship, partnership and marriage, public spaces (such as parks, libraries, sport) and cyberspace. We concluded that most people do not go out of their way to seek out people and experiences that are different, and that there are environments and social models that encourage and exacerbate the tendency to aversion. However, evidence also points to some environments being more conducive to interaction than others and that strategic interventions can transform avoidance and indifference into engagement and cooperation. Our conclusion is that if we want an intercultural city, we cannot leave it to chance.

We make no apology for offering the reader an extensive grounding in both theory and evidence. However, the true purpose of this book is to influence the policy-maker and to offer guidance to the practitioner. So, at the business end of the book, we described how cities may implement strategies that are both informed by and seek to instigate an intercultural environment. First, we looked at the prize that is there to be claimed by cities that become more progressive – the release of *diversity advantage* through intercultural innovation. In planning and consultation we seek a heightened cultural literacy among practitioners, that is, the ability to read, understand and find the significance of diverse cultures and, as a consequence, to be able to evaluate, compare and decode the varied cultures that are interwoven in a place. When consultation is conducted in a context of wider cultural literacy, the process of consultation becomes an end in itself and not just a means to an end. We then asked that city institutions, policy-makers, planners and professional practitioners reconceive their role through an *intercultural lens*.

We also examined what a new intercultural citizenship might look like. In the process we critiqued the multicultural model that, in the UK at least, has seen local government form alliances with (often self-appointed) ethnic community leaders. These alliances have often heightened divisions by reifying the idea of distinct ethnic groups and there was little incentive for cross-cultural polity. Intercultural citizenship should be at once local and international, recognizing the ever-increasing global connectedness of things while acknowledging the importance of bottom-up autonomy. It may even fall on cities to take an independent lead in matters of citizenship.

In the intercultural city, conflict is not necessarily something to be avoided and certainly not to be glossed over. Conflict can be interesting and a site of creativity. We follow Chantal Mouffe (2000) in believing that a healthy *agonism* between adversaries can replace *antagonism* between enemies. We finished Chapter 8 with a look at some examples of intercultural leaders and citizens we ourselves have encountered in our work.

As we showed in Chapter 9, interculturalism is something that, to a lesser or greater extent, we can measure. Beyond finding out how ethnically diverse a city is (which can be answered by recourse to census and other market data), we should also investigate mixing between groups, the ease of movement between different groups and institutional networks, and actual collaboration. More specifically, indicators like intermarriage, crossover networks and products, and the value placed on multilingualism may point to an intercultural city.

FIVE PRINCIPLES OF AN INTERCULTURAL CITY

Before we finish, we consider five key areas: leadership, city-making, city management, citizenship and bridging and mixing.

The leader with an intercultural perspective has some characteristics. To start with, they will be willing to take the risk of switching the focus from diversity deficit to diversity advantage. They will stick their neck out. This is already courageous even though it seems innocuous. But by being honest about the fears and misgivings of all parties in their city, they will have shown the strength to open out debate. They will initiate a bigger picture conversation. It is always easier to live in the certainties of prejudice rather than in the realm of the 'to be discussed, understood and negotiated'. They will try to retell the evolving story of their city with a sense of hope so that the gains override the perceived losses of the new diversity. They will need to set in train a paced and purposeful action plan in the knowledge that the change in self-identification takes more than one political term of office. They will find a way of making everyone feel welcome so that people can be encouraged to be makers, shapers and co-creators of their evolving city.

Typical projects such a leader might champion include: setting up an institute of intercultural excellence, perhaps in their city or helping to create one nationally; they might provide professional support; monitor good examples; do an intercultural skills audit and fill gaps that are recognized or help professional bodies like the Royal Town Planning Institute to learn about cultural literacy; the leader might establish creativity programmes where schools with different cultural mixes jointly work together or they might be bold enough to set up an explicit 'anti-extremism budget'.

City-making with an intercultural perspective takes its lead from the leadership grouping that needs to legitimize looking at the city through an intercultural lens. Only then will the implications, say on masterplanning or new forms of consultation, be taken seriously. Too often new agendas are taken on board by an enlightened leadership but get lost as they are translated or watered down in the process of being delivered at a lower level in the organization. The 'lens' analysis provides a rich and potentially vast set of things to work on from adjusting the school curriculum, looking again at housing types, to reframing economic incentives or cultural programming.

City management is where the ideas turn into action. The problem that immediately confronts us is that the rules have not been created for nor are concerned with an intercultural outcome. Instead they are concerned with an aspect such as social affairs, health, safety, privacy, road guidelines, traffic flow or the environment. The rules are designed for simpler single issues rather than a complex thing like interculturalism. Indeed there is no division concerned with 'relations between people'. A central question is, do you create a special section to deal with a single topic, do you try to embed the thinking throughout or do you do both? Initially, at least, it seems a task force approach might be right to get the issue onto the agenda, raise awareness and provide professional help.

One point to consider is the difference between multidisciplinary and interdisciplinary working. Intercultural initiatives should be run much more on interdisciplinary or transdisciplinary lines where skills intermesh, joint solutions emerge and perspectives change through working together, rather than in multidisciplinary ways where we share information and knowledge from the position of the expert, but are less likely to transform our thinking. In the interdisciplinary world, the aim and intent, say helping your city be more intercultural, is central and continually in focus. The only question then is how the expert discipline can help that goal. This will involve much more self-consciously putting mixed teams together with different skill sets and mindsets.

Because nation states make the rules but cities are the lived reality of our multiethnic mix, there is an increasing strain emerging. The city should conceive of itself and behave as if it were a state or a nation, as cities in their collectivity drive national economies. Only then will the city be able to maximize opportunities for its own citizens and create spin-off benefits for others. Nation states are increasingly unable to deliver what cities need: jobs, good design, well functioning services and strategic positioning.

Cities, then, require foreign policies, cultural diplomacy and trade strategies and need to project their view of the world.

This in turn implies the need for a new form of *citizenship*. Many people, migrants or not, find it increasingly difficult to find common cause with or loyalty for a national state that does not recognize them and that pursues an aggressive or dubious foreign policy abroad; but they do identify with the city where they live, work and interact. Increasingly, people are going to be demanding and taking upon themselves a 'glocal citizenship' guaranteeing basic rights for everybody, based on the social bond of belonging to and participating in the local community.

Finally, while we know that large political, cultural and economic forces have a powerful sway over power relations and the prospects for antagonism, avoidance or cooperation between ethnic groups in our cities, we should not overlook the power of individuals to make a difference: the *bridgers and mixers* who we have found in every place we have looked and who – often at some risk to themselves – have reached out to overcome barriers or divides that others take for granted. Among these are some remarkable people but this should not intimidate us into thinking that they are somehow different from the rest of us. Just as remarkable people can envision an intercultural city, so very many more people can contribute simply by behaving a little remarkably within their local context, from an open gesture and warm smile or sharing a common concern or celebration to beginning to see life through the eyes of another and just altering routine to accommodate this. A million small accommodations amount to a movement that can shift a city. This is the place where we want to live – the city that the people themselves made intercultural because it works for them.

TEN STEPS TO AN INTERCULTURAL CITY POLICY

So what are the intercultural cities of the early 21st century? There is no uniform model, nor should there be, but from looking at Amsterdam and Rotterdam, Toronto and Vancouver, Stuttgart and Århus, Leicester and London, Singapore and Auckland and others some common themes recur. This could be the basis of a policy:

1   Make a public statement that the city explicitly understands and is adopting an intercultural approach. Take an iconic action to symbolize the transition to a new era, for example, through making atonement for a past misdeed or designating a day devoted to intercultural understanding.
2   Initiate an exercise to review the main functions of the city 'through an intercultural lens', and establish some flagship trial projects, for example:

- In *education*, establish a few schools/colleges as intercultural flagships, with high investment in staff training, intercultural curriculum, cooperative learning models, closer links with parents/community, twinning links with monocultural schools, and citizenship education – as has been done in Huddersfield.
- In the *public realm*, identify a number of key public spaces (formal and informal) and invest in discrete redesign, animation and maintenance to raise levels of usage and interaction by all ethnic groups; develop a better understanding of how different groups use space and incorporate into planning and design guidelines.
- In *housing*, trial programmes in allocation and publicity that give ethnic groups confidence and information enabling them to consider taking housing opportunities outside traditional enclaves, as has been done in Bradford.
- In *neighbourhoods*, designate key facilities as intercultural community centres, containing key services such as health, maternity, childcare and library, as has been done in Århus and Vancouver.
- Rethink the role of frontline *police* officers in key areas to act primarily as agents of intercultural integration.
- In *business and economy*, take extra effort to ensure migrants find jobs appropriate to their skills, ensuring recognition of accreditation; explore trade opportunities through diasporic networks of local migrants; assist migrant businesses to break out into multiethnic markets.
- In *sport and the arts*, initiate tournaments and festivals that bring together young people from different parts of the city and train multiethnic youngsters as sports and arts leaders, as in Oldham.

3   Explore and learn from best practice elsewhere through taking politicians and policy-makers to other places. Also take multi-ethnic groups of young community leaders, as in Belfast and Derry.

4   Invest heavily in language training to ensure that all migrants are able to converse in the majority language, but also enable

members of the majority to learn minority languages, as in Delft.

5   Establish awards or other schemes to reward and acknowledge single acts or lives devoted to building intercultural trust and understanding.

6   Establish a city international relations office (as in Chicago) that:
    - creates an independent international profile for the city;
    - establishes independent trade and policy links with partner cities;
    - establishes independent links with key countries of origin of migrant population;
    - monitors and develops new models of local/global citizenship.

7   Establish an intercultural observatory (as has been done in Madrid) that:
    - monitors good practice;
    - gathers and processes local information and data;
    - conducts research into quantity/quality and outcomes of interaction;
    - establishes and monitors intercultural indicators;
    - dispenses advice and expertise and facilitates local learning networks.

8   Initiate a programme of intercultural awareness training for politicians and key policy and public interface staff in public sector agencies. Encourage the private sector to participate, as has been done in Stuttgart.

9   Establish a city-wide interfaith consultative forum and within neighbourhoods establish cross-cultural consultation exercises wherever possible, as has been done in Leicester

10 Initiate welcoming initiatives and urban exploration projects whereby new arrivals (temporary and permanent) but – equally importantly – local citizens, can visit parts of the city to which they have not previously been, hosted by people of different cultures, as has been done in Rotterdam.

There is no prescription for cities to do all of these things at once or in this order. As we conclude this book on the eve of 2008, which has been designated the European Year of Intercultural Dialogue, we would simply say that the most important thing of all is to start.

BEING INTERCULTURAL

Box 10.1 Mostar: The Youth Cultural Centre Abrasevic

The destruction of the ancient and beautiful Mostar bridge in Bosnia-Herzegovina was emblematic of everything dreadful in the Balkans, where ethnic cleansing raised its ugly head again in the 1990s. In Mostar the three ethnic groups – Bosniacs and especially Croats as well as Serbs faced each other across the Neretva river. In a climate of suspicion and misgivings there was barely any communication across the divides. In 2003 a group of 11 NGOs, associations and individuals who were largely young wanted change. They joined together to demand a communal space from the local authority where all groups could meet, have fun, talk and play music. One of the groups was involved in an Intercultural Festival and others in music promotion, community arts and cultural exchange activities and they initiated the Short Film Festival Mostar. They wanted to break down not only physical but also mental borders.

Out of this came the Youth Cultural Centre Abrasevic. Initially this was housed in a set of old containers covered by a tent within an old, small sports stadium that had been shot to pieces in the war.

Later they moved to an even more significant site – a set of buildings at the former frontline where the bullets and graffiti still pockmark the walls. The group caught the eye of the Swiss Cultural Programme South-East Europe and Ukraine – a joint initiative of the Arts Council of Switzerland and Pro Helvetia and the Swiss Agency for Development and Cooperation who now fund them. The aim of this programme is to help independent organizations like Abrasevic become more self-sufficient by building capacity.

Bibliography

Abrams, D. and Hogg, M. A. (eds) (1990) *Social Identity Theory: Constructive and Critical Advances*. London: Harvester Wheatsheaf

Adler, N. (1997) *International Dimensions of Organizational Behavior*. Cincinnati: South-Western College Publishing

Alesina, A. and La Ferrara, E. (2004) 'Ethnic diversity and economic performance'. NBER Working Paper. Cambridge, MA: National Bureau of Economic Research

Alesina, A. and La Ferrara, E. (2005) 'Ethnic diversity and economic performance'. *Journal of Economic Literature*, 43(3), 762–800

Alexander, M. (2001) 'Comparing local policies towards migrants: A proposed analytical framework and preliminary survey results'. Paper presented to the Metropolis 2001 Conference,Rotterdam, 26–30 November

Alexander, M. (2003) 'Local policies towards migrants as an expression of host-stranger relations: A proposed typology'. *Journal of Ethnic and Migration Studies*, 29(3), 411–430

Alexander, M. (2006) *Cities and Labour Migration: Comparing Policy Responses in Amsterdam, Paris, Rome and Tel Aviv*. Aldershot: Ashgate

Alibhai-Brown, Y. (1999) *True Colours*. London: Institute for Public Policy Research

Alibhai-Brown, Y. (2000) *Beyond Multiculturalism*. London: Foreign Policy Centre

Alibhai-Brown, Y. (2001) *Who Do We Think We Are? Imagining the New Britain*. London: Penguin.

Allen, J. and Cars, G. (2001) 'Multiculturalism and governing neighbourhoods'. *Urban Studies*, 38(12), 2195–2209

Allen, T. and Eade, J. (eds) *Divided Europeans: Understanding Ethnicities in Conflict*. Amsterdam: Kluwer

Allison, P. (ed) (2006) *David Adjaye: Making Public Buildings*. London: Whitechapel Gallery

Allport, G. W. (1954) *The Nature of Prejudice*. Reading, MA: Addison-Wesley

Amin, A. (2002) 'Ethnicity and the Multicultural City: Living with Diversity'. *Environment and Planning A*, 34(6), 959–980

Amin, A. (2006) 'The Good City'. *Urban Studies*, 43(5–6), 1009–1023

Amin, A. and Thrift, N. (2002) *Cities: Reimagining the Urban.* Cambridge: Polity Press

Andersen, T. and Van Kempen, R. (eds) (2001) *Governing European Cities: Social Fragmentation, Social Exclusion and Urban Governance.* Aldershot: Ashgate

Anderson, E. and Massey, D. S. (eds) (2001) *Problem of the Century: Racial Stratification in the United States.* New York: Russell Sage Foundation

Ang, I., Brand, J., Noble, G. and Wilding, D. (2002) *Living Diversity: Australia's Multicultural Future.* Artamon, NSW: Special Broadcasting Services Corporation

Antal, A. B. and Friedman, V. (2003) 'Negotiating Reality as An Approach to Inter-cultural Competence'. Discussion Paper SP III 2003-101. Berlin: Wissenschafts-zentrum Berlin für Sozialforschung

Appold, S. and Chua, K. H. (2006) 'Crossing Life Domains: Can Workplace Affirmative Action Achieve Social Peace in Urban Neighborhoods?'. Paper presented at the annual meeting of the American Sociological Association, Montreal Convention Center, Montreal, Quebec, Canada, 10 August, www.unc.edu/~appolds/research/progress/AANeignborhoodsASA.pdf

Arbabzadeh, N. (2004) 'Multiculturalism in Mediaeval Islam', www.opendemocracy.net/arts-multiculturalism/article_2263.jsp

Atkinson, R. (2006) 'Padding the bunker: Strategies of middle-class disaffiliation and colonisation in the city'. *Urban Studies*, 43(4), 819–832

Audunson, R. (2005) 'The public library as a meeting-place in a multicultural and digital context'. *Journal of Documentation*, 61(3), 429–441

Axelrod, R. (1997) *The Complexity of Cooperation: Agent-Based Models of Competition and Collaboration.* Princeton: Princeton University Press

Aycan, Z. (1997) 'Expatriate adjustment as a multifaceted phenomenon: Individual and organisational level predictors'. *The International Journal of Human Resource Management*, 8, 434–456

Babiker, I. E., Cox, J. L. and Miller, P. (1980) 'The measurement of cultural distance and its relationship to medical consultations, symptomatology, and examination performance of overseas students at Edinburgh University'. *Social Psychiatry*, 15, 109–116

Back, L. (1996) *New Ethnicities and Urban Culture.* London: UCL Press

Bailey, B. (2000) 'Communicative behavior and conflict between African-American customers and Korean immigrant retailers in Los Angeles'. *Discourse & Society*, 11(1), 86–108

Bairoch, P. (1988) *Cities and Economic Development: From the Dawn of History to the Present.* Oxford: Oxford University Press

Barham, K. and Wills, S. (1992) *Management Across Frontiers.* Berkhamsted: Ashridge Management Research Group and Foundation for Management Education

Baubock, R. (2003) 'Reinventing urban citizenship'. *Citizenship Studies*, 7(2), 139–160

Beckman, N. (2006) 'Creativity, ethnic communities and the curious case of museums'. *Aotearoa Ethnic Network Journal*, 1(2), 41–44

Bennett, M. J. (ed) (1998) *Basic Concepts of Intercultural Communication: Selected Readings*. Yarmouth, ME: Intercultural Press

Berger, A. (2002) 'Recent trends in library services for ethnic minorities: The Danish experience'. *Library Management*, 23(1–2), 79–87

Berry, J. W. (1990) 'Psychology of acculturation: Understanding individuals moving between cultures'. In R. Brislin (ed) *Applied Cross-cultural Psychology*. Newbury Park, CA: Sage

Binnie, J., Holloway, J., Millington, S. and Young, C. (eds) (2006) *Cosmopolitan Urbanism*. London: Routledge.

Bloomfield, J. (2003) '"Made in Berlin" – multicultural conceptual confusion and intercultural reality'. *Journal of International Cultural Policy*, 9(2), 167–184

Bloomfield, J. and Bianchini, F. (2004) *Planning for the Intercultural City*. Stroud: Comedia

Bochner, S. (1979) 'Cultural diversity: Implications for modernisation and international education'. In K. Kumar (ed) *Bonds Without Bondage: Explorations in Transcultural Interactions*. Honolulu; University of Hawaii Press

Bochner, S., Hutnik, N. and Furnham, A. (1985) 'The friendship patterns of overseas and host students in an Oxford student residence'. *Journal of Social Psychology*, 125, 689–694

Bond, M. H. (1986) 'Mutual stereotypes and the facilitation of interaction across cultural lines'. *International Journal of Intercultural Relations*, 10, 259–276

Bore, A. (2001) 'Urban social transformations and the impact of migration on metropolitan areas'. Paper presented at the Urban Futures seminar, Södertälje, Sweden, 9–12 May, www.storstad.gov.se/urbanfutures/

Borjas, G. (1995) 'The economic benefits of immigration'. *Journal of Economic Perspectives*, 9, 3–22

Borjas, G. (1999) *Heaven's Doors*. Princeton: Princeton University Press

Bozon, M. and Heran, F. (1989) 'Finding a spouse: A survey of how French couples meet'. *Population*, 44, 91–212

Braker, S. and Haertel, C. (2004) 'Intercultural service encounters: An exploratory study of customer experiences'. *Cross Cultural Management*, 11(1), 3–14

Brecknock Consulting (2006a) 'A Meeting of People, a Well-Spring of Ideas', www.interculturalcity.com/city_case.htm#auckland

Brecknock Consulting (2006b) 'Intercultural City: Logan Case Study', www.interculturalcity.com/city_case.htm#logan

Brecknock, R. (2006) *More Than Just a Bridge: Planning and Designing Culturally*. Stroud: Comedia

Brecknock, R. and Howell, A. (2005) *Knowing Lewisham*. Stroud: Comedia

Briggs, X. de S. (2004) 'Civilization in color: The multicultural city in three millennia'. *City and Community*, 3(4), 311–342

Brislin, R. and Yoshida, Y (1994) *Intercultural Communication Training: An Introduction*. Thousand Oaks: Sage

Brown, K. T., Brown, T. N., Jackson, J. S., Sellers, R. M. and Manuel, W. J. (2003) 'Teammates on and off the field? Contact with Black teammates and the racial attitudes of White student athletes'. *Journal of Applied Social Psychology*, 33(7), 1379–1403

Browne, A. (2003) 'Some truths about immigration'. *The Spectator*, 2 August

Brubaker, R. W. (1992) *Citizenship and Nationhood in France and Germany*. Cambridge, MA: Harvard University Press

Bruegel, I. (2006) *Social Capital, Diversity and Education Policy*. Families & Social Capital ESRC Research Group. London: South Bank University

Buonfino, A. with Geissendorfer, L. (2007) *Mapping Rural Needs*. London: Young Foundation, www.youngfoundation.org.uk/files/images/final_rural_needs_report_ppt.pdf

Burayidi, M. (ed) (2000) *Urban Planning in a Multicultural Society*. Westport, CT: Praeger

Burgess, S., Wilson, D. and Lupton, R. (2005) 'Parallel lives? Ethnic segregation in schools and neighbourhoods'. *Urban Studies*, 42(7), 1027–1056

Burrows, R., Ellison, N. and Woods, B. (2005) *Neighbourhoods on the Net: The Nature and Impact of Internet-based Neighbourhood Information Systems*. York: Joseph Rowntree Foundation

Byram, M. (1997) *Teaching and Assessing Intercultural Communicative Competence*. Clevedon, England: Multilingual Matters

Byrne, D. (1969) 'Attitudes and attraction'. In L. Berkowitz (ed) *Advances in Experimental Social Psychology, Volume 4*. New York: Academic Press

CABE (Commission for Architecture and the Built Environment) (2005) *Creating Successful Neighbourhoods: Lessons and Actions for Housing Market Renewal*. London: CABE

CABE (2006) *Decent Parks, Decent Behaviour: The Link Between the Quality of Parks and User Behaviour*. London: CABE

Canadian National Settlement Conference (2003) 'The Small Centre Strategy: The Regional Dispersal and Retention of Immigrants', http://integration-net.ca/inet/english/vsi-isb/conference2/pdf/p02.pdf

Cantle, T. (2001) *Community Cohesion: A Report of the Independent Review Team*. London: Home Office

Cantle, T. (2005) *Community Cohesion: A New Framework for Race and Diversity*. Basingstoke: Palgrave

Cantle, T. (2006) *Challenging Local Communities to Change Oldham*. Coventry: Institute of Community Cohesion

Capra, F. (1982) *The Turning Point: Science, Society, and the Rising Culture*. New York: Simon and Schuster

Card, D. and Di Nardo, J. (2000) 'Do immigrant inflows lead to native outflows?' *American Economic Review*, 90, 360–367

Castells, M. (1994) 'European cities, the informational society and the global economy'. *New Left Review*, 1(204), 18–32

Castells, M. (1997) *The Power of Identity*. Oxford: Blackwell Publishing

Castro, R. (1994) *Civilisation Urbaine ou Barbarie*. Paris: Pion

CEEDR (2003) *Playing it Right: Asian Creative Industries in London*. London: Greater London Assembly

Chen Yinke (1996) *Chen Yinke's Scholarly and Cultural Works*. Beijing: Zhongguo Qingnian Chubanse

Cheung, G. C. K. (2004) 'Chinese diaspora as a virtual nation: Interactive roles between economic and social capital'. *Political Studies*, 52, 664–684

Chih Hoong Sin (2002) 'The quest for a balanced ethnic mix: Singapore's ethnic quota policy examined'. *Urban Studies*, 39(8), 1347–1374

Chirot, D. (1994) *How Societies Change*. Thousand Oaks: Pine Forge Press

Clack, B., Dixon, J. and Tredoux, C. (2005) 'Eating together apart: Patterns of segregation in a multi-ethnic cafeteria'. *Journal of Community and Applied Psychology*, 15, 1–16

COE/CLRAE (2006) 'Effective access to social rights for immigrants: The role of local and regional authorities'. Explanatory Memorandum from the 13th Plenary Session of the Congress, 30 May–1 June

Cohen, W. M. and Levinthal, D. A. (1989) 'Innovation and learning: The two faces of R&D'. *The Economic Journal*, 99, 569–596

Cohn, N. (2005) 'Politics of the ghetto'. *The Observer*, 30 October

Coleman, T. (1995) 'Managing diversity'. *Local Government Management*, October, 30–34

Coles, M. and Vincent, R. (2006) *The Role of Schools in the Intercultural City*. Stroud: Comedia, www.interculturalcity.com/

Collier, P. (2001) 'Implications of ethnic diversity'. *Economic Policy*, 0, 127–55

Comedia (1995) *Park Life: Urban Parks and Social Renewal*. Stroud: Comedia

Comedia (2005) *The Attraction and Retention of Migrants to the Tyne and Wear City Region*. Newcastle: One North East

Comedia (2006) *Planning and Engaging With Intercultural Communities*. Leeds: Academy for Sustainable Communities

Comedia (2006a) 'How open is Bristol?' www.interculturalcity.com/city_case.htm#bristol

Comedia (2007) 'Knowing Lewisham', www.interculturalcity.com/city_case.htm#lewisham

Commission for Racial Equality (1993) *Housing Allocations in Oldham: Report of a Formal Investigation*. London: CRE

Commission on Integration and Cohesion (2007a) *Our Shared Future*. Wetherby: Commission on Integration and Cohesion

Commission on Integration and Cohesion (2007b) *Integration and Cohesion Case Studies*. Wetherby: Commission on Integration and Cohesion

Commission for Racial Equality (2006) *Common Ground: Equality, Good Race Relations and Sites for Gypsies and Irish Travellers*. Report of a CRE enquiry in England and Wales. London: CRE

Cooper, C. (2004) 'Mix up the Indian with all the Patwa: Rajamuffin sounds in "Cool" Britannia'. *Language and Intercultural Communication*, 4(1–2), 81–99

Cova, B. and Cova, V. (2002) 'Tribal marketing: The tribalisation of society and its impact on the conduct of marketing'. *European Journal of Marketing*, 5(6), 595–620

Cox, T., Jr. (1994) *Cultural Diversity in Organizations: Theory, Research and Practice.* San Francisco: Berrett-Koelher

Cox, T. H. and Blake, S. (1991) 'Managing cultural diversity: Implications for organisational competitiveness'. *Academy of Management Executive*, 5(3), 45–56

CRC (Commission for Rural Communities) (2005) *State of the Countryside, 2005.* Cheltenham: Commission for Rural Communities

Cross, M. and Waldinger, R. (1992) 'Migrants, minorities and the ethnic divisions of labor'. In S. S. Fanstein, I. Gordon and M. Harloe (eds) *Divided Cities: New York and London in the Contemporary World.* Oxford: Blackwell

Cutler, D. and Glaeser, E. (1997) 'Are ghettos good or bad?' *Quarterly Journal of Economics*, 112, 827–872

Dansereau, F. (2003) 'Social mix as public policy and private experience'. Paper presented to the Challenging Urban Identities conference, International Sociological Association Research Committee 21, Milan, 25–27 September

Davis, K. (1997) *Exploring the Interface Between Cultural Competency and Managed Behavioural Care Policy: Implications for State and County Health Agencies.* Alexandria, VD: National Technical Assistance Center for State Mental Health Planning

Davis, M., Seibert, R. and Breed, W. (1966) 'Interracial seating patterns on New Orleans public transit'. *Social Problems*, 13(3), 298–306

Dawkins, R. (1976) *The Selfish Gene.* Oxford: Oxford University Press

Department for Communities and Local Government (2007) *Preventing Violent Extremism: Winning Hearts and Minds.* London: HMSO

DeVoretz, D. (2003) *Canadian Regional Immigration Initiative in the 21st Century: A Candle in the Wind?* Vancouver: RIIM Commentary Series #03-01, Simon Fraser University

Dhaliwal, S. (1997) 'Silent contributors – Asian female entrepreneurs.' Paper presented at the 20th ISBA National Research and Policy Conference, Belfast, 19–21 November

Di Cicco, P. G. (2007) *Municipal Mind: Manifestos for the Creative City.* Toronto: Mansfield Press

DIMIA (Department of Immigration and Multiculturalism and Indigenous Affairs) (2002) *The Innovation and Learning Advantage from Diversity: A Business Model for Diversity Management.* Canberra: DIMIA

Dines, N., Cattell, V., Gesler, W. and Curtis, S. (2006) *Public Spaces, Social Relations and Well-being in East London.* Bristol: The Policy Press

Dixon, J. and Durrheim, K. (2003) 'Contact and the ecology of racial division: some varieties of informal segregation'. *British Journal of Social Psychology*, 42(1), 1–23

Dixon, J., Durrheim, K. and Tredoux, C. (2005a) 'Beyond the optimal contact strategy: A reality check for the contact hypothesis'. *Amercian Psychologist*, 60(7), 697–711

Dixon, J., Tredoux, C. and Clack, B. (2005b) 'On the micro-ecology of racial division: A neglected dimension of segregation'. *South African Journal of Psychology*, 35(3), 395–411

Dompierre, S. and Lavallée, M. (1990) 'Degré de contact et stress acculturatif dans le processus d'adaption des réfugiés Africains'. *International Journal of Psychology*, 25, 417–437

Donà, G. and Berry, J. W. (1994) 'Acculturation attitudes and acculturational stress of Central American refugees'. *International Journal of Psychology*, 29, 57–70

DTZ Pieda Consulting (2004) *The Economic Impact of Inward Investment on the London Economy*. London: DTZ Pieda Consulting

Dumas, M.-C. (2001) 'Immigration and Urban Management in the 21st Century: Balancing local issues and global trends'. Paper presented at the Urban Futures seminar, Södertälje, Sweden, 9–12 May, www.storstad.gov.se/urbanfutures/

Dupont, F. (1992) *Daily Life in Ancient Rome*. Oxford: Blackwell

Duranton, G. and Puga, D. (2001) 'Nursery cities: Urban diversity, process innovation, and the life cycle of products'. *American Economic Review*, 91(5), 1454–1477

Dustmann, C., Fabbri, F., Preston, I. and Wadsworth, J. (2003) *The Local Labour Market Effects of Immigration in the UK*. London: Home Office

Edgar, D. (2005a) 'Speech to the Graduation Class of ACS International School', London: ACS International School

Edgar, D. (2005b). *Playing with Fire*. London: Nick Hern Books

EFILWC (European Foundation for the Improvement of Living and Working Conditions) (2007) *Local Integration Policies for Migrants in Europe*. Dublin: EFILWC

Eisenberger, R., Fasolo, P., and Davis-LaMastro, V. (1990) 'Perceived organizational support and employee diligence, commitment and innovation'. *Journal of Applied Psychology*, 75, 51–59

Eisenbruch, M. (1991) 'From posttraumatic stress disorder to cultural bereavement: Diagnosis of South East Asian refugees'. *Social Science and Medicine*, 33, 673–680

Ellis, M., Wright, R. and Parks, V. (2004) 'Work together, live apart? Geographies of racial and ethnic segregation at home and work'. *Annals of the Association of American Geographers*, 94(3), 620–637

Entzinger, H. (1994) 'A future for the Dutch "ethnic minorities" model?' In B. Lewis and D. Schnapper (eds) *Muslims in Europe*. London /New York: Pinter

Eslund, C. (2005) 'Working together: Crossing color lines at work'. *Labor History*, 46(1), 79–98

Espin, O. M. (1987) 'Psychological impact of migration on Latinas'. *Psychology of Women Quarterly*, 11, 489–503

Eun Young Kim and Youn-Kyung Kim (2005) 'The effects of ethnicity and gender on teens' mall shopping motivations'. *Clothing and Textiles Research Journal*, 23(2), 65–77

Ezard, J. (2004) 'British libraries could shut by 2020'. *The Guardian*, 28 April

Fairlie, R. W. (2005) *Are We Really a Nation Online? Ethnic and Racial Disparities in Access to Technology and Their Consequences*. Santa Cruz and Michigan: University of California and National Poverty Center, University of Michigan

Farley, R. (1999) 'Racial issues: Recent trends in residential patterns and intermarriage'. In N. Smelser and J. Alexander (eds) *Diversity and its Discontents*. Princeton, NJ: Princeton University Press

Favell, A. (1998) *Philiosophies of Integration: Immigration and the Idea of Citizenship in France and Britain*. London: Macmillan

Favell, A. (2001) 'Multi-ethnic Britain: An exception in Europe?' *Patterns of Prejudice*, 35(1) 35–58

Feldman, M. P. and Audretsch, D. B. (1999) 'Innovation in cities: Science based diversity, specialization and localized competition'. *European Economic Review*, 43, 409–429

Fernandez, J. and Barr, M. (1993) *The Diversity Advantage: How American Business Can Out-Perform Japanese and European Companies in the Global Marketplace*. New York: Maxwell Macmillan International

Fine, R. and Cohen, R. (2002) 'Four cosmopolitan moments'. In S. Vertovec and R. Cohen (eds) *Conceiving Cosmopolitanism: Theory, Context and Practice*. Oxford: Oxford University Press

Fischer, G. (1998) *E-mail in Foreign Language Teaching. Towards the Creation of Virtual Classrooms*. Tübingen, Germany: Stauffenburg Medien

Fisher, G. (1997) *Mindsets: The Role of Culture and Perception in International Relations*. 2nd edition. Yarmouth, ME: Intercultural Press Inc

Fiske, J. (1983) 'Surfalism and sandiotics: The beach in Oz popular culture'. *Australian Journal of Cultural Studies*, 1(2), 120–149

Fleming, T. (2006) *London Borough of Tower Hamlets: Intercultural Consultation for a Global City District*. Stroud: Comedia

Florida, R. (2002a) 'Bohemia and economic geography'. *Journal of Economic Geography*, 2, 55–71

Florida, R. (2002b) *The Rise of the Creative Class: And How It's Transforming Work, Leisure and Everyday life*. New York: Basic Books

Florida, R. (2003) *Boho Britain*. London: Demos

Florida, R. (2005) *The Flight of the Creative Class*. New York: Harper Business

Florida, R. and Tinagli, I. (2004) 'Europe in the Creative Age'. London: Demos, http://www.creativeclass.org/acrobat/Europe_in_the_Creative_Age_2004.pdf

Foot, J. (2001) *Milan Since the Miracle: City, Culture and Identity*. Oxford: Berg

Forbes, H. (1997) *Ethnic Conflict: Commerce, Culture and the Contact Hypothesis*. New Haven, CT: Tale University Press

Ford, R. G. (1950) 'Population succession in Chicago'. *American Journal of Sociology*, 56, 151–160

Friedmann, J. (2002) *The Prospect of Cities*. Minneapolis: University of Minnesota Press

Furnham, A. (1986) *Culture Shock: Psychological Reactions to Unfamiliar Environments*. London: Routledge

Gaines, S., Jr. and Leaver, J. (2002) 'Interracial relationships'. In R. Goodwin and D. Cramer (eds) *Inappropriate Relationships: The Unconventional, the Disapproved and the Forbidden*. Mahwaj, NJ: Lawrence Erlbaum Associated

Gans, H. J. (1961*)* 'The balanced community: Homogeneity or heterogeneity in residential areas?' *American Institute of Planners Journal*, 27(3), 176–184

Ghilardi, L. (2006) *The Contribution of Outsiders to Entrepreneurship and Innovation in Cities: The UK Case*. Stroud: Comedia. www.interculturalcity.com/thematic_studies.htm#Case5

Gil, A., Vega, W. and Dimas, J. (1994) 'Acculturative stress and personal adjustment among Hispanic adolescent boys'. *Journal of Community Psychology*, 22, 42–54

Gilroy, P. (1987) *There Ain't no Black in the Union Jack: The Cultural Politics of Race and Nation*. London: Hutchinson

Gilroy, P. (2000) *Between Camps*. London: Penguin

Gladwell, M. (2000) *Tipping Point: How Little Things can Make a Big Difference*. London: Abacus

Glaeser, E. L., Kallal, H. D., Scheinkman J. A. and Shleifer A. (1992) 'Growth in cities'. *Journal of Political Economy*, 100(6), 1126–1152

Gobster, P. (1998) 'Urban parks as green walls or green magnets? Interracial relations in neighbourhood boundary parks'. *Landscape and Urban Planning*, 41, 43–55.

Golden, J. (1987) 'Acculturation, biculturalism and marginality: A study of Korean-American high school students'. *Dissertation Abstracts International*, 48, 1135A. University Microfilms No. DA8716257

Goodchild, B. and Cole, I. (2001) 'Social balance and mixed neighbourhoods in Britain since 1979: A review of discourse and practice'. *Social Housing, Environment and Planning (D): Society and Space*, 19(1), 103–121

Goodhart, D. (2004) 'Too diverse?' *Prospect*, February, 30–37

Graham, S. (2005) 'Software-sorted geographies'. *Progress in Human Geography*, 29(5), 562–580

Grenier, P. and Wright, K. (2006) 'Social capital in Britain: Exploring the Hall paradox'. *Policy Studies*, 27(1), 27–53

Grossman, R. (2000) 'Is diversity working?' *HR Magazine,* 45(3), 47–50

Grove, A. (2001) *Swimming Across: A Memoir*. New York: Warner Books

Gustafson, P. (2001) 'Retirement migration and transnational lifestyles'. *Ageing and Society*, 21, 371–394

Hajer, M. and Reijndorp, A. (2002) *In Search of the New Public Domain*. Rotterdam: Nai Publishers

Halfmann, J. (1998) 'Citizenship universalism, migration and the risks of exclusion'. *British Journal of Sociology*, 49(4), 513–533

Hall, E. T. (1990) *The Hidden Dimension*. New York: Anchor Books

Hall, E. T. and Hall, M. R. (1990) *Understanding Cultural Differences*. Yarmouth, ME: Intercultural Press Inc

Hall, P. (1998) *Cities in Civilisation*. London: Weidenfield & Nicholson

Hall, P. and Landry, C. (1997) *Innovative and Sustainable Cities*. Dublin: European Foundation for the Improvement of Living and Working Conditions

Hallinan, M. and Smith, S. (1985) 'The effects of classroom racial composition on students' interracial friendliness'. *Social Psychology Quarterly*, 48, 3–16

Hallinan, M. and Williams, R. A. (1990) 'Students' characteristics and the peer-influence process'. *Sociology of Education*, 63, 122–132

Hambrick, D. C. (1994) 'Top management groups: A conceptual integration and reconsideration of the team label'. In B. M. Staw (ed) *Research in Organizational Behavior 16*. Greenwich, CT: JAI Press

Hannerz, U. (1996) *Transnational Connections: Culture, People, Places*. London: Routledge

Hansson, R. and Skog, T. (2001) 'The LoveBomb: Encouraging the communication of emotions in public spaces'. Paper for the Conference on Human Factors in Computing Systems. New York: ACM Press, 333–343

Harris, P. R. and Moran, R. T. (1991) *Managing Cultural Differences*. 3rd edition. Houston: Gulf Publishing

Hart, W. (1998) 'Intercultural computer-mediated communication'. *The Edge: E-Journal of Intercultural Relations*, 1(4), www.interculturalrelations.com/Resources/TheEdge.htm

Hartley, J. (2005) 'Tower Hamlets' Idea Stores: Are They Working?' A study submitted in partial fulfilment of the requirements for the degree of Master of Arts in Librarianship. Sheffield: University of Sheffield

Hartley, J. and Green, J. (2006) 'The public sphere on the beach'. *European Journal of Cultural Studies*, 9(3), 341–362

Heaton, T. and Jacobson, C. (2000) 'Intergroup marriage: An examination of opportunity structures'. *Sociological Inquiry*, 70, 30–41

Hellerstein, J. and Neumark, D. (2003) 'Workplace Segregation in the United States'. Draft paper presented at the Harvard Color Lines Conference, Cambridge, MA, 1–2 September

Henry, I., Amara, M., Aquilina, D., Argent, E., Betzer-Tayar, M. and Coalter, F. (2005) *The Roles of Sport and Education in the Social Inclusion of Asylum Seekers and Refugees: An Evaluation of Policy and Practice in the UK*. Loughborough: Institute of Sport and Leisure Policy, Loughborough University and Stirling University

Henry, N., McEwan, C. and Pollard, J. S. (2002) 'Globalization from below: Birmingham – post-colonial workshop of the world?' *Area*, 34(2), 117–127

Herrick, C. (2006) *Celebrating Diversity: An Evaluation of a Twinning Project between Ethnically Different Schools from Kirklees and Wakefield.* Huddersfield: University of Huddersfield, Nationwide Children's Research Centre

Herschlag, M. (1996) 'Cultural Imperialism on the Net: Policymakers from Around the World Express Concern over US Role'. Paper from Harvard University Conference on the Internet and Society, May 28-31; Virtual Press Room, Harvard, MA, www3.uakron.edu/hfrance/archives/mm1301.htm

HM Government (2006) *Countering International Terrorism: The United Kingdom's Strategy.* London: HMSO

Hofstede, G. (1991) *Cultures and Organizations. Software of the Mind.* Maidenhead: McGraw-Hill

Hollander, S. (2002) 'Retailers as creatures and creators of the social order'. *International Journal of Retail and Distributive Management*, 30(11), 514

Holme, J. J., Wells, A. S. and Revilla, A. T. (2005) 'Learning through experience: What graduates gained by attending desegregated high schools'. *Equity & Excellence in Education*, 38(1), 14–24

Home Office (2001) *Building Cohesive Communities: A Report of the Ministerial Group on Public Order and Community Cohesion.* London: Home Office

Hopkins, S., Hopkins, W. and Hoffman, K. (2005) 'Domestic inter-cultural service encounters: An integrated model'. *Managing Service Quality*, 15(4), 329–343

Houston, S., Wright, R., Ellis, M., Holloway, S. and Hudson, M. (2005) 'Places of possibility: Where mixed-race partners meet'. *Progress in Human Geography*, 29(6), 700–717

Hunter, L. and Elias, M. J. (1999) 'Interracial friendships, multicultural sensitivity, and social competence: How are they related?' *Journal of Applied Developmental Psychology*, 20, 551–573

Huntington, S. P. (1996) *The Clash of Civilizations and the Remaking of World Order.* New York: Simon and Schuster

Huskinson, J. (1999) *Experiencing Rome: Culture, Identity and Power in Ancient Rome.* London: Routledge

Hye-Kyung Ryoo (2005) 'Achieving friendly interactions: A study of service encounters between Korean shopkeepers and African-Amercian customers'. *Discourse & Society*, 16(1), 79–105

Hylarides, P. C. (2005) 'Multiculturalism in the Netherlands and the murder of Theo van Gogh'. *Contemporary Review*, February, 73–78

Iles, P. and Hayers, P. K. (1997) 'Managing diversity in transnational project teams: A tentative model and case study'. *Journal of Managerial Psychology*, 12(2), 95–117

Imber, C. (2002) *The Ottoman Empire, 1300–1650: The Structure of Power.* Basingstoke: Palgrave Macmillan

Independent Review Team (2001) *Community Cohesion: A Report of the Independent Review Team, chaired by Ted Cantle.* London: Home Office

Institute of Community Cohesion (2006) *The Power of Sport: Sport and Cohesion Best Practice.* Coventry: IcoCo

Ipsos MORI (2006) *Race Relations 2006: A Research Study*. London: Ipsos MORI

Ipsos MORI (2007) *'What Works' in Community Cohesion*. London: Department for Communities and Local Government

Isbister, J. (1996) *The Immigration Debate: Remaking America*. West Hartford, CT: Kumarian Press

Jackman, M. R. and Crane, M. (1986) '"Some of my best friends are Black...": Interracial friendship and Whites' racial attitudes'. *Public Opinion Quarterly*, 50, 459–486

Jackson, S. E., May, K. E. and Whitney, K. (1995) 'Understanding the dynamics of diversity in decision-making teams'. In R. Guzzo, E. Salas and Associates (eds) *Team Effectiveness in Decision Making in Organizations*. San Francisco: Jossey-Bass

Jacobs, J. (1961) *The Death and Life of Great American Cities*. London: Pimlico

Jacobs, J. (1969) *The Economy of Cities*. New York: Random House

Jamal, A. (2003) 'Retailing in a multicultural world: The interplay of retailing, ethnic identity and consumption'. *Journal of Retailing and Consumer Services*, 10, 1–11

Jameson, D. and O'Mara, J. (1991) *Managing Workforce 2000: Gaining the Diversity Advantage*. Somerset, New Jersey: Wiley

Jayasuriya, L. (1997) *Immigration and Multiculturalism in Australia*. Perth: School of Social Work and Social Administration, University of Western Australia

Johansson, F. (2004) *The Medici Effect: Breakthrough Insights at the Intersection of Ideas, Concepts and Cultures*. Boston: Harvard Business School Press

Jones-Correa, M. (2001) *Governing American Cities: Inter-ethnic Coalitions, Competition, and Conflict*. New York: Russell Sage Foundation

Joyner, K. and Kao, G. (2000) 'School racial composition and adolescent racial homophily'. *Social Science Quarterly*, 81, 810–825

Kagan, H. and Cohen, J. (1990) 'Cultural adjustment of international students'. *Psychological Science*, 1, 133–137

Kang, J. (2000) 'Cyber race'. *Harvard Law Review*, 113(5), 1130–1209

Kant, I. 1963 [1784] 'Ideas towards a universal history from a cosmopolitan point of view'. In L. W. Beck (ed) *On History*. Indianapolis: Bobbs-Merrill, pp11–27

Kaplan, P. and Fugate, D. (1972) 'Pilot study of racial interaction in a public place: Northern and Southern settings compared'. *International Journal of Group Tensions*, 2, 63–79

Karnes, M. and Blade, T. (1998) *Ethnic Barriers and Biases: How to Become an Agent for Change*. New York: National Training Associates

Kaye, S. (1999) 'Some proven ways to promote the exchange of ideas'. *Quality Progress*, March, 29–33

Kearns, A. and Parkes, A. (2003) 'Living in and leaving poor neighbourhood conditions in England'. *Housing Studies*, 18(6), 827–851

Kee, P. (1994) 'Unravelling the global Chinese business networks'. *BIPR Bulletin*, 11, 9–12

Kelley, C. and Meyers, J. (1989) *CCAI: Cross-Cultural Adaptability Inventory*. Minneapolis: National Computer Systems

Kelley, N. and Trebilcock, M. J. (1998) *The Making of the Mosaic: A History of Canadian Immigration Policy*. Toronto: University of Toronto Press

Khakee, A., Somma, P. and Thomas, H. (eds) (1999) *Urban Renewal, Ethnicity and Social Exclusion in Europe*. Aldershot: Ashgate

King, R. and Black, R. (eds) (1997) *Southern Europe and the New Migration*. Brighton: Sussex Academic Press

King, R., Warnes, A. and Williams, A. (2000) *Sunset Lives: British Retirement Migration to the Mediterranean*. Oxford: Berg

Kivisto, P. (2002) *Multiculturalism in a Global Society*. Oxford: Blackwell

Kloosterman, R. and Rath, J. (2003) *Immigrant Entrepreneurs: Venturing Abroad in the Age of Globalization*. Oxford: Berg

Kochan, T., Bezrukoval, K., Ely, R., Jackson, S., Joshi, A., Jehn, K., Leonard, J., Levine D. and Thomas, D. (2003) 'The effects of diversity on business performance: Report of the Diversity Network'. *Human Resource Management*, 42(1), 3–21

Kohls, L. R. and Knight, J. M. (1994) *Developing Intercultural Awareness: A Cross-cultural Training Handbook*. Yarmouth, ME: Intercultural Press

Krishnarayan, V. and Thomas, H. (1993) *Ethnic Minorities and The Planning System*. London: Royal Town Planning Institute

Kumar, K. (2003) *The Making of English National Identity*. Cambridge: Cambridge University Press

Kurthen, H., Fijalkowski, J. and Wagner G. (eds) (1998) *Immigration, Citizenship and the Welfare State in Germany and the United States: Welfare Policies and Immigrants' Citizenship*. Stamford, CT: JAI Press

Kyambi, S. (2005) *Beyond Black and White: Mapping New Immigrant Communities*. London: Institute for Public Policy Research

Kymlicka, W. (2003) 'Multicultural states and intercultural citizens'. *Theory and Research in Education*, 1(2), 147–169

Kymlicka, W. and Norman, W. (eds) (2000) *Citizenship in Diverse Societies*. Oxford: Oxford University Press

Lamont, M. and Aksartova, S. (2002) 'Ordinary cosmopolitans: Strategies for bridging racial boundaries among working class men'. *Theory, Culture & Society*, 19(4), 1–25

Landry, C. (2000) *The Creative City: A Toolkit for Urban Innovators*. London: Earthscan

Landry, C. (2004) *Riding the Rapids: Urban Life in an Age of Complexity*. London: CABE/RIBA/Comedia

Landry, C. (2006) *The Art of City Making*. London: Earthscan

Larner, J. (1999) *Marco Polo and the Discovery of the World*. New Haven: Yale University Press

Larsen, J. I., Jacobs, D. L. and van Vlimmeren, T. (2004) *Cultural Diversity: How Public Libraries Can Serve the Diversity of the Community*. Gutersloh: Bertelsmann Stiftung

Law, B. (1999) *Oldham Brave Oldham: An Illustrated History of Oldham*. Oldham: Oldham Metropolitan Borough Council

Lazear, E. (1995) 'Culture and language'. NBER Working Paper no. 5249. Cambridge, MA: National Bureau of Economic Research.

Lee, D. (1998) 'Mail fantasy: Global sexual exploitation in the mail-order bride industry and proposed legal solutions'. *Asian Law Journal*, 5, 139–179

Lee, J. (2002) *Civility in the City: Blacks, Jews, and Koreans in Urban America*. Cambridge, MA: Harvard University Press

Leong, C.-H. and Ward, C. (2000) 'Identity conflict in sojourners'. *International Journal of Intercultural Relations*, 24, 763–776

Li, P. (2003) 'Deconstructing Canada's Discourse of Immigrant Integration'. PCERII Working Paper WP04-03. Edmonton: PCERII

Lian, B. and Oneal, J. (1997) 'Cultural diversity and economic development: A cross-national study of 98 Countries, 1960–1985'. *Economic Development and Cultural Change*, 46, 61–77

Lichfield, J. (2005) 'Sarkozy blames French "model" for riots'. *The Independent*, 16 November

Liddle, R. (2004) 'How Islam killed multiculturalism'. *The Spectator*, 1 May

Light, I. and Bhachu, P. (eds) (2004) *Immigration and Entrepreneurship: Culture, Capital and Ethnic Networks*. New Brunswick: Transaction Publishers

Light, I. and Gold, S. (2000) *Ethnic Economies*. Orlando: Academic Press

Lixl-Purcell, A. (1995) 'Foreign language acquisition and technology', www.uncg. edu/~lixlpurc/publications/MLAtech.html

Low, S., Taplin, D. and Scheld, S. (2005) *Rethinking Urban Parks: Public Space and Cultural Diversity*. Austin: University of Texas Press

Lucas, R. E. (1988) 'On the mechanisms of economic development'. *Journal of Monetary Economics*, 22, 3–42

Lynch, F. (1997) *The Diversity Machine*. New York: The Free Press

McGuigan, J. (2005) 'The cultural public sphere'. *European Journal of Cultural Studies*, 8(4), 427–443

Mackintosh-Smith, T. (ed) (2003) *The Travels of Ibn Battutah*. London: Picador

McLeod, P. L., Lobel, S. A. and Cox, T. H., Jr. (1996) 'Ethnic diversity and creativity in small groups'. *Small Group Research*, 27, 246–264

Macpherson of Cluny, W. (1999) *The Stephen Lawrence Enquiry*. London: HMSO

Maffesoli, M. (1996) *The Time of the Tribes: The Decline of Individualism in Mass Society*. London: Sage

Maignan, C., Ottaviano, G., Pinelli, D. and Rullano, F. (2003) *Bio-Ecological Diversity vs Socio-Economic Diversity: A Comparison of Existing Measures*. Milan: ENGIME nota di lavoro

Malanga, S. (2004) 'The curse of the creative class'. *City Journal*, Winter, www.city-journal.org/html/14_1_the_curse.html

Malik, K. (2002) 'Against multiculturalism'. *New Humanist*, 117(2), 14–16

Mann, V. and Glick, T. (eds) (1992) *Convivencia: Jews, Muslims and Christians in Mediaeval Spain*. New York: George Braziller

Marcuse, P. (2001) 'Enclaves Yes, Ghettoes, No: Segregation and the State'. Paper presented at the International Seminar on Segregation in the City. Lincoln Institute, 26–28 July

Marcuse, P. (2002) 'The partitioned city in history'. In P. Marcuse and R. van Kempen (eds) *Of States and Cities: The Partitioning of Urban Space*. Oxford: Oxford University Press

Marks, K. (2005) 'The end of innocence at Bondi beach'. *The Independent*, 26 December

Marx, E. (1999) *Breaking Through Culture Shock: What You Need to Succeed in International Business*. London: Nicholas Brealey

Maslow, Abraham. (1943) 'A theory of human motivation'. *Psychological Review*, 50, 370–396

Matarasso, F. (1998) *Beyond Book Issues: The Social Potential of Library Projects*. Stroud: Comedia

Meagher, M. and Castaños, F. (1996) 'Perceptions of American culture: The impact of an electronically-mediated cultural exchange program on Mexican high school students'. In S. Herring (ed) *Computer Mediated Communication. Linguistic, Social and Cross-cultural Perspectives*. Amsterdam: John Benjamins Publishing Company

Menocal, M. R. (2002) *The Ornament of the World: How Jews, Christians and Muslims Created a Culture of Tolerance in Mediaeval Spain*. New York: Little Brown and Company

Menzies, G. (2002) *1421, The Year China Discovered the World*. London: Bantam Press

Metcalf, H., Modood, T. and Virdee, S. (1996) *Asian Self-Employment: The Interaction of Culture and Economics in England*. London: Policy Studies Institute

Michon, R. and Chebat, J.-C. (2004) 'Cross-cultural mall shopping values and habitats: A comparison between English- and French-speaking Canadians'. *Journal of Business Research*, 57, 883–892

Milgram, S. (1977) *The Individual in a Social World: Essays and Experiments*. Reading, MA: Addison

Modood, T. (2005) 'Remaking multiculturalism after 7/7'. *Open Democracy*, 29, 7

Modood, T. and Werbner, P. (1997) *The Politics of Multiculturalism in the New Europe: Racism, Identity and Community*. London: Zed Books

Mokyr, J. (1990) *The Lever of Riches. Technological Creativity and Economic Progress*. New York: Oxford University Press

Montes, T. (2000) 'The diversity challenge'. *Ashridge Journal*, Summer, 18–21

Moss, K. (2003) *The Color of Class: Poor Whites and the Paradox of Privilege*. Pennsylvania: University of Pennsylvania Press

Mouffe, C. (2000) *Deliberative Democracy or Agonistic Pluralism.* Vienna: Institut für Höhere Studien (IHS)

Mumford, L. (1938) *The Culture of Cities.* New York: Harcourt, Brace, and World

Mumford, L. (1961) *The City in History.* New York: Harcourt, Brace, and World

Musterd, S. (2003) 'Segregation and integration: A contested relationship'. *Journal of Ethnic and Migration Studies,* 29(4), 623–641

Musterd, S. (2005) 'Social and ethnic segregation in Europe: Levels, causes and effects'. *Journal of Urban Affairs,* 27(3), 331–348

Musterd, S. and Andersson, R. (2005) 'Housing mix, social mix, and social opportunities'. *Urban Affairs Review,* 40(6), 761–790

Nagel, J. (2003) *Race, Ethnicity and Sexuality: Intimate Intersections, Forbidden Frontiers.* Oxford: Oxford University Press

Nairn, T. (2000) *After Britain.* London: Granta

Neal, S. and Agyeman, J. (eds) (2006) *The New Countryside? Ethnicity, Nation and Exclusion in Contemporary Britain.* Bristol: The Policy Press

Neuliep, J. W. and Ryan, D. J. (1998) 'The influence of intercultural communication apprehension and socio-communicative orientation on uncertainty reduction during initial cross-cultural interaction'. *Communication Quarterly,* 46, 88–99

Newman, K. S. (1999) *No Shame in My Game: The Working Poor in the Inner City.* New York: Alfred A. Knopf and Russell Sage Foundation

Niman, M. (2005) 'Katrina's America: Failure, racism, and profiteering'. *Humanist,* 65(6), 11–15

Niner, P. (2002) *The Provision and Condition of Local Authority Gypsy and Traveller Sites in England.* Birmingham: University of Birmingham

Oberg, K. (1960) 'Cultural shock: Adjustment to new cultural environments'. *Practical Anthropology,* 7, 177–182

O'Dowd, R. (2001) 'In Search of a Truly Global Network: The Opportunities and Challenges of On-line Intercultural Communication,' CALL-EJ Online, 3(1), www.clec.ritsumei.ac.jp/english/callejonline/6-1/o_dowd.html

O'Dowd, R. (2003) 'Understanding "The Other Side": Intercultural learning in a Spanish-English e-mail exchange'. *Language Learning & Technology,* 7(2), 118–144

Ogbu, J. (1995) 'Cultural problems in minority education: Their interpretations and consequences'. *Urban Review,* 27, 271–297.

Oldenburg, R. (1989) *The Great Good Place: Cafés, Coffee Shops, Bookstores, Bars, Hair Salons, and other Hangouts at the Heart of a Community.* New York: Marlowe and Co.

ONS (Office of National Statistics) (2001) *2001 Census.* London: ONS

O'Reilly, C. A., Caldwell, D. F. and Barnett, W. P. (1989) 'Work group demography, social integration and turnover'. *Administrative Science Quarterly,* 34, 21–37

O'Reilly, K. (2002) 'Britain in Europe/the British in Spain: Exploring Britain's changing relationship to the other through the attitudes of its emigrants'. *Nations and Nationalism,* 8(2), 179–193

O'Reilly, K. (2007) 'Intra-European migration and mobility – enclosure dialectic'. *Sociology*, 41(2), 277–293

Ottaviano, G. and Peri, G. (2004) *The Economic Value of Cultural Diversity: Evidence from US cities*. Milan: FEEM

Ottaviano, G. and Peri, G. (2005) 'Rethinking the Gains from Immigration: Theory and Evidence from the US'. NBER Working Paper, 11672. Cambridge, MA: National Bureau of Economic Research

Ouseley, H. (2001) *Community Pride Not Prejudice*. Bradford: Bradford Vision

Owen, D., Green, A. E., McLeod, M., Law, I., Challis, T. and Wilkinson, D. (2003) *The Use and Attitudes Towards Information and Communication Technologies (ICT) by People from Black and Minority Ethnic Groups Living in Deprived Areas*. Department for Education and Skills, Research Report 450. London: Department for Education and Skills

Pacino, J. (2007) 'Multicultural Discussions Inside Second Life', http://ext.sac.edu/faculty_staff/pacino_joe/slmulticul/slmulticuldiscussion.htm#overview

Page, S. E. (2007) *The Difference: How the Power of Diversity Creates Better Groups, Firms, Schools and Societies*. Princeton: Princeton University Press

Pahl, R. (2006) 'On respect: The social strains of social change'. In A. Buonfina and G. Mulgan (eds) *Porcupines in Winter: The Pleasures and Pains of Living Together in Modern Britain*. London: Young Foundation

Parekh, B. (2000) *The Future of Multiethnic Britain*. London: Runnymede Trust

Parekh, B. (2006) *Rethinking Multiculturalism: Cultural Diversity and Political Theory*. 2nd edition. Basingstoke: Palgrave Macmillan

Park, R. (1926) 'The urban community as a special pattern and a moral order'. In E. E. Burgess (ed) *The Urban Community*. Chicago: University of Chicago

Park, R., Burgess, E. and McKenzie, R. (eds) (1925) *The City*. Chicago: University of Chicago Press

Patil, G. P. and Taillie, C. (1982) 'Diversity as a concept and its measurement'. *Journal of the American Statistical Association*, 77(379), 548–561

Paulos, E. and Goodman, E. (2004) 'The familiar stranger: Anxiety, comfort, and play in public places'. Proceedings of the SIGCHI conference on Human factors in computing systems, 24–29 April, Vienna, Austria, 223–230

Paulos, E., Anderson, K. and Townsend, A. (2004) 'UbiComp in the urban frontier'. In Urban Computing Workshop Proceedings. September, Nottingham, UK

Peach, C. (1980) 'Ethnic segregation and intermarriage'. *Annals of the Association of American Geographers*, 70, 371–381

Peach, C. (1996) 'Good segregation, bad segregation'. *Planning Perspectives*, 11, 379–398

Peach, C. (2001) 'The ghetto and the ethnic enclave'. Paper presented at the International Seminar on Segregation in the City, Lincoln Institute, 26–28 July

Pearce, P. L. (1982) 'Tourists and their hosts: Some social and psychological effects of intercultural contact'. In S. Bochner (ed) *Cultures in Contact: Studies in Cross-cultural Interaction*. Oxford: Pergamon

Pearman, H. (2001) 'Terence Conran: The Super-ego Who Changed a Nation's Taste', www.hughpearman.com/articles2/conran.html

Penaloza, L. (1994) 'Altravesando Fronteras/Border Crossings: A critical ethnographic exploration of the consumer acculturation of Mexican immigrants'. *Journal of Consumer Research*, 21, 289–294

Perez de Cuellar, J. et al (1995). *Our Creative Diversity. Report of the World Commission on Culture and Development*. Paris: UNESCO Publishing

Peters, P. (1996) *Invented in the USA: Immigrants, Patents and Jobs*. Arlington, VA: Alexis de Tocqueville Institute

Pettigrew, T. F. (1998) 'Intergroup contact theory'. *Annual Review of Psychology*, 49, 65–85

Pettigrew, T. F. and Tropp, L. R. (2000) 'Does intergroup contact reduce prejudice? Recent meta-analytic findings'. In S. Oskamp (ed) *Reducing Prejudice and Discrimination, The Claremont Symposium on Applied Social Psychology*. Mahwah, NJ: Lawrence Erlbaum Associates

Philipp, S. (1999) 'Are we welcome? African American racial acceptance in leisure activities and the importance given to children's leisure'. *Journal of Leisure Research*, 31, 385–403

Phillips, D., Butt, F. and David, C. (2002) 'The racialisation of space in Bradford'. *Regional Review*, July, 9–10

Phillips, T. (2004) Speech at the Civil Service Race Equality Network Annual Lecture, 26 April

Phillips, T. (2005) 'After 7/7: Sleepwalking to segregation'. Speech given at the Manchester Council for Community Relations, 22 September

Phizacklea, A. and Ram, M. (1995) 'Ethnic entrepreneurship in comparative perspective'. *International Journal of Entrepreneurial Behaviour and Research*, 1(1), 48–58

Pickering, P. (2006) 'Generating social capital for bridging ethnic divisions in the Balkans: The case of Bosniak-dominated urban Bosnia'. *Ethnic and Racial Studies*, 19(1), 79–103

Pinelli, D., Ottaviano, G. and Maignan, C. (2003) *Economic Growth, Innovation and Cultural Diversity: What Are We All Talking About? A Critical Survey of the State-of-the-art*. Milan: FEEM

Po-Chia Hsia, R. and van Nierop, H. (2002) *Calvinism and Religious Toleration in the Dutch Golden Age*. Cambridge: Cambridge University Press

Popkin, S., Katz, B., Cunningham, M., Brown, K., Gustafson, J. and Turner, M. (2004) 'A decade of hope VI: Research findings and policy challenges'. Washington, DC: The Urban Institute and The Brookings Institution.

Porter, M. E. (1998) *The Competitive Advantage of Nations*. London: Macmillan

Portes, A. and Sensenbrenner J. (1993) 'Embeddedness and immigration: Notes on the social determinants of economic action'. *American Journal of Sociology*, 98, 1320–1350

Priem, R., Harrison, D. and Muir, N. (1995) 'Structured conflict and consensus outcomes in group decision making'. *Journal of Management*, 21, 691–710

Pugh, R. (2004) 'Responding to rural racism: Delivering local services'. In N. Chakraborti and J. Garland (eds) *Rural Racism*. Cullompton, Devon: Willan Publishing

Putnam, R. (1993) *Making Democracy Work*. New York: Basic Books

Putnam, R. (2000) *Bowling Alone: The Collapse and Revival of American Community*. New York: Simon and Schuster

Pyong Gap Min (1996) *Caught in the Middle: Korean Communities in New York and Los Angeles*. Berkeley: University of California Press

Qadeer, M. (1997) 'Pluralistic planning for multicultural cities'. *Journal of the American Planning Association*, 63(4), 481–94

Quigley, J. M. (1998) 'Urban diversity and economic growth'. *Journal of Economic Perspectives*, 12(2), 127–138

Ram, M. and Smallbone, D. (2001) *Ethnic Minority Enterprise: Policy in Practice*. Final report. Sheffield: Small Business Service

Ram, M., Smallbone, D. and Linneker, B. (2002*) Assessing the Potential of Supplier Diversity Initiatives as a Means of Promoting Diversification Amongst Ethnic Minority Businesses in the UK*. Final Report. Sheffield: Small Business Service

Rath, J. and Kloosterman, R. (2000) 'Outsiders' business: A critical review of research on immigrant entrepreneurship'. *International Migration Review*, 34(3), 657–681

Raw, A. (2006) *Schools Linking Project 2005–06: Full Final Evaluation Report*. Bradford: Education Bradford

Raybourn, E. (1997) 'Intercultural Communication, Simulation Games and Computer Game Technology.' Paper presented at the 1997 Association for Business Simulation and Experiential Learning (ABSEL) Conference, New Orleans, Louisiana, 19–21 March

Reitman, M. (2006) 'Uncovering the white place: Whitewashing at work'. *Social and Cultural Geography*, 7(2), 267–282

Remy, E. and Kopel, S. (2002) 'Social linking and human resources management in the service sector'. *The Services Industries Journal*, 22(1), 35–56

Rex, J. and Moore, R. (1967) *Race, Community and Conflict*. Oxford: Oxford University Press

Richard, O. C. (2000). 'Racial diversity, business strategy and firm performance: A resource based view'. *Academy of Management Journal*, 43(2), 164–177

Robinson, D. (2005) 'The search for community cohesion: Key themes and dominant concepts for the public policy agenda'. *Urban Studies*, 42(8), 1411–1428

Robinson, D., Coward, S., Fordham, T., Green, S. and Reeve, K. (2004) *How Housing Management Can Contribute to Community Cohesion*. Coventry: Chartered Institute of Housing

Robinson, G. and Dechant, K. (1997). 'Building a business case for diversity'. *Academy of Management Executive*, 11(3), 21–37

Rodriquez, V. and Salva-Tomas, P. (2001) 'Northern Europeans and the Mediterranean: A New California or a New Florida?' In J. M. Beck (ed) *Geography, Environment and Development in the Mediterranean*. Brighton: Sussex Academic Press

Rogers, E. M. (2003) *Diffusion of Innovations*. 5th edition. New York: Free Press

Rogers, E. M. and Steinfatt, T. M. (1999) *Intercultural Communication*. Prospect Heights: Waveland Press

Rogers, R. and Power, A. (2000) *Cities for a Small Country*. London: Faber and Faber

Romer, P. M. (1990) 'Endogenous technological change'. *Journal of Political Economy*, 98, 71–102

Rossell, C. H. (1990) *The Carrot or the Stick for School Desegregation Policy. Magnet Schools or Forced Bussing*. Philadelphia: Temple University Press

Rotheram-Borus, M. (1993) 'Biculturalism among adults'. In M. Bernal and G. Knight (eds) *Ethnic Identity*. Albany: State University of New York Press, 81–102

Sager, M. (2000) 'What I've learned: Andy Grove'. *Esquire Magazine*, 1 May.

Sandercock, L. (1998) *Towards Cosmopolis*. Chichester: John Wiley

Sandercock, L. (2003a) *Cosmopolis 2: Mongrel Cities of the 21st Century*. New York: Continuum

Sandercock, L. (2003b) 'Integrating Immigrants: The Challenge for Cities, City Governments and the City-building Professions'. Vancouver Centre of Excellence RIIM Working Paper 03-20. Vancouver: Simon Fraser University

Sandercock, L. (2004) 'Reconsidering multiculturalism: Towards an intercultural project'. In P. Wood (ed) *The Intercultural City Reader*. Stroud: Comedia

Sardar, Z. (2006) 'Three lives – one identity'. *The Observer Sport Monthly*, February

Sarkissian, W. (1976) 'The idea of social mix in town planning: An historical review'. *Urban Studies*, 13, 231–246

Sassen, S. (1994) *Cities in a World Economy*. Thousand Oaks: Pine Forge Press

Sassen, S. (2000) *Women in the Global City: Exploitation and Empowerment*. Lola Press @ www.lolapress.org/elec1/artenglish/sass_e.htm

Saxenian, A. (1999) *Silicon Valley's New Immigrant Entrepreneurs*. San Francisco: Public Policy Institute of California

Schaefer, L. (2006) 'Spades and Trowels Help Immigrants Feel At Home', www.stiftung-interkultur.de/eng/me_dw.pdf

Schill, M. H. (1994) 'Race, the underclass and public policy'. *Law and Social Enquiry*, 19(2), 433–456

Schnell, I. and Yoav, B. (2001) 'The sociospatial isolation of agents in everyday life spaces as an aspect of segregation'. *Annals of the Association of Amercian Geographers*, 91(4), 622–636

Scott, K. A. (2004) 'African-American and White girls' friendships'. *Feminism and Psychology*, 14, 383–388

Sher, P. (2003) 'Ethnic innovation networks (EIN): A strategic linkage explanation for intellectual advantage in international business'. *Taiwan Academy of Management Journal*, 3(1), 41–58

SHM Ltd (forthcoming) 'Promoting Interaction Between People from Different Ethnic Backgrounds,' London: Commission for Racial Equality.

Sigelman, L. and Welch, S. (1993) 'The contact hypothesis revisited: Black-White interaction and positive racial attitudes'. *Social Forces*, 71, 781–795

Sigelman, L., Bledsoe, T., Welch, S. and Combs, M. (1996) 'Making contact? Black-white social interaction in an urban setting'. *American Journal of Sociology*, 101, 1306–1332

Simons, G. (1998) 'Meeting the intercultural challenges of virtual work'. *Language and Intercultural Learning*, 16(1), 13–15

Simpson, L. (2007) 'Ghettoes of the mind: The empirical behaviour of indices of segregation and diversity'. *Journal of the Royal Statistical Society: Series A*, 170(2), 405–424

Sisk, D. (1995) 'Simulation games as training tools'. In S. M. Flowers and M. M. Mumford (eds) *Intercultural Sourcebook: Cross-cultural training methods, Volume 1*. Yarmouth, Maine: Intercultural Press

Sizoo, S., Plank, R., Iskat, W. and Serrie, H. (2005) 'The effect of intercultural sensitivity on employee performance in cross-cultural service encounters'. *The Journal of Service Marketing*, 19(4), 245–255

Skerry, P. (2002) 'Beyond Sushiology: Does diversity work?' *The Brookings Review*, 20(1), 20–23

Slavin, R. E. and Cooper, R. (1999) 'Improving intergroup relations: Lessons learned from cooperative learning programs'. *Journal of Social Issues*, 55, 647–633

Smallbone, D., Athayde, R. and Kitching, J. (2005) *Ethnic and Linguistic Diversity and Competitive Advantage*. Report for the London Development Agency. London: Small Business Research Centre, Kingston University

SOLACE (UK Society of Local Authority Chief Executives and Senior Managers) (2004) *Diversity and Innovation*. London: SOLACE, www.solace.org.uk/downloads/DiversityAndInnovation.pdf

Solé, C. and Parella, S. (2002) 'The labour market and racial discrimination in Spain'. *Journal of Ethnic and Migration Studies*, 29(1), 121–140

Soysal, Y. (1996) 'Boundaries and identity: Immigrants in Europe'. *EUI Working Papers*, 96(3), 1–15

Spackova, L. and Stefkova, J. (2006) *Libraries as Gateways to the Integration of Immigrants in the EU*. Prague: Multicultural Center Prague

Spencer, C. (2003) *British Food: An Extraordinary Thousand Years of History*. New York: Columbia University Press

Spencer, R. G. (1997) *British Immigration Policy Since 1939*. London/New York: Routledge

Spitz, J. and Thom, M. (2003) *Urban Network: Museums embracing communities*. Chicago: The Field Museum

Stam, D. (2005) 'A clog-dance with diversity: Past, present and future of the multi-cultural Netherlands'. *Zeitschrift für Feministische Geschichtswissenschaft*, 16(2), 105–112

Stark, E. E. (2003) 'Undelivered promises from the HR profession: A plea to return to a more defensible motivation for embracing diversity'. *The Journal of Behavioral and Applied Management*, 4(3), 299–317

Strategy Unit (2003) *Ethnic Minorities and the Labour Market*. London: Cabinet Office Strategy Unit, HM Government, www.strategy.gov.uk/output/page3672. asp

Sue, D. W., Ivey, A. and Pedersen, P. B. (1996) *A Theory of Multicultural Counselling and Therapy*. Pacific Grove, CA: Brooks/Cole

Tajfel, H. (ed) (1978) *Differentiation between Social Groups: Studies in the Psychology of Intergroup Relations*. London: Academic Press

Tatjer, L. C. (2003) 'Multiculturalism in the City: Managing Diversity'. Paper presented to the Congress of the European Regional Science Association, Jyväskylä, Finland, 27–30 August

Terrill, R. (2003) *The New Chinese Empire*. New York: Basic Books

Thornton, M. (2005) 'The Museum as Intercultural Site'. Paper presented at Museums Australia Conference Sydney, Australia 1–4 May, www.mia.id.au/text/mthornton_ma.pdf, 10/01/07

Tredoux, C., Dixon, J., Underwood, S., Nunez, D. and Finchilescu, G. (2005) 'Preserving spatial and temporal dimensions in observational data of segregation'. *South African Journal of Psychology*, 35(3), 412–432

Triandis, H. (1990) 'Theoretical concepts that are applicable to the analysis of ethnocentrism'. In R. W. Brislin (ed) *Applied Cross-cultural Psychology*. Newbury Park, CA: Sage

Trompenaars, F. and Hampden-Turner, C. (1997) *Riding the Waves of Culture*. 2nd edition. London: Nicholas Brealey Publishing

Tropp, L. R. and Bianchi, R. A. (2006) 'Valuing diversity and interest in intergroup contact'. *Journal of Social Issues*, 62(3), 533–551

Turgeon, L. and Pastinelli, M. (2002) '"Eat the world": Postcolonial encounters in Quebec City's ethnic restaurants'. *Journal of American Folklore*, 115, 247–268

Turner, T. (2005) *Garden History: Philosophy and Design, 2000BC–2000AD*. London: Spon Press

Turok, I., Kearns, A., Fitch, D., Flint, J., McKenzie, C. and Abbotts, J. (2006) *The State of the English Cities: Social Cohesion*. London: Department for Communities and Local Government

Tyler, K. (2006) 'Village People: Race, Class, Nation and the Community Spirit'. In S. Neal and J. Agyeman (eds) *The New Countryside? Ethnicity, Nation, and Exclusion in Contemporary Rural Britain*. Bristol: Policy Press

Uitermark, J., Rossi, U. and van Houtum, H. (2005) 'Reinventing multiculturalism: Urban citizenship in the negotiation of ethnic diversity in Amsterdam'. *International Journal of Urban and Regional Research*, 29(3), 622–640

UNHCR (2005) *Statistical Yearbook.* Geneva: UNHCR

United Nations (2005) *Development Programme Report.* New York: UN

University of Auckland (1998) *The Integration of Highly Skilled Migrants into the Labour Market: Implications for New Zealand Business.* Report prepared for the New Zealand Immigration Service. Auckland: University of Auckland

Valente, T. W. and Barnett, G. (eds) (1995) *Network Models of the Diffusion of Innovations.* Cresskill, NJ: Hampton Press

Varshney, A. (2002) *Ethnic Conflict and Civic Life: Hindus and Muslims in India.* New Haven, CT: Yale University Press

Vellas, F. and Becherel, L. (1995) *International Tourism: An Economic Perspective.* London: Macmillan

Vermeulen, H. and Penninx, R. (eds) (2000) *Immigrant Integration: The Dutch Case.* Amsterdam: Het Spinhuis

Vertovec, S. (1995) 'Berlin Multikulti: Germany, "foreigners" and "world-openness"'. *New Community,* 22(3), 381–400

Vertovec, S. and Cohen, R. (2002) *Conceiving Cosmopolitanism.* Oxford: Oxford University Press

Wadhwa, V., Saxenian, A., Rissing, B. and Gereffi, G. (2007) *America's New Immigrant Entrepreneurs.* Master of Engineering Management Program, Duke University. Berkeley, CA: School of Information, U.C. Berkeley

Waldinger, R. (1996) 'Ethnicity and opportunity in the plural city'. In R. Waldinger and M. Bozorgmehr (eds) *Ethnic Los Angeles.* New York: Russell Sage Foundation

Ward, C., Bochner, S. and Furnham, A. (2001) *The Psychology of Culture Shock.* London: Routledge

Ward, D. (2003) 'Culture class: Contact theory could help children cross the racial divide'. *The Guardian,* 14 January

Ward, G. C. and Burns, K. (2000) *Jazz: A History of America's Music.* New York: Alfred A. Knopf

Warde, A., Martens, L. and Olsen, W. (1999) 'Consumption and the problem of variety: Cultural omnivorousness, social distinction and dining out'. *Sociology,* 33(1), 105–127

Warschauer, M. (2000) 'Language, identity, and the Internet'. In B. Kolko, L. Nakamura and G. Rodman (eds) *Race in Cyberspace.* New York: Routledge

Watson, P. (2005) *Ideas: A History of Thought and Invention from Fire to Freud.* London: HarperCollins

Watson, S. with Studdert, D. (2006) *Markets as Sites for Social Interaction: Spaces of Diversity.* Bristol: Policy Press

Watson, W. E., Kumar, K. and Michaelsen, L. K. (1993) 'Cultural diversity's impact on interaction process and performance: Comparing homogeneous and diverse task groups'. *Academy of Management Journal,* 36, 590–602

Weimann, G. (2004) *How Modern Terrorism Uses the Internet.* Special Report 116. Washington, DC: United States Institute of Peace.

Weisehofer, J. (2001) *Ancient Persia*. London: Tauris

Welz, G. (2003) 'The cultural swirl: Anthropological perspectives on innovation'. *Global Networks*, 3, 255–270

Williams, A. and Dourish, P. (2006) 'Imagining the city: The cultural dimensions of urban computing'. *Computer*, 39(9), 38–43

Williams, A. and Hall, C. (2002) 'Tourism, migration, circulation and mobility: The contingencies of time and place'. In A. Williams and C. Hall (eds) *Tourism and Migration: New Relationships Between Production and Consumption*. London: Kluwer Academic Publishers

Williams, K. and O'Reilly, C. (1998) 'The complexity of diversity: A review of forty years of research'. In D. Gruenfeld and M. Neale (eds) *Research in Managing in Groups and Teams*. Vol. 20. Greenwich, CT: JAI Press

Winder, R. (2004) *Bloody Foreigners: The Story of Immigration to Britain*. London: Abacus

Wirth, L. (ed) (1964) *On Cities and Social Life*. Chicago: University of Chicago Press

Wood, P. (ed) (2004) *The Intercultural City Reader*. Stroud: Comedia

Wood, P., Landry, C. and Bloomfield, J. (2006) *Cultural Diversity in Britain: A Toolkit for Cross-cultural Co-operation*. Published for the Joseph Rowntree Foundation. Bristol: Policy Press

World Bank (2005) *2005 World Development Indicators*. Washington DC: World Bank Group

Wrench, J. and Modood, T. (2000) *The Effectiveness of Employment Equality Policies in Relation to Immigrants and Ethnic Minorities in the UK*. Geneva: International Labour Office

Wright, S. C., Aron, A., McLaughlin-Volpe, T. and Ropp, S. A. (1997) 'The extended contact effect: Knowledge of cross-group friendships and prejudice'. *Journal of Personality and Social Psychology*, 73, 73–90

Zachary, G. P. (2003) *The Diversity Advantage: Multicultural Identity in the New World Economy*. Boulder, CO: Westview Press

Zachary, G. P. (2005) *When Immigrants Revive a City and When They Don't: Lessons from American Cities*. Stroud: Comedia, www.interculturalcity.com/thematic_studies.htm#Case2

Zheng, X. and Berry, J. W. (1991) 'Psychological adaptation of Chinese sojourners in Canada'. *International Journal of Psychology*, 26, 451–470

Appendix

Masterplanning and Interculturalism: The Knowledge Questions

Indicative discussions with the community groups might evolve around the following categories.

TALKING ABOUT THE SIZE AND COMPOSITION OF AVERAGE FAMILIES

- Are they intergenerational?
- Do extended families share or wish to share houses?
- What are their physical space requirements?

TALKING ABOUT RITUALS AND NEEDS ASSOCIATED WITH FOOD PREPARATION AND CONSUMPTION

- What are the main rituals and celebrations through the year or rites of passage that involve significant food preparation and sharing?
- What size group will gather to celebrate and where do the celebrations take place?

- What are the special needs associated with such rituals that might relate to the design of private and public places?

Talking About the Appropriateness of Current Housing Stock

- How well do existing houses meet the needs of community members in terms of family size, community gatherings, and room layouts?
- How well do existing houses meet needs for internal privacy?
- How well do existing houses contribute to a sense of community – that is, meet needs for interaction with neighbours and people in the street?
- What are the different family roles and relationships from a cultural, gender or age perspective that impact on the nature of housing design?

Talking About Family, Religious or Community Events or Celebrations

- What are the important cultural considerations in planning such events?
- What are the domestic and public space requirements?
- What events are considered appropriate to share with the broader community?

Talking About Daily Routine Outside the Home

- What are the patterns of shopping, working, visiting friends or worship during the week?
- What are the differences between weekday and weekend public life?

- What are the cultural, gender or generational sensitivities associated with public life that need to be understood by council planners?

Talking About Young People

- Are there specific cultural differences between the ways young people use public space?
- Are young people respected and catered for in the planning and design of public space?
- What are the key gathering places for young people to meet and interact?

Talking About How Appropriate Local Parks Are in Meeting the Needs of the Community

- What are the qualities that make you feel safe and comfortable in the local parks?
- Do your local parks provide the right park furniture and facilities to meet your community's needs?
- How do you and your community use the parks for personal or communal activities – that is, are they gathering places for communal gatherings or for personal quiet time away from family or peer groups?

Talking About How Safe or Welcoming the Streets and Public Places Feel

- What are the qualities that make you feel comfortable in public spaces and shops?
- How well do the existing public spaces, streets, parks and shopping centres meet your needs?
- What are the issues with being in the streets and public spaces during the day, evening and night?

- Is the public street a place to be seen and enjoy promenading or a place to use only for essential activities such as shopping or going to work?

Talking About the Design of Public Space Such as Footpaths, Plazas, Shopping Centres and Market Squares

- Do you have a preference for large open spaces or for more crowded smaller spaces and busy footpaths?
- Are there activities such as meeting and gathering with friends that are not currently catered for in the public spaces you frequent?
- Would you use public seating in quite public nodes associated with streets and squares?

Talking About Retail Needs and Experience

- How well do the local retailers cater for culturally appropriate products?
- What are the qualities that make you feel comfortable using local shops?
- Are there cultural preferences associated with shopping in the small shops of main street as opposed to a shopping mall?

Talking About Festivals and Markets in Public Places

- Do you take part in and enjoy cultural festivals and street markets?
- How important are cultural festivals and such like in providing your culture with recognition and respect from the broader community?
- Do the existing public squares and streets adequately meet the needs of local events?

Talking About Interaction with People from Different Cultures

- What factors encourage or make possible interaction?
- What sort of places and or activities are important in bringing people together in a safe and sharing environment?
- How much cross-cultural interaction takes place in shops and at markets?

Talking About Cultural Expression

- Do you feel that your physical environment expresses the cultural diversity of the local community – that is, are there artwork, designs, signs and decorations that celebrate cultures?
- Are there colours, designs and symbols that you would like to use on your homes or businesses that would help to express your culture?
- Are there barriers to cultural expression that you have experienced with regard to your home, business or local public environments?

Index